# WALK-ON©

MY RELUCTANT JOURNEY TO INTEGRATION
AT AUBURN UNIVERSITY

A MEMOIR

THOM GOSSOM, JR.

Walk-On©

ISBN: 978-0-9890865-1-6

Best Gurl, inc.

PO Box 4235

Fort Walton Beach FL 32549

This 2nd Edition is published by Best Gurl, inc.

First Edition published by State Street Press 2008

Cover photo: Les King

Cover Design: Frank Rivera

For my Mom and Dad

# FROM THE AUTHOR

I've reread *Walk-On* several times since it was first published in September 2008. Five years later and over forty years since the events described in this memoir, I am still brought to tears, reflection, and occasional laughter.

*Walk-On* has touched people from all over the world. Many have contacted me through email, Facebook, phone calls, and the U.S. Mail to tell me that something within these pages resonated with them, whether their own lives or feelings of empathy for those of us who were racial pioneers. I am most grateful.

I am most proud of The Auburn Nation, Alumni, teammates, friends, administrators, and students who have and continue to embrace *Walk-On*. More knowledgeable persons from that era have written me beautiful letters and notes of understanding. Some of those who lived through those days, but through ignorance or absorption in their own worlds, have expressed surprise and amazement. Current students who continually invite me to campus for lectures look on in awe, their admiration often bringing me tears and a huge dose of humility.

Finally I say to all, stay awake and aware. History is made everyday and often repeats.

# FOREWORD

I was honored when Thom Gossom asked me to contribute the foreword to his memoir *Walk-On*. I've known Thom since our high school days. I wish I could say I knew him better back then, but I didn't. I knew him in passing, the way a senior knows a sophomore, from a distance. After we were both at Auburn, I knew him a little better. He was a redshirt sophomore on the team during my senior year.

What I remember is Thom walked on the field without a scholarship and announced he wanted to play. The Auburn coaches recognizing a jewel had fallen into their laps were curious as to who and where this young black man had come from. They asked me and the other guys on our team from our old high school, John Carroll Catholic. I told them what I knew, which wasn't much. He was fast. He had been a good athlete on bad teams in high school. He played basketball, had integrated the football team and everyone thought a lot of him. Also, we'd discovered we both loved the same disc jockey at the all black radio station in our hometown of Birmingham.

Undaunted by the challenge of resistance to the coming changes in our society, Thom earned a scholarship, becoming the first black player to do so successfully in Auburn's and maybe Southeast Conference history. He made the travel squad my senior year, becoming an eager teammate, then started three years and became Auburn's first black athlete to graduate.

Thom has written a memoir that captures the beginning of the biggest cultural change the southern sports landscape has experienced. Back then, I was aware of some of the changes taking place in our society, but traditions, and culture distance made what had been normal in a segregated society, abnormal in the changing south and the United States. Thom and James Owens, the other black player on our team were facing everyday obstacles that many of us were not aware of or took for granted.

Today, as a coach I try and instill in our players some of the lessons from those times; the journey of life, the foundation a young man can lay for his own future. I use Thom Gossom, as an example of a man who had a dream, a vision of himself that he never gave up on against all odds and in doing so he made that same journey possible for the many who have followed the trail he blazed.

As time has moved us all farther down the road to a clearer understanding of our own humanity, I have come to know him as a man of dignity, character, and understanding. More importantly I'm come to know him as my friend.

Pat Sullivan
Head Football Coach-Samford University
1971 Heisman Trophy Winner

# WALK-ON

[ 2002 ]

# THE AMAZINS

My car roared north up the beautiful stretch of I-85 that lies between Auburn University and home. It was one of those perfect Alabama fall days, the air was crisp, not yet cold. The trees put on a colorful show with their leaves of red and yellow. Just past the line of trees, open fields zoomed by. As we left Auburn, the familiar green blur of highway signs raced past: *Tuskegee, 19 miles.*

Without warning, a rush of tears started streaming down my face. They spilled over my cheeks and onto the new Auburn University t-shirt I bought the day before. It was like someone turned a spigot on and I tried to move my face so that my wife would not see.

Don't get me wrong. I wasn't hiding my tears because of some macho thing. I'm an actor. I cry for money, on cue when I must. However, this was private.

"What is it?" My wife asked. I couldn't tell her. Not that I didn't want to. It's just that the pain came right from my gut, like it was being ripped out. Only once before did pent-up emotions rise up on me like this. I was in Los Angeles, about three months after my mom died; and was overcome by grief while stopped at a red light at Robertson and Pico.

This pain was different, though. I wasn't angry or grieving; it was a cleansing process. I was letting go of three decades of pent-up anger and hurt.

The look on my wife's face let me know I needed to say something. I pulled the car over to the side of the interstate. After a few moments, I said, "It's taken me thirty years, but I finally feel like part of the team."

It started back in March 2002. My wife, joyce (she spells her name with a lowercase "J"), at our home in Florida, called me in Los Angeles where I was on the set. "You got a letter from Terry Henley." Terry "Henlo" Henley was one of my college teammates from my days at Auburn University.

He was inviting me back to Auburn for a reunion.

March 28, 2002

Dear Teammate:

Thirty years ago this spring, we stepped onto the football field to try and show everybody in the country we were better than they said we were. No one will ever know, unless they participated that spring, what a rough and tough physical undertaking it was to complete that task. Once we were finished, I think everyone knew when we walked off the field what kind of team and season we were going to have. I know each of us is proud to know that Coach Jordan recognized the 1972 team as his favorite. Today, thirty years later, you go out and talk to people or pick up books and the 1972 team is still discussed among a very elite group. It has to make us all very proud.

The (Auburn) Athletic Department has telephoned to tell me they are going to recognize the 1972 team on its thirtieth anniversary at the Arkansas ball game during the upcoming football season. That game will be played on October 12 and we will all be introduced before the game.

Many people have asked that we get together Friday night before the game. The media wants to interview us.

...The media has been especially anxious to talk to all of you.

I hope everybody looks forward to this. It's bound to be a very enjoyable evening. I'm anxious to hear from all of you. Hope to see you all soon.

Yours truly,

Terry Henley

My first thought was, "I'm not going!" Mixed emotions stumbled over themselves as they raced through my mind. It wasn't that I didn't love my alma mater. Auburn and I had a complicated history, but I'd made my peace. I had forgiven so much, but I hadn't totally shaken the pain of those years. I didn't want to open old wounds.

I called James. "You going?" I asked him over the long distance line from Los Angeles to Auburn.

"I was going to call you," he said. "I talked to Terry. Told him I'll be there."

James Curtis Owens' smooth melodious voice was as soothing as always. A minister now, James still has the same calming effect he had on us when we were students. Us black kids on campus always called him "Daddy Owens," because he was always so calm and serene.

Our lives had taken divergent roads. James and I were the first two black players to play football at Auburn. For the first three years of my career we were inseparable, and not just because we were the only blacks on the team. We respected and liked each other.

All these years later, James lives just a few miles from Auburn University's Jordan-Hare stadium, where we played our games. I ended up on the West Coast.

"You're going?" I asked, surprised that James was ready to cross the bridge to our past. I was worried about going back to see guys with whom I'd shared one of the most special times in my life.

In Alabama, college football legacies last a lifetime. Enthusiasts, talk show callers, and bloggers can quote plays, situations, names, coaching decisions, and legends from decades ago. Time had not dimmed their enthusiasm for the team that had been dubbed "The Amazins."

We were always underdogs; favored in only two games. We didn't have any stars, rarely threw the ball, and on most Saturdays we were not the physically superior team. Despite all that, we won, game after game after game, against all odds.

Ten out of eleven games we walked off the field victorious. After the horn sounded, the other team and coaches would claim they were better and should have won.

The scoreboard would tell a different story. We outscored our opponents 209-141. We beat three Top Ten teams. We ended the nation's longest winning streak, twice. We worked harder. We worked smarter. We grew to be special. We ended up ranked number five in the country. It's a legacy we will carry to our graves. "The Amazins."

My wife had never been to Auburn. She'd never experienced a football Saturday in the loveliest village on the plains. She'd never seen the eagle flying around the stadium before kickoff, the hordes of tailgaters, the fans all dressed up in orange and blue, lining the sidewalk by the thousands, for the players in the "Tiger Walk."

I hadn't been back since 1995. Living in Florida while working in Los Angeles didn't make it easy. I'd only been to a handful of games since the last game I played in the 1974 Gator Bowl. I moved on when I moved on.

I was the first black athlete to graduate from Auburn in 1975, but there was no alumni network for me. There were fewer than 100 black Auburn alumni total, and only one in my hometown. In the mid-eighties, I was invited as the only black to sit on the inaugural board of directors of the Auburn Football Lettermen Club. In the middle of a meeting one of the guys dropped "the 'N' word." The meeting ended uncomfortably for all. I wasn't invited back.

# WALK-ON

Now I was going back to a reunion.

Other than my teammates and the other black guys on campus, I didn't have many friends. Practices, school, games, and the newness of having black students in class made it hard for me to get to know my fellow students. Still, it would be good to see the guys I played with. We shared a common bond. We were warriors. We accepted the challenges the coaches laid before us. We worked in heat, cold, rain, outdoors, indoors, and under the stadium. We sacrificed for the greater good of the team. No individual identities. We were Coach Ralph "Shug" Jordan's boys. We forged a bond that was still strong thirty years later.

On the field, we experienced success and a feeling of togetherness. Off the field, James and I experienced loneliness, isolation, anger, and racism. Being a trailblazer didn't seem so glamorous at the time.

The night of the reunion came and joyce and I were riding an elevator up to the opening reception. I've played ball in front of 70,000 people. I've done live theater. I've done television shows that have been seen by millions. Films I've acted in have played all over the world. I'm never nervous. I always know I can perform when called upon. Except for this night. I was nervous.

The elevator door opened and there he stood, the 1972 Most Valuable Player in the Southeastern Conference, Terry Henley. His infectious smile froze me. Then other guys rushed up to us and I was caught up in a sea of well meaning former teammates.

A murmur went through the crowd as the Reverend James Owens and his wife Gloria stepped out and into the room. The most beloved member of the 1972 team, the guys gathered around James like he was a rock star. One of the guys called James out by his old football nickname, proudly proclaiming, "The 'Big O' is in the house!"

What a night! I ran into coaches, trainers, news reporters, managers, and teammates. There were plenty of laughs, lies, and stories. We posed for photos and signed footballs for charity.

I realized something that night. All of us had lived through a time of change in our society. It was not just James and I who had lived in and through a painful era. We all had.

Things would never be the way they were. Odds are, a coach will never stay at Auburn twenty-five years like Coach Jordan. Also, it would be the last time Auburn would field a team with only two black players. That night, James and I received the respect for the contribution we made to Auburn football.

After a while, I was so giddy I didn't mind when a reporter, eager for a quote, came up to me and said, "James, let me ask you about that punt you ran back against Florida." I laughed and corrected him, "I'm not James, I'm the other one."

As the night ended, my teammates went out of their way to make James and me feel that we belonged. The conclusion to this story had finally been written. It had taken thirty years.

[ 1970 ]

# CHAPTER 1

# TO PLAY FOOTBALL AT AUBURN UNIVERSITY

Midnight, New Year's Day, 1970, Daddy raised the old double-barrel shotgun, aimed at the night sky and fired. With a loud "boom" the buckshot tore into the woods behind our house. He waited a couple of seconds. He looked at me with a grin, his white teeth gleaming in the dark. "Boom." Another round of buckshot tore from the gun.

The gun had been my great-grandfather's. It had been passed down to his son to his son, and one day it would belong to me.

"You want to shoot?" my dad asked. "Nah," I answered.

When I was twelve, I begged to shoot that gun. "Daddy, Daddy, let me shoot," I would plead. "Nah," he answered. "The kick is too strong." Yet, when I protested long enough, he gave in. "Okay." He handed the big, heavy gun over.

"Boom!" The old double-barrel's kick lifted me off my feet, sent me reeling into the side of the house. I couldn't feel my numbed shoulder, but I pretended I wasn't hurt. "You want to shoot the other barrel?" Dad asked. "No, that's okay." Lesson learned.

It was a Birmingham tradition in black neighborhoods all over town to erupt in good-natured gunfire at midnight on New Year's Eve. All up and down our street, people blasted into the air over the woods. Traditionally, you shot out the old, and brought in the new.

Fireworks and shotguns went off everywhere.

On New Year's Day, children played in the streets with their still new, shiny Christmas bicycles, wagons, black dolls, white dolls, cowboy outfits, and for me, my football uniform.

It was also a day filled with family and friends. Uncles, aunts, and cousins came by in a steady stream all day. We wouldn't see them again until the next holiday season and my dad would buy a bottle of whiskey for the occasion.

Mom spent all day in the kitchen, assisted by my sisters. The aroma of fried chicken and cornbread coming from the kitchen was deliciously thick. I ran back and forth all morning asking "Is it ready yet?"

Dad chopped a block of ice and he and I hand cranked our old ice cream maker filled with cream, sugar, ice, and vanilla.

That afternoon was filled with crispy fried chicken, buttery cornbread, and macaroni and cheese. Mom cooked black-eyed peas for health and collared greens for money. Homemade vanilla ice cream was joined by dark, rich, chocolate cake.

After dinner, we kicked back and enjoyed college football's biggest day. The games in 1970 on New Year's Day were the Sugar Bowl, Rose Bowl, Orange Bowl, and Cotton Bowl. I watched all of them.

But it was the game the night before that had really held my interest. I'd watched the University of Houston put a 36-7 whupping on my favorite team, the Auburn Tigers, in the Bluebonnet Bowl.

I loved watching and listening to Auburn games. That New Year's Eve, I had a resolution. Each year, Mom would always insist we write our resolutions down. "Set your goals. That way you know you can't fall short."

This year I had a secret resolution. I went into my room and shut the door. "Write it down," rang in my ears. Pen and paper in hand, I pondered. Dare I write it? If I wrote it, I'd have to do it.

I'd been planning to do it since the fourth grade, but I knew plenty of reasons I would not get to. Racism, lack of money, segregation, and fear were all good reasons for me to back down.

I scribbled the words down. I looked on them with pride. I buried the paper deep in my brown wallet. Didn't tell Mama. Didn't tell Daddy. They would be afraid for me. I figured they'd know soon enough. That piece of paper would remain in my wallet for the next four years.

Naiveté can be a beautiful thing. The fact that I'd grown up in the fiercely segregated south of Birmingham, Alabama never deterred me. Nothing ever made me think I couldn't do what I wanted.

Why would it? I'd grown up a Rover Boy.

In the tiny library of Our Lady of Fatima Catholic School, I'd gotten hooked on The Rover Boys, a series of books by Arthur M. Winfield about life in the early 1900s. I first met The Rover Boys in *The Rover Boys at School*. When I discovered these three brothers, I would spend long afternoons on trips around the world while never leaving home. I soon journeyed alongside the boys in the rest of the books, *The Rover Boys on the Ocean, The Rover Boys in the Jungle, The Rover Boys Out West*.

Tom, Dick, Sam, and I got to be buddies. Every adventure they had, I traveled along with them. They didn't merely have adventures; their lives were adventures. So why not mine? I figured the only difference between me and the Rover Boys was they were rich.

While books and an education gave me a taste of what was possible, they were not the only reasons for my confidence. Even though we were deep in the dark ages of segregation and racism, my parents, relatives, and neighborhood showered me with affection and support. I was allowed to dream. Our neighborhood of blue-collar, hard-working people, primarily from rural Alabama towns, could see "times were changing."

The civil rights movement, the women's liberation movement, and the Vietnam War protests were broadcast daily into our living rooms. Watching the evening news, we saw the body bags from Vietnam, we saw the war protesters being bullied by National Guardsmen, we saw children in Birmingham being hit with water bursts from fire hoses and attacked by police dogs. Television brought us somber photos of Emmett Till, the young black boy in Mississippi killed for whistling at a white woman. I remember watching the chilling scene of the Chicago dormitory where Richard Speck killed eight student nurses. Assassinations, murders, wars, sit-ins, and presidential debates were all brought into our living rooms nightly through the power of television; first in black and white, then in color.

Slowly, grudgingly, the changes came to the South and our small community of Rosalind Heights. When the prodding of the federal government and a determined citizenry came knocking in Birmingham, doors swung open. Black people could explore options never before possible. They were able to govern their own lives.

The elders of my community fought the civil rights fight for us younger ones. We were charged to take the baton of change and run headlong into the New South with it.

Dad worked three jobs most of my life. He did what it took for my two sisters and me to attend Catholic schools for twelve years, then college. My mom sewed our clothes, made creative dinners, and ruled the house; ensuring that we would be good citizens and make positive contributions to our community and country. My parents insisted that we were going to college. It wasn't a hope or a suggestion. It was mandatory.

My sisters and I attended Our Lady of Fatima, an all-black school with black lay teachers, white nuns, a white priest, and mass every morning. There were no sports teams. No physical education. No band or debate teams; nothing but school and the little library.

After school, the boys would organize games on the big empty field a block from the school. After I ripped a tear in the knee of my blue uniform pants, I started bringing an extra pair of old pants for our games.

Upon graduation from Our Lady of Fatima, I fought my mom to go to the public high school with my neighborhood buddies, Cool, Duck, Pat, and Bubba, but Mama would have none of it.

Mama felt we'd get a better education at the Catholic school. When my friends at the black public school received their books, they would already be signed with another kid's name. The books were hand-me-downs from the white kids. Many of the materials and equipment in the black public schools were used and had been passed down from the white public schools.

Going to Catholic schools in my white shirt and navy blue pants, earned me the nickname "white boy" from some of the kids in our neighborhood. Mama knew we'd be criticized for our educational and religious choices and she prepared me for the criticism "that comes with getting ahead."

Come fall of 1966, I left the comfort of segregation for the discomfort of integration.

In 1966, the newly expanded "American Dream" opened up for me. Worlds that had previously existed in parallel universes came together because of Mama's determination to give us the best education possible. That year, I became one of six black freshmen to attend John Carroll High School. John Carroll, an oasis in a sea of racial swirl, was a Catholic school of white, Italian, Middle Eastern, and Greek students, plus fifteen black students.

I fought my parents for weeks about going to the "white school" across town. I wanted no part of it. Mama had attended Immaculata, the Catholic high school her father helped build for black students in Birmingham. I, along with my sisters, had attended a Catholic elementary school for blacks since first grade. There were at least three white Catholic schools between our home and our school, but they were not integrated. "Why did we have to go to a school so far away?" I would ask.

Attending John Carroll meant we had to take four city buses a day to go back and forth. Mama convinced Daddy the education we'd receive was worth it. Daddy got an extra job to pay the tuition and bus fares, so we went. My sisters made the daily trips fun. We played games from the back seat of the bus.

John Carroll was the best thing that ever happened to me. I learned early to survive, then to thrive in two separate worlds; between my black neighborhood and my white classmates.

John Carroll was located high on a hill across from a well-kept city park in a beautiful part of town. The school consisted of three buildings: the nuns' residence, the school, and the gym. The city bus would stop right in front of the school.

My two worlds never collided. I traveled between them. I was the lone ambassador so it became easy to maneuver back and forth. I spoke the language of my neighborhood, which gave me black credibility. I spoke the language of the whites I went to school with. I learned to understand the rationale of their culture. I learned how the system works for the majority. I learned about options and opportunities. My education went far beyond books. It was my first taste of another world and I drank fully from that cup.

At John Carroll, the teachers were all white. Still, I was nurtured, treated fairly, even loved. A popular three-sport athlete, I wrote for the school newspaper, became a student government representative, and made many friends.

My favorite teacher, Miss Hilda Horn, a legendary John Carroll educator, became my friend. She was someone I could talk to and she encouraged my growth. A speech teacher, she challenged me to pursue my talents. She started with a serious critique to a silly speech I'd given on how to fry a hot dog. Everyone in the class laughed except her. She kept me after class. "You know you can be good at this," she told me. She shared her notes with me, pointed out my strengths and things I needed to work on. She concluded by saying, "You have talent. What do you want to do with it?" Before long, with her encouragement, I was writing for the school newspaper.

Miss Horn later cast me in a small role in the school play. It was my first time being on stage. Miss Horn and I were friends until her death. A dedicated educator, she died at the school on July 12, 2002. Her photo is in my office. It always will be.

Socially, things started to get awkward. My junior year, a white girl and I developed a friendship. We would talk on the phone for long hours at night, flirt during the day. Miss Horn encouraged our "fondness." One day, she encouraged me to ask her out. "I can't do that," I said. "Why?" she would ask in return. What could I say? The girl and I could talk on the phone, but we both knew that at that time, there were still limits.

One evening in downtown Birmingham, I got off the bus with some of my John Carroll friends after football practice. We were laughing and talking when suddenly, I saw my dad across the street sweeping the entrance to the City Federal Building. I told the guys I had to go and left them on the street corner.

I knew most of the kids in our school came from working-class families, but I still wanted to keep my worlds separate. I told myself I wasn't ashamed of my dad; all the men in our neighborhood had a "side hustle" to make ends meet. I just didn't want my friends to know my dad did janitorial work to afford to pay my tuition. I remember being speechless, confused, and embarrassed.

I was ashamed to see my dad sweeping and I was ashamed of myself for feeling that way.

When I talked to Daddy about it later, he understood. That was why he wanted me to go to college; so I wouldn't have to sweep up behind people. I felt better after talking about it, but I know it hurt when I told him.

Later, when the cleaning service made him a supervisor, my dad got me a job cleaning. I didn't last long. It did not take long for me to see that for years he had put up with things I would not stand for. In one office I cleaned, the occupant would throw his daily bag of roasted peanut shells on the floor. Everyday. Every shell. There would not be one shell in the garbage can. Not one. My pride would not allow me to stand for it. Plus, I didn't have to. But my dad did. If he had not taken the crap he took, my sisters and I would never have had the opportunities we did. He did what he had to do for us. All he asked in return was that we take advantage of the opportunities he was providing.

John Carroll was my first chance to play organized sports. I tried out for the freshman basketball team along with two other black students, Marion Humphrey and John Mardis. Our coach, Richard Porter, also coached the varsity featuring Pat Sullivan, who would later win the Heisman Trophy at Auburn.

Coach Porter taught us the fundamentals of the game. He taught me to use my body underneath the bucket and how to use my left hand. Most importantly, he taught me how to cope with my new world.

In late fall of 1966, the freshmen were scheduled to play our first two games. The opponents would be all-white Mountain Brook High School and Berry High School. They were known to us blacks as the "over the mountain" teams, because Birmingham is divided by a small mountain range that separates the more affluent suburban communities from Birmingham's mostly black and working-class neighborhoods.

None of that stuff mattered to our team; we were ready to play ball. It turns out they weren't.

A day before the first game, Coach Porter summoned the three black freshmen, Marion, John, and me for a talk. He cut right to the chase. The two schools refused to play if any black athletes played. The games were being held in their gyms and we would not be allowed to participate.

At the time, there was a huge backlash in Alabama to anything mandated by the federal government. Civil rights sparked the biggest backlash. When the federal courts ruled that the city of Montgomery had to integrate its library, city officials had all of the chairs taken out so that people could use the books but they could not sit to read. When the courts decreed that Montgomery must integrate the rest rooms at the municipal airport, they simply locked them.

Despite federal orders, Birmingham still had not desegregated its schools. It still refused to integrate its public parks. That meant no interaction between whites and blacks on playing fields. There were games for whites and there were games for blacks.

Coach Porter told us that if we wanted, the school would refuse to play. We were pleased to hear that and thought it was a good idea, until we thought of our teammates. They had worked as hard as we had. They would be deprived of playing too. What were we supposed to do? It was a dilemma that Coach Porter and Birmingham society asked three black fourteen-year-olds to decide.

We told the coach that if we couldn't play we'd go and cheer for our teammates.

That suggestion was greeted by silence. We didn't get it. We couldn't show our faces in their gym. Period! Ouch!

I don't remember the exact words Coach Porter used to explain, but he informed us that we were now involved in a more important issue than a basketball game. We were changing a way of life in Birmingham. He did promise we would beat the hell out of them when we played in our gym.

At the time, it was cold comfort and yeah, we did kick their asses later, but being left out still hurt.

I didn't know what to say to my friends in the neighborhood. Balancing two worlds at fourteen is quite an undertaking. "You didn't make the team?" they asked. "Yeah, well I made it, but... it's a long story," was my response. "Told you them white folks wouldn't let you play," my friend, Bubba said. What else could I say? My parents quietly, helplessly, watched my disappointment.

THOM GOSSOM JR.

Once I was able to get on the basketball court, Coach made me his defensive stopper. He'd put me on their star players and I'd shut them down. I prided myself on it.

On a cold evening at Tarrant High School, I was all over this boy, denying him the ball, beating him to his spots. He was a good basketball player, but I was the better athlete.

A redneck in the stands didn't like it and he cut loose on me unmercifully. "Hey ref," he shouted. "Get that shine off of the white boy." There weren't many fans in the stands. His voice bounced all over the gym. "Ref, call off the monkey," he shouted. "You know that white boy can't outplay that baboon." My teammates looked at me with concern. I kept my eyes down, pretended I didn't hear him. "The white boy ain't got a chance against that coon," he continued.

At last, Coach Porter called a time out. It was obvious neither the officials nor the school administrators were going to do anything about the guy. I still remember Coach's words to me. "I can take you out and he wins," he said, referring to the redneck, "or leave you in there and you keep shutting the boy down. Don't let him score a point." With tears in my eyes, I said, "Leave me in coach." I shut the boy down. So much so that the redneck got flustered and left the gym.

Unfortunately, Coach Porter didn't stick around for my last two years of high school. Neither did Coach Hugh Craig, the varsity football coach. Good Catholic schools didn't pay much money. I never got the same respect from the new coaches, James "Mac" McNally in football and Charles Rea in basketball.

I had been groomed by the previous coaches to be a star. Yet, Coach Mac only let me play because I was too talented to keep off the field.

The first game of my senior year we were playing Shades Valley High School, a team we never could beat, even when we had the great Pat Sullivan. Before the game, Coach Mac went around the locker room, "firing each of us up," individually. When he got to John and me he said,

"Mardis, you and Gossom can go out there tonight and do something for your people." I guess we didn't represent our people very well. We were beaten 31-7.

Things got so bad with the coach that my dad, who had just started to come to my games, asked me if I wanted to transfer to another school. Daddy was far more concerned with my education than my being a football star. But he could see that Coach Mac didn't care for me. I told him no, I'd stay.

Initially, my parents had not come to my high school games. Dad was a baseball man. For the longest time, like most Southern black men his age, he loved the Dodgers (first Brooklyn, then Los Angeles). Why? Jackie Robinson had integrated major league baseball with the Dodgers. Dad would sit up late into the night, listening to his radio, trying to hear a Dodger game above the static coming from a West Coast broadcast.

Like most mothers, my mom was afraid I'd get hurt, but she understood my passion. She did learn the game, but she was only interested in football when I was playing.

Another reason my parents did not come to my games was the attitude they would have to face from the white crowds. It was one thing for me to be comfortable being the only black on the field; it was another for my parents to be the only blacks in the stands. They were uncomfortable. Neither had ever been the only black person in a sea of whites faces. Integration was not yet a part of their world.

The John Carroll parents and boosters tried to make my parents feel welcome; a part of the Carroll family. We laugh now at some of the well-meaning parents who would sit down next to my dad, survey the field of all white kids and me, and then ask, "Which one is your son?"

After my senior season, Coach Mac asked John and me about playing college ball. He'd gotten inquiries from a couple of small black colleges. Instead, we expressed interest in playing for either Auburn or Alabama. He looked at us with disgust and walked away. He never mentioned college ball again.

Other than the two coaches, I encountered very little overt racism. My teammates and I partied together and had tons of fun. One evening at Billy Johnson's "over the mountain" Vestavia home, I was invited to stay over. Billy's parents respected our friendship. So did mine. Though the two sets of parents never met, Billy and I got them to agree.

I befriended several girls as well who would call me at home. We'd spend long teenage hours on the phone, talking, talking, and talking. That got my mom's attention. She would demand to know why the white girls were calling me. Again, so much fear surrounded anything to do with integration. I would try to reassure my mom; told her the girls were my friends. Unconvinced, she got Daddy to talk to me. "You know you got to be careful," he said. "Something happen between you and one of those white girls and you know who's going to get into trouble." I tried to assure him things were cool, that I wasn't doing anything that would get me in trouble. "We're just friends, Daddy." He looked at me long and hard, wanting more. I didn't offer any more than that. He accepted my explanation, but he knew better. He walked away shaking his head.

Although I fought Mama not to go to John Carroll, she was right. It was one of the best times of my life.

I was ready for the next step.

As the oldest, I would be the first to go to college. Interested colleges from the Northeast sent me letters. I found it intriguing. Some college "in the North" knew who I was. Me. Living in the blue-collar community of Rosalind Heights outside Birmingham.

That wasn't enough. Why should I have to go to a prestigious college up north? I pulled the folded paper from my wallet and read my New Year's resolution for 1970. "To play football at Auburn University."

CHAPTER 2

# DOC AND CAT

It was one of those rare snow days in Birmingham in the early 1970s. I called home to check on my parents. "There's snow everywhere," Mom said. "Roads frozen, everything closed, the whole town is shut down."

I asked to speak to Dad. "He's gone to work," Mom told me over the phone line.

"Gone to work? How?" I asked.

"He left here walking about three this morning," she answered.

"Damn," I murmured.

My parent's driveway is a steep incline. When it snows it's impossible to get out. Dad, determined not to miss a day of work at ACIPCO Pipe and Foundry, set out on foot three hours before his 6:30 a.m. shift. When Mama protested he said, "Don't work, they don't pay you. " Off he went in the dark of the snowy morning.

That afternoon *The Birmingham News* ran a photo of a solitary man walking between the snowy railroad tracks. Just the man, the railroad tracks, and lots of snow, a poignant shot. We cut out the photo and saved it.

Born "in the country" outside Wetumpka, Alabama, in 1925, my dad, Tom "Doc" Gossom, was the fifth of thirteen children. A child sharecropper until he left home for the Army at eighteen, Dad didn't miss work, ever. In thirty-five years at ACIPCO he missed six days, three of which he was in the hospital, in traction. He worked outdoors in the loading yard in all weather; rain, sun, snow, heat, and cold.

Each day at 2:30 p.m., after he got off his day job, he came home to eat dinner. Within an hour, he was gone again to his second job at a janitorial service in Birmingham's downtown buildings. After cleaning for several years, he was made a supervisor.

During the week, Dad and I rarely saw each other. We never had time to play catch, or do the father-son things I saw on television. Each day, I caught the school bus to get back to school from our football practice field. I then caught a city bus to downtown where I transferred to the #20 bus to get home. I rarely got home before 9:00 in the evening. Dad would get home between 10:30 and 11:00 and we would only get a few minutes to talk before heading to bed to do it again the next day.

On Saturdays, my dad did plumbing with his friend and mentor, Willie "Goat" Stewart. Goat was not a licensed plumber, but he could fix any plumbing problem for half the cost of a regular plumber. He taught Dad his trade and they would crawl under old houses with low, damp, crawl spaces and old clay pipes. They'd fix the plumbing problem and that evening, Dad would bring home a few extra bucks.

Sundays, Dad stayed home. It was the only day he didn't work, and we would all go to Our Lady of Fatima Catholic Church. After church there was a big family meal and lots of conversation. Those afternoons, Dad talked a lot about education.

Dad liked to tell us stories that reminded us why we kids were expected to work so hard at school. "Growing up," Dad would tell us, "we were really poor. We ate what we grew or killed. I knew an education could get me a better life. I liked school. But every time my brother Acon and me got started in school, Papa would take us out of school to work. He rented us out to local farmers. He could get fifty cents a day for us."

Dad would shake his head, "All we ever did was work the fields. We could never get ahead. Once we'd get the crops in, Mr. Fitzpatrick, the white man whose land we sharecropped, always figured the numbers up where we never made any money. We always owed him. One time he figured things up and Papa came out ahead by $44. He refigured things and said we owed him money. Papa never got any money.

"My brother Sonny left when he was eighteen and signed up for the army. He served in three wars. When I turned eighteen, I'd never been farther than downtown Wetumpka, but I was ready to leave. I signed up too."

Mom also believed in education, but for different reasons. One of seven children and known affectionately as "Cat" by her family, Catherine Tankersley attended twelve years of Catholic school. She pleased her domineering father by making straight A's throughout high school, and by "staying out of trouble." Eventually she would graduate from Business College. She knew that smart, young, black women in Birmingham with a degree could become a secretary, or a receptionist in a medical office.

My mother's father, James "Tank" Tankersley, was a tough little man who owned a service station and rental apartments. He was a light skinned man. Back then, light-skinned blacks were considered closer to "being white." Many thought of themselves as a step above dark-skinned blacks.

Tank ran a tight ship at home with his children, particularly his girls. Light-skinned and freckled, my mom defied her father by falling in love with the dark-skinned country boy who climbed trees for the city, my dad. With no other choice, they eloped.

My mom made sure we were well-rounded citizens within our financial constraints. She would join book clubs and there were always books and magazines in the house. She joined record clubs and we all got to choose the records. We kids chose the Supremes, Temptations, Aretha Franklin, James Brown, and other soul crooners. Mom got us to listen to Robert Goulet, Lena Horne, Johnny Mathias, Frank Sinatra, Perry Como, Nancy Wilson, and Neal Diamond. She would sing along with the records. We collected a set of Bill Cosby comedy albums; Mom would sit and laugh at Cosby with us.

By the mid-1960s, my parents had three children and had saved enough money to buy a modest house in a community northeast of the Birmingham Airport called Rosalind Heights.

Like a lot of Southern blacks, my parents thought about following the black migration to the promised lands of Los Angeles, Chicago, and Detroit. Several of my dad's and my mom's sisters and brothers struck out for Los Angeles, where black people "could get a fair shake." Others we knew took out for Chicago and Detroit and the promise of a "good job" in a meatpacking plant or automobile factory. My mom and dad decided that they loved being around family and friends in Birmingham and Dad already had a good job.

"The Heights" was a paradise for me, but its location was inconvenient for my parents. In those pre-freeway, one-car-to-a-family days, getting to work, school, and balancing the daily chores of life required some juggling. Dad usually drove the car to work. The children caught the daily city buses to get across town to school. Mama, who ran the home and our lives, kept the car when she needed it.

The Heights was filled with blue-collar, working-class families; it was a churchgoing, gossiping, neighbor-watching, home-owning, normal, prejudiced neighborhood of Alabamians in the 1960s. The men, who had mainly migrated from the rural areas of Alabama, hitched their belts up every day and went out to provide for their families and the women took care of the homes, finances, and children.

All the money Dad brought home went to necessities. The Catholic school tuition took priority. We never went to bed hungry, but funds were always tight. If we wanted something beyond our needs, Dad would work during his vacation.

We always had plenty of food. My parents would buy a cow with one of their friends. We got half and the other family got half. The meat would be prepared at a packinghouse in Bessemer, a city west of

Birmingham. We'd pick it up. The meat would be cut, packaged, and labeled into steaks, hamburger, etc. We stored it away in our freezer. We would have beef for days. Mama would do the same with vegetables she got from the farmers' market. She'd buy a bunch of vegetables. We all had to help shuck, cut, pull, or whatever needed to be done. We'd pack the vegetables in plastic and store them in the freezer.

Our small yellow house had three bedrooms and a carport. Dad literally dug out the basement with a pick, shovel, and wheelbarrow to create a storage space underneath the house. He built a barbeque pit for cookouts and a doghouse for my dog Tippy. Of course, on all his work adventures around the house, I was drafted as his reluctant assistant.

Occasionally, my sisters and I would hear my parents arguing. Money would be at the root of many of them. If Mama bought a nicety rather than a necessity it could light Daddy's fuse, but Mama would make sure he found out too late to do anything about it. They had a couple of loud arguments over Daddy getting home later than his usual time from his second job. Our little home wasn't perfect, but when Daddy finally came home at night, and the family was intact, we felt safe, loved.

In the Heights, integration was something people fought for on television. The only time we saw white people in our neighborhood was when they came to sell insurance, encyclopedias, or something for the house. There would also be the occasional slow drive through the neighborhood by the sheriff.

Throughout the Heights, ran a deep skepticism about anything white people had to say. When the U.S. went to the moon and the astronauts did a moonwalk, the elders in the Heights said it was bull----. "It's television," they declared. "Tommy, don't believe it," an elderly Mr. Deloach told me. "Those people are in some television studio somewhere." Mr. Burke, another neighbor, said it was a trick to get black people to leave the earth. He insisted the white people were going to the moon and were going to leave the black people on earth. To that idea, some said, "Good riddance."

If it seems they spent an inordinate amount of time thinking and worrying about white people, you're right. Black people in the South learned early to live in two worlds. The one with Mr. Charley, white men were always referred to as "Mr. Charley," and the one without. Most of the people in our neighborhood were pawns in the white world. They had no standing. In Alabama, the white world still required a black man to have a "good white man" to negotiate the white world. The sponsoring white man could vouch for his black's standing, credit worthiness, and any legal matter that might arise.

My dad had several, and Mr. Funk, who ran the service station where my dad traded, was one. The man who ran the Western Auto would give my dad credit. My dad also met a lawyer while cleaning the downtown offices. Other than the white priests and nuns at our church and school, these were the only white people we knew. Most of the black folks preferred the safety of the all black world.

Very little civil rights activism took place in the Heights. Some of the kids from the public school participated in the downtown marches, but none of my friends did.

My parents did not encourage or discourage activist thinking. We were encouraged to think for ourselves. We were readers. Everyone in our house read the newspaper. We had political and social discussions at the weekend breakfast table. Daddy believed in the Democrats. In his lifetime, he said, "Democrats have always been for the little man."

Progressive activist talk from me would lead my dad to give me one of his cautionary talks about, "The white man kicking the black man's ass in Elmore County," where he grew up. Mama would always pooh-pooh this talk, telling Dad not to discourage me. "He can do and be anything he wants," she would tell Dad.

As soon as we boys could, we followed the examples of our fathers and got jobs. At twelve, I borrowed my dad's lawnmower and gas can. My friend, Cool, and I cut grass all summer.

As teenagers, my friends and I loved going to downtown Birmingham. We'd make a little money, get dressed up, catch a bus for town with our money burning a hole in our pockets, and hit the town.

My favorite part of these trips was going to the movies. While Cool and the guys went for the fashions, in the shops along Fourth Avenue, I had to set aside part of my money to buy uniforms for school; another one of Mama's rules.

The Carver and the Famous theaters were the two black movie theaters in the bustling black downtown business district. White downtown was starting to integrate its stores, but black downtown still thrived. The Carver and Famous were like the nice theater palaces of the era with lights, posters, and red velvet curtains.

My uncle, James Tankersley, was a projectionist at the Famous Theater. He was a movie buff by virtue of having seen every movie that was ever released into the theater where he worked. He knew any and all movie trivia. "Hey Tommy," he'd say, "What movie did Joan Crawford win the Oscar for?" I'd say I don't know. He would announce, "*Mildred Pierce* released in 1945." He'd immediately start with another question. "What year was *Cabin in the Sky* released?"

A half block from the Famous Theatre was the Carver. I loved passing by the giant marquee. Looking at the posters of coming attractions. Getting swept up in the welcoming blinking lights. Once inside, in the darkness of the theater, we would see two movies, a short feature, a cartoon, and previews of loud action-packed coming attractions. I was transported away to another world.

Up until the so-called Blaxploitation movies of the seventies, black theaters showed mainly movies featuring white actors. I maxed out on John Wayne, Elvis, and Tarzan. It was always strange to witness a theater full of black folks cheering on Tarzan kicking the native's ass. One white man could kick a whole jungle full of Africans.

By 1970, I ventured into the Alabama Theater on Third Avenue North in white downtown Birmingham. "The Showplace of the South," as it was called, had integrated and this was my first visit. I was alone. I've always liked going to movies alone. I checked out the coming attraction posters and stepped inside.

The theater was beautiful. There was a huge pipe organ on stage. Beautiful red curtains and velvet everywhere. The theater was half full. I chose a seat away from everybody. No one bothered me. There were no stares. No incidents. When the lights went down, I enjoyed the film.

At home, my New Year's secret was out. I applied to Auburn and was accepted.

"Why Auburn?" Mom wanted to know. I didn't know anybody there. I didn't apply to any other schools. While she did research on the school and its academic programs, my dad looked it up on the map. Finding it was in the country, he wondered aloud if I'd lost my mind. My dad was worried for me. He'd grown up around rural whites.

I'd decided to major in either journalism or TV/Radio/Film. Auburn did not have a great program, but by going there, I could play for my favorite team and study what I enjoyed learning. My mind was made up. I was going to play football even though I still had not talked to anyone connected to Auburn about that. They didn't know I existed.

"Did I get any mail?" I asked daily. "Not yet," would be the response from Mom. Every day we hoped for some money for college. Daddy was already working two jobs and taking on more plumbing with Goat. I worked at Shoney's Big Boy™ Restaurant on weekends and saved my money.

Two important pieces of paper were delivered to our mailbox on the same day. They both held good news.

The first was my deferment from military service. Like all young men in the country, at the time, within six months of turning eighteen, I had to register with the Selective Service. Thousands of young men were being drafted every month and most ended up in Vietnam. As long as I was in college, I would be deferred from military service.

The second piece of mail I'd received would help keep me in school. We'd gotten the money! I was given a loan and a grant, totaling $1,500. That total was divided into a $750 loan and a $750 grant. The money would cover my tuition, books, and rent. I would use my savings and whatever my parents could give me in spending money to pay for food and other incidentals. I was guaranteed one year of school.

In August, our 1965 lavender Chevy Impala headed down I-85 toward Auburn. Doc and Cat in the front seat of the car were quiet. I was in the back seat. Occasionally, I'd catch my dad looking at me in the rearview mirror. They were taking their son to college. They were proud and nervous. There were no life roadmaps to help them negotiate this critical family event. No one in our family or extended family had gone off to one of the big, white, state universities before.

We drove 150 miles southeast of Birmingham. Finally, we passed Exit 32 for Tuskegee-Franklin. We were getting close. Shortly thereafter, I announced, "There's the exit sign." I pointed. "Auburn University."

The road from the freeway to campus was bordered by acres and acres of farmland, large tracts as far as you could see with cows, horses, and white fences. "Looks like the plantations from down home," Daddy said sourly.

We crossed into the city limits of Auburn and drove onto the majestic campus. I remember well the look of satisfaction on Mom's face, the look of nervous determination on Dad's. I would get to live their dream, but the rest was up to me.

# CHAPTER 3

# AUBURN AND INTEGRATION COLLIDE

**TELEGRAM**

March 22, 1965.

TO: Dr. Ralph Draughon, President of Auburn University.

The march on Montgomery to end discriminating in voting and police brutality is one of the historic events in the realization of democracy in the state of Alabama.

STOP.

I am calling on all students of colleges and universities of this state to join with us in building a new south where men of all races might live together.

STOP.

I am asking in justice and brotherhood that faculty and students of Tuskegee Institute, Selma University, Alabama State College, University of Alabama, Auburn University, Talladega College, Stillman College, Miles College and Birmingham Southern, join us in the dramatic attempt to lay the cornerstone of a true democracy at the state Capitol Thursday, March 25 at noon where we will join men of all faiths and democratic principle from all over the nation.

STOP.

Signed: Dr. Martin Luther King Jr.

President Southern Leadership Conference

---

This telegram arrived on Dr. Draughon's desk while Auburn was already preoccupied with its own attempts to participate in the building of a new South.

In 1963, Harold Franklin became the first black student to file an application of admission to Auburn University. Franklin, a graduate of the all black Alabama State College (today, Alabama State University), was denied admission because "he had not attended and/or graduated from an accredited college," a requirement of all candidates for admission to Graduate School. Franklin, represented by Alabama civil rights attorney Fred Gray, went to court. The U.S. District court of Alabama found that "Within the state of Alabama, Mr. Franklin could not meet such a requirement since the state did not offer higher education available to Negro students in an accredited college."

On November 5, 1963, Judge Frank Johnson ordered that Franklin be admitted to Auburn. The Auburn president, Dr. Draughon, and the board of trustees filed a counter suit in an effort to block Franklin's admission, but they were denied.

On November 28, the Auburn trustees accepting the inevitable, voted to accept Franklin as a student "for the welfare of the university community."

Dean James Foy was the most recognizable face of the administration during the time. Today, even after his death in 2010, the former dean of men is still an Auburn legend and favorite. After retiring in 1980, he continued to reign as the grand marshal of the student pajama parade, pajamas and all. Dean Foy was called on as recently as the 2007 football season to lead a pep rally of students.

He recalled Franklin's admission. "As Dean of Men and all students, really, I got a call from the judge's office telling me we would be served with the petition telling us Auburn had to integrate. The man drove up from Montgomery. He arrived at my door. He had his little boy with him. He was a white man. He handed me the petition and said, 'I thought you wouldn't be home. That's why I called, so you could leave and not accept this if you didn't want to.'"

Dean Foy accepted the petition because he knew he had to. The Auburn University officials did not want a spectacle. On June 11, 1963, Governor George Wallace attracted national attention when he stood in the doorway at the University of Alabama to symbolically block the way to integration. The black students were able to register over Wallace's televised objections, but the governor got what he wanted: national publicity. Wallace would use the pulpit of television to rail against the northern liberal media, commanding enough attention to be a factor in presidential politics for the next ten years. Regardless of his presidential aspirations, the televised schoolhouse stand was an embarrassment to many in the state of Alabama.

The country watched in disbelief in September of 1963, as riots erupted in Oxford, Mississippi. James Meredith, a black man, had been admitted to the University of Mississippi over the objections of state officials. The backlash was so intense that President John F. Kennedy had to call out the National Guard and two people were killed. Meredith himself was wounded by a gunshot.

In Auburn, plans were put in place to ensure there would be no similar incidents. Powers McLeod, the pastor at Auburn Methodist Church, in his book *Southern Accents, Different Voices* described the Auburn community that autumn as "tense." Mike Warren, McLeod's son-in-law and a 1968 graduate of Auburn, tells the story. "My father-in-law was contacted by the Justice Department and the FBI about Franklin coming to Auburn. The feds wanted to talk to some of the leaders in the community to ensure nothing would happen along the lines of what happened at the University of Alabama or the University of Mississippi. There were rumors that the university gathered everyone in the stadium to prep for the black students' coming."

Dean Foy confirmed the rumor. "Everyone did meet in the stadium. It was after we realized integration was inevitable and that we had better start preparing people for it. Dr. Draughon told everyone, 'We are not in favor of integration, but we are going to do it. We follow the law. We follow the Auburn Creed. Next fall if you find that you can't do that you need to transfer right now, faculty or student.'"

According to *The Plainsman*, the student newspaper, the meeting in the stadium asked for cooperation in the face of Auburn's forced integration.

Draughon, faculty members, and student leaders addressed the mass gathering of students, explaining the situation, and asking the student body to protect Auburn University's good name.

All students were required to sign a pledge that they would "refrain from any conduct, which would in any fashion contribute to disorder and to avoid all activities, which would be in conflict with the high standards expected of Auburn students."

As an added precaution, university policy prohibited students from having "weapons in their rooms, in their cars, or on their person." Possession of a firearm under this edict would result in immediate expulsion.

At Auburn's request, Judge Johnson agreed to postpone the enrollment until January. The university wanted as much time as possible to prepare everyone at the school and in the white community. Auburn was getting tremendous pressure from Governor Wallace. A wild card, Wallace could turn the admission into another spectacle. Auburn officials knew that Wallace was prepared to come down to Auburn to defend the ideals of segregation; on the other side stood the federal government and the law.

Franklin would enroll on January 4, 1964.

Through emissaries, the white ministers of the local community were quietly approached by the university and asked to make contact with Judge Johnson's office, Franklin's attorney, Fred Gray, and with the Department of Justice. Their mission would be to speak with influential persons in their respective churches to "prepare the way in the community for Franklin's admission." This work had to be done in secrecy and "without the university's official knowledge." Friends and neighbors soon turned against each other. A routine trip to the grocery store or the post office for the pro integrationist meant being ignored by former close friends who were staunch segregationists. In schools, students whose parents were segregationists ridiculed children of professors who were pro-integration.

The ministers were certain state officials tapped their phones. Dr. McLeod and others tested their theory by making phone calls to each other announcing that Dr. Martin Luther King was coming to Auburn for a meeting with the ministers. When the police and others knew about the details of the fake meeting and made plans to intercept Dr. King, the ministers knew for sure they were being monitored by phone and followed.

Dr. John Jeffers, of Auburn and former pastor of Auburn Baptist, remembers that time, "I was a product of my upbringing," says Dr. Jeffers, "but as a pastor I had to be everybody's pastor and help people to come together. We were talking about a change in culture. Most of the membership was professors and so I could be more aggressive. We had some die-hards who wanted to maintain the old Southern system, but time would make them change their minds. The stance of the ministers was unanimous in that position."

Christmas 1963: Tension rose as the day for Franklin's admission neared. Dr. McLeod became Auburn's point man with the Justice Department and with John Doer of the Justice Department's Civil Rights division. Dr. McLeod tells the story in *Southern Accents, Different Voices*.

"On the day before Franklin's admission, John Doer called to say that he and his assistant, John Douglas, were unable to find a place to stay in Auburn. I invited Doer to stay with me, and we arranged for John Douglas to stay with Dr. John Evans, the pastor of the Presbyterian Church. On the evening of January 3, which was the day before Harold Franklin was to enter the university, we went to bed with great apprehension."

According to Dr. McLeod, the next morning unfolded quietly into history.

"In the church parking lot was the Justice Department's communications car. Mr. Douglas could talk to anyone in the country from that car. They weren't taking chances. They could have taken over Auburn, both the university and the city, in twenty minutes.

"Mr. Douglas and Mr. Doer went down to the highway where the new student (Franklin) and Mr. Gray were to come into Auburn. The routes they were to use had been agreed on with the state troopers, and everyone knew that the roads would be carefully watched for unauthorized persons.

"The announced plan had been to place barriers on Highway 29 as it came into Auburn so that the meeting of Harold Franklin and his attorney with local authorities would occur before he reached the campus, but the agent said that the barriers had been unexpectedly moved to a spot inside the campus, where a wooded area could offer concealment for people other than the troopers, the plan being to arrest Mr. Gray for coming on the campus. In the confusion, someone would be able to plant a gun or a knife in Mr. Franklin's baggage. We knew that this is what had happened to James Meredith in his room at the University of Mississippi.

"John Douglas looked at me and said, 'That's a trap. They can't go that way.' 'Okay bring them here,' I said. He replied, 'I'm going to ask for two FBI agents and I want them to search Franklin and go through his luggage here before he leaves for the campus. That way, no one can accuse him of having a concealed weapon.' Thus it was that I met Harold

Franklin for the first time, there in my office with everyone on edge. He seemed to be as nervous as the rest of us; he had every reason to be even more so. He didn't strike me as a guy who was hostile enough to be a radical or arrogant enough to be a troublemaker. He was a young man who wanted to break down barriers and have a voice in making a difference."

Harold Franklin's admission into graduate school at Auburn University under a court order, in January 1964, marked the legal end of racial segregation at the university. The national news media descended on Auburn. Seventy-four newsmen from *Newsweek*, The *New York Times*, ABC, CBS, the Associated Press, and United Press International found their way to campus, yet the admission was conducted quietly and without incident. Franklin was heavily monitored and under constant guard.

Franklin's integration would do little to change de facto segregation at the university. Franklin was installed all by himself in one whole wing of the largest dormitory on the campus, kept isolated from the other 11,000 students on campus. The floors below him and above him were kept empty. His isolation negated any positive effect his integration could have had. Franklin said, "I always felt like a guest of the university. That's what I like to refer to it as. Now you can look back on it and laugh. I was angry. I'll make no bones about it. Why couldn't I be put with the rest of the students? I wasn't going to harm them."

Franklin eventually left Auburn to attend the University of Denver. His isolation and disputes with faculty over his choice of a thesis topic are reasons he cites for leaving. "See, I was told what to write on. I didn't have a choice. I wanted to write on something on the concept of civil disobedience, which is one thing I really loved. The people in the history department told me that was too controversial. They instructed me to write on the history of Alabama State College because it had never been written before."

Three weeks after Franklin's departure, the ban on firearms was lifted at the university.

By 1970, not many black people in the state wanted to attend Auburn. Harry Philpott, who would become president in 1965, said in his oral history, "We had a very difficult time in attracting blacks to Auburn." Among the many reasons cited was the lack of a professional black community, Auburn's location in rural southeast Alabama, and the all-black Tuskegee Institute (today, Tuskegee University) was nearby. Long held social customs and traditions were also a contributing factor.

Auburn social life, like most major Southern institutions, has long revolved around the fraternity and sorority system. Traditionally, male students dressed in coat and tie for football games. Corsages and dresses for female students. Women lived on campus in dormitories with enforced curfews. If you were late you found the door locked. Many a teammate had to sneak their Friday night dates into the dorm with the help of a girl already in for the night. The old Southern double standard stood tall. Men could live in fraternity houses, apartments, and the one on campus male dorm, Magnolia Hall. There were no curfews for men.

Among my non-football friends from Auburn are actor Michael "Michael O" O'Neill, who is white, and businessman Henry Michael Ford, who is black. They're both Alabama natives who attended Auburn in the 1970s. Their stories are literally as different as black and white.

"I'd been steered to Auburn all my life," says Michael O. "I have a vivid memory of attending a game with my dad. All these people sitting in the bright sun on a beautiful day watching a team they loved. I got to run out on the field after the game.

"After I arrived on campus as a student I got involved in student government, working with Dr. Philpott and the administration and just had the time of my life."

Michael O remembers a black student that he and some of his fraternity brothers befriended.

"Several of us tried to rush him. We knew there was no chance of getting him to pledge, but we made the effort. It's funny, because most of our guys were indifferent. But there was a vocal hard-core minority who were adamant. Their answer was an absolute no.

"Socially, it was 'not happening' between the majority of blacks and whites. It was tough. In my junior high school in Montgomery there was one black guy in the school. I liked him. I would nod to him and speak. But I admit today, I was not brave enough to befriend him. I would have been ostracized."

Henry began his Auburn journey in 1971. He's from Birmingham and although our fathers both worked for ACIPCO, we didn't meet until we were at Auburn. Henry had no experience with integration. His school, Hayes High, was all black.

"When the high schools started to integrate, I wanted to go to a white school, but my parents said no. They wanted me to go to the school right up the street from our house. A recruiter from Auburn came to my school and I was hooked. The recruiter made me feel like they would welcome black students. So, when I got the chance again, I took it. The pioneer spirit has always been in me. I didn't know one white person in the whole world, but I relished the opportunity to be a pioneer. It excited me."

Coming from an all-black environment, Auburn was an eye-opener for Henry.

"After I got there, there were no black people. I'd never seen anything like that. There was no welcome. It was like I was like everyone else, but of course I wasn't. They sure didn't treat me like everyone else. I didn't want to be in awe, but I was overwhelmed by that experience.

"Every year a few black kids would be admitted but it didn't take long for them to drop out. Either the academics or the lack of a social life got them," he said. "There were still some things like Old South Day where the Kappa Alphas dressed up like Confederates. They would parade through campus on horseback. The girls dressed like Southern belles. This big Confederate flag hung from their porch. It was huge."

There were also blackface parties. In the 1969 issue of the *Glomerata*, the Auburn University annual, there are several photos of the Phi Gamma Delta "jungle" or "island" party on display. Everyone's body was covered in black. Their eye areas are the only white spots on their white bodies.

It should be noted that not everyone on campus belonged to the frat system, or even wanted to. There was a vocal fringe of hippies or "long hairs," as they were called. I gravitated to this group as they followed the examples of students at universities from across the country. They were determined to protest the United States involvement in Vietnam. Peace rallies were small but got a lot of local press and campus-wide attention. Still, the hippies' thinking so thoroughly deviated from the Auburn political norm they were dismissed by critics as cowards just afraid of getting drafted.

For the most part though, we were set apart. Henry remembers, "I believe the administration's intention was to treat us all the same. For that they were to be commended. But you can't legislate someone's heart. Those kids wanted nothing to do with us. There was some overt racism. Off campus, I had an incident with the Klan. On campus there was a professor who was notorious for failing black students. I took his class as a challenge. Studied hard. Knew my stuff. I thought I'd aced the test. I failed. I know I didn't fail. What could I do? I dropped the class. Took it the next quarter from another professor and passed."

Parallel lives existed on campus between most black and white students. The fraternity and sorority system ruled separate and unequal. Those who tried to push for change were rebuffed.

Gloria Owens, wife of team member James Owens, recalls, "My first year in the dorm, I checked into my room. I was moving my stuff in when my roommate showed up. It was a white girl. I said hi. She turned around and walked out. She went downstairs and got them to change her room. I never saw her again."

The situation became a little better when the first black fraternity was started. "In 1972, after the Omegas were chartered," Henry shares, "there were enough blacks to have a party in a tiny apartment. The apartment would be full with maybe twenty people. Sometimes we would have to get girls from the community to come. Those parties were major happenings during that time."

Throughout those early years at Auburn, the few black students on campus did make attempts to integrate themselves into the school social system. Several of the young women tried out for cheerleader. None made it. Guys like George Smith, from Birmingham, got involved in student government. Henry, Clayton Kellum, and John Mardis tried out for the football team. All could play, but none of them received a formal scholarship.

Anthony Copeland was elected vice president of the student body. He was the first black student to hold a general campus office. According to Dr. Philpott, "Unfortunately, the other black students felt that he was currying favor with the whites and looked upon him as something of a Uncle Tom, which distressed him tremendously. I think he left school during that year. He never did graduate."

In spite of Auburn's less-than-glorious history with desegregation, Auburn University was the school I was determined to attend. As a child, I'd first decided to be the first black player to play for the legendary University of Alabama football coach, Bear Bryant. The challenge excited me. I imagined it as another Rover Boy adventure, but the more I watched, the more I listened, I began to fall in love with the Auburn Tigers. Something about Auburn resonated with a little black boy growing up outside Birmingham, Alabama. Why not be the first black player at Auburn?

I didn't know one black person at Auburn before arriving there. I did not know the courage of Harold Franklin. What I knew of Auburn University, I learned from the radio listening to football games.

Auburn became special in my eyes. The University of Alabama would win national championships but Auburn became my team.

On Saturdays, I would let the radio broadcast of Auburn games carry me away. I imagined myself being there on a crisp fall day. I imagined the crowd, the colors. There was another quirk to listening to games on the radio. There was no skin color. It didn't matter. I'd never been to a game, so I could imagine it anyway I wanted. I could dream of being on the receiving end of one of those Pat Sullivan bombs. I could dream of making a difference.

When the NFLs Washington team became the last in the league to integrate, Bobby Mitchell, a versatile runner and receiver, was the player they selected. I admired him and patterned my game after him. I never told the equipment manager, the coaches, or any of the players at Auburn why I chose to wear number 49. It wasn't a cool number like 22, 44, and 88. I wore 49 in honor of Bobby Mitchell.

I was ready to make history at Auburn, but someone else would beat me to it.

As significant as Harold Franklin's forced integration is to Auburn's history, Auburn University administrators would make a more daring and ironic volunteer move just four years later when they took the bold lead to sign the first black athletes in the Deep South. With the signings, Auburn University and the Southern sports landscape would be forever altered.

# CHAPTER 4

---

# HENRY AND THE BIG O

When Henry Harris pulled on his number 25 Auburn University basketball jersey, he was usually smiling with his tight Afro, gleaming teeth, taut muscles, and his six-foot-three-inch frame crouched in the ready position. He found his freedom in basketball. He controlled the court. He was the captain, the best player and, on the court, he was happy.

In 1968, Henry became Auburn's first black athlete and the first black athlete in the Deep South.

According to Dr. Philpott, who was president when Auburn signed Henry, "We had a lunch for the board of trustees at my home. I told them that we were about to sign our first black athlete. One of the trustees spoke up and said, 'Oh, we can't do that. The state is not ready for that.' Auburn's athletic recruiter responded by saying that he had taken a black athlete to dinner trying to help coaches recruit him to Auburn. The trustee was very surprised at that. When others told him that this was inevitable, he said, 'All right. I won't say anything more. It probably is time.'"

Henry came to Auburn from the one-traffic-light town of Boligee, Alabama. "Nothing to do but walk and play basketball," he told me. A born storyteller, Henry would keep us laughing with poor man stories of his hometown; but on the basketball court, Henry Harris became an Auburn star. As a freshman, he dropped forty-two points on Kentucky's freshman team. He led Auburn's freshman team in scoring, averaging 20.5 points and 9.7 rebounds. He led Auburn to victory in the Vanderbilt Classic and made the All-Tournament team.

Early on, Henry was the heart and soul of the team, but during his sophomore year, he blew his knee out and needed season ending surgery. The team needed him though and surgery was postponed. He continued to play with his knee bandaged so tightly he could hardly bend it. His team needed him at forward. While others played his natural guard position, he became a workhorse, battling much bigger men for rebounds. He played on his bum knee throughout the rest of the season and because of that, he was never the same.

His averages dropped. He limped his way through junior and senior seasons, but still made third team All-Conference. Even with the injury, on most nights, Henry was still the best player on the court. He ended up averaging 11.8 points along with 6.7 rebounds for his career.

On the court he was as smooth as silk. Off the court was a different story. No effort was made to assimilate Henry into university life. No social organization offered to smooth Henry's transition. He was on his own.

Lonely and isolated, Henry lived the way he played. He was like a cat, moving in and out of spaces, quietly, unhappy, and most of the time alone. In his first year, he was the only black athlete in the athletic dormitory of more than a hundred athletes. He never had a roommate.

Perry Wallace, the first black athlete in the Southeastern Conference, at Vanderbilt University in 1967-68 explained it this way, "I have been there myself. It's a very lonesome thing. People knew my name but weren't interested in knowing me."

Henry never had a car but managed to get where he wanted to go. He never had many visitors. No family at his games. He passed the classes he needed to pass to remain eligible for basketball. Henry's happy moments were few and far between. He was happiest "across the tracks," where the black folks lived. There, he was the hero who had integrated Auburn athletics. Back at school, he was the dirt-poor student who sold his books, clothing, and food to earn spending money.

Once, I asked Henry why come to Auburn. Why be the pioneer if it made him so unhappy? I'll never forget his answer. "I did it for the old folks."

In 1969, James "Big O" Owens became Auburn's first black football player and the first black football player at a major state institution in Alabama, Georgia, the Carolinas, Mississippi, and Louisiana.

At six-foot-three, James was 215 pounds of lean muscle. He was recruited by Nebraska, Tennessee, Oklahoma, Kentucky, Ohio State, as well as many others; about sixty in all. "Recruiting was exciting. Like a dream," James recalls. "I was a poor boy. I got a chance to go visit places that I never dreamed of. I only heard about them. And it felt good to be pampered."

What made James Owens so attractive? In addition to his size he was blessed with great speed. In high school he scored twenty-one touchdowns, made All-Metro, All-State, and All-American. In basketball, he averaged sixteen rebounds and fourteen points a game. In track, Owens ran legs on the 220 and 440-yard relay teams. He finished third in the state in the high jump. To top it all off, he was a courteous, respectful, religious young man. Most evenings after practice he could be found either in the television room of the dorm or in his room reading the Bible. He was a coach's dream.

James says, "I never really thought about it, being the first black. I looked forward to the level of the game. I was the first black to play at my high school. You saw these things on television. But you didn't imagine the day-to-day of going through integration. I guess it was the Lord's will.

"I didn't realize at first I would be a pioneer," James tells me. "I just didn't focus on that. I did not know what to expect. I wanted people to like me but I wanted respect more. The biggest thing was to get respect. After I got there I realized how much I was under the spotlight. You know, everyone went out of his or her way to be nice. People on campus were excited. They were anxious to see what their first black could do.

"Besides the normal things of being away from home and making my own decisions, I had to deal with the black-white thing. Right after I arrived on campus, I was told by the coaches to get a haircut. You know, my hair has never been long, but I went downtown to a barber who told me, 'Son, please get out of here, you will ruin my business.' He was terrified someone would see me in his shop. That kind of set the tone for me."

The first two black athletes formed a friendship; a year later, I would join them. "Henry came a year before me," Owens remembers. "And he was a big brother type to me because that was the first time I had been away from home. I think it was Henry's first time being away. He taught me. He encouraged me. There was no one there to teach him or encourage him. If Henry hadn't been there, I probably would have left Auburn."

The administration, both academic and athletic, saw their role as making sure no differences existed between the students. The problem was that we were different, in a state that had always treated us as different. We were left on our own to build bridges with a culture that did not want bridges. The dominant culture did not include us, and there were not enough of us to either demand diversification or diversify on our own.

After I arrived at Auburn, Henry and James became my big brothers. Henry would take me around town; he liked going to Vans, the nightclub on the black side of town with patrons as old as my parents. Henry and I resembled each other and some people thought we were brothers. Henry introduced me to the few black students on campus and some of the girls in the community. We found our way to Tuskegee Institute, the black college twenty miles down Highway 29.

James was our spiritual guide. We all looked up to him. In later years when the number of blacks in the athletic dormitory increased, we all referred to James as, "Daddy Owens." I still call him Daddy O. He was like our fathers; strong, quiet, didn't complain.

Henry and James were highly recruited stars. On the other hand, I came to Auburn to get an education. The biggest difference was in our educational backgrounds. I had a great fundamental elementary and high school education. I was already familiar with the freshman schoolwork at Auburn.

James and Henry had come from a different background. Sports were their ticket. Lack of academic preparedness, no social life, and no economic means had to be conquered through the world of sports. If they made it through, professional sports waited on the other side. If only they could get there.

I was more suited for the pioneer role. I'd done it before. Having lived in two worlds since I was fourteen, it didn't bother me as much to not fit in. In some ways, the only thing James, Henry, and I initially had in common was that we were black athletes at Auburn.

The beautiful thing about our relationship was that we thoroughly supported each other. We knew we were on a journey. To successfully complete our journey we would need each other. They supported my going to school. They knew I wanted to graduate. If that happened, I would be the first.

Some days James would wake me. Make sure I headed off to class. I'd ask, "You coming?" He'd say, "I'll be on." I knew he wouldn't. It's frustrating and embarrassing to be a hero in one facet of life and not be able to conquer another.

James tells me, "I knew getting an education was your dream. That was the thing that was going to get you ahead in life. We weren't going to let that go lacking."

# CHAPTER 5

---

# FRESHMAN YEAR

Auburn University's academic schedule, set up on a quarter system, wouldn't start until the third week of September. The varsity football team was to play two games before the students were even officially on campus and football practice for freshmen would start in mid-August.

On the first day of orientation, with a bounce in my stride, I passed Cliff Hare Stadium (today, Jordan Hare Stadium). The huge cement structure stood empty. The gate was flung open and no one was around. I hesitated, looked around, then wandered in. I walked past the tunnel to the player's locker room and out onto the field.

It was a gorgeous summer day and the stadium looked like a postcard you'd send home. The beautiful green grass, the empty stands, the scoreboard overhead. It was not hard to imagine 60,000 screaming fans in the stands, and me streaking toward the end zone, ball in tow. An imaginary "Touchdown Auburn" rang in my ears. I pulled my New Year's resolution from my wallet and read it again. I was ready.

"Come in, son," Coach Tom Jones welcomed me into his office and we went through the nice-to-meet-you formalities. He was a pleasant man with a slight build, wearing a cap and had some chew in his jaw. "What can I do for you?" he asked.

I cut to the chase. "I came down here to play football. I mean, I came down here to go to school and play football."

He pulled a pad from his desk drawer and waded right in. He asked my name, where I was from, and my high school. After giving him my name, I informed him I was from Birmingham and had gone to John Carroll. "John Carroll," he murmured. He made some notes, wondering why he'd never heard of me from the Auburn coaches who recruited at John Carroll. Maybe one of the other coaches would know who I was.

"You seem to have good height and weight."

"I'm six feet, 185" I responded, bumping it up ten pounds.

He continued writing down my vitals. "Your position?"

"At John Carroll I played receiver and running back."

"You fast?" he wanted to know.

"Faster than anyone on our team," I responded.

Coach reached into his top desk drawer and pulled out a little tin cup of tobacco. He slipped a fresh piece of the brown chew in his jaw. The phone rang and he picked it up. "Be right there," he said into the phone. "Excuse me," he said. He got up and left. I sank deeper into the orange and blue chair. I checked out the office.

Everything in the office was Auburn orange and blue. Framed photos covered the walls, with Governor George Wallace, Auburn Quarterback Pat Sullivan, Coach Ralph "Shug" Jordan, and President Richard Nixon. There were many others of players and coaches. Some signed, others not.

On a wall facing the coach's desk was a large orange bulletin board. In bright colors was the heading, "Freshmen 1970." Underneath the heading were the names of the incoming scholarship freshmen. Some of the names jumped out at me: Rusty Fuller, David Langner, Mike Gates, and Virgil Pearson.

"Sorry it took so long." Coach Jones made his way back into the room. "When 'The Man' wants you, you have to go." He shuffled some papers. "Now let's see, I have some information here you can use to get ready for camp. Starts in late August." I floated out of his office.

On my very first day of practice, I quickly realized this was not high school. In the hot August sun, I would have to prove my worth every day. We practiced in the heat of the day, twice. Two and a half hours in wet, stinking, heavy pads. You could not remove your helmet and your chinstrap had to be fastened. There was one water break. During it, I got down on my hands and knees to capture the precious water shooting downward from a faucet that protruded about six inches from the ground. We were still only a few years removed from legally designated "white and colored" water fountains and I was too tired to care. After I drank, two guys behind me decided they were not thirsty.

The team had about forty scholarship freshmen and almost as many walk-ons. As it turned out, everyone would make the freshman team. The coaches would keep all of us around for tackling dummies and to keep the scholarship athletes from getting hurt.

Most of the freshmen were small town guys and most of the towns, I'd never heard of. We had guys from Brundidge, Letohatchee, Pisgah, Scottsboro, Childersburg, and Opelika, not to mention a few guys from small towns in Florida and Georgia. There were also a few guys from Birmingham.

In a meeting of the freshman players, Coach Jones outlined our mission. "Number one… we help prepare the varsity for their season and every individual game.

"Number two… we want to have a good season ourselves.

"Number three… we want to get each of you ready for the varsity next spring. Each one of you will get a shot at impressing the varsity coaches. That means scholarship or no scholarship, we don't play favorites."

They did play favorites.

The scholarship guys got the best equipment: shiny helmets, new shoulder pads. The walk-ons got the leftovers. Mr. Thurston, the equipment manager, handed me a set of hip pads from the leather helmet days. The shoes were older than I was. I looked at him but he just grunted, and moved along to the next guy. Maybe he figured I wouldn't be around very long.

Many of the walk-ons from big-time high school programs, had been unofficially invited to try out by the Auburn coaches. That way, the coach could see what the kid had without having to invest any money in him. These walk-ons were under the impression they'd get a shot at a scholarship. They were treated a little better. At least they had a coach who knew their name; who'd seen them play before.

Roger Mitchell, a defensive back, walked on the same year I did. He recalled his experience: "I had to drive back to my high school, to get equipment that fit; and then drove back to Auburn. Sure, I used my stuff from high school. At least it fit."

Walk-ons were placed in a different locker room from the scholarship players. Scholarship guys were given nice lockers. Their lockers had numbers. They were assigned jersey numbers in practice. Walk-ons were placed in a little dingy room called "the ghetto." We weren't assigned locker numbers or numbers on the field. You had to earn a number.

Practices were grind-it-out days. Most days, we walk-ons spent our practice time as dummies for the varsity, either being hit, blocked, tackled, or cussed out. When the freshman team gathered to run our own plays the walk-ons stood on the sideline while the high-priced guys showed their stuff.

Coach Gene Lorendo, the varsity offensive coordinator, was fair; he treated all the walk-ons like dirt. He had been with Coach Jordan since the 50s. He had a deep, booming, scary voice. He could spit words that would make you piss your pants. He stood six-feet-four-inches with white hair and weighed around 250 pounds, a Nordic Viking. A scary Nordic Viking. He was intimidating and he liked being that way. He believed in breaking you down and remolding you in his likeness. If you were going to play offense, you had to learn to handle Coach Lorendo and his intimidating ways.

During one grinding practice, Coach Lorendo motioned in my direction and barked, "Hey you, you, you, and you, get over here."

I scrambled over to Coach Lorendo, panting. "Yes coach, yes coach, yes coach." My name was written on a piece of tape stuck across the front of my helmet; it read "GOSSOM." "Yes, sir?" I asked.

His pipe jutted from his mouth and he purposely mispronounced my name. "GOOSSEM," he growled, "You and your buddies get over there and warm up those quarterbacks." He pointed at the varsity offensive field where quarterbacks Pat Sullivan and Ralph Brock were limbering up for passing drills.

The drill was simple. Go out five yards and run a slant route by cutting back into the middle of the field. We'd all done it thousands of times before. But there was a catch. We quickly found out why the varsity receivers didn't warm up their own quarterbacks. Ralph could throw a rocket. He walked around with one of those hand squeezers that built up your forearms. He had huge Popeye forearms and biceps. When he threw the ball, it whistled. I learned that day that you'd better get your head around quickly and get your hands up. If you didn't, you'd get drilled in the head. Bam! Guys would go down, get up woozy, stumbling around. That's why they used walk-on receivers. Walk-ons were dispensable.

The first time I lined up, Ralph faked the hike from center. "Hut." I ran my route. Ralph let it go. Whoosh! The ball, a zinging missile, hit my hands. Crack! One of my fingers was dislocated. Pain shot through my body. My finger was bent in an ugly, painful, grotesque shape. I held my bent hand with my good one. The pain had me hopping up and down wishing for some help. The trainer came over and calmly snapped the dislocated finger back into its original position. Crack! He slapped a couple of strips of tape on two of my fingers. Back in line I went.

The scholarship freshmen were constantly told that they were the best of the best and we were the rest of the rest.

One guy in particular hated walk-ons. For a while we fought almost every day.

He let me know that I didn't belong every chance he got. Not only was I a walk-on, I was "the 'N' word" walk-on. He liked slinging "the 'N' word" at me. I'd catch a pass and know instinctively to get my head around. He'd be coming like a heat seeking missile. The guy didn't tackle with his shoulders and arms. He went through you like a torpedo.

After, a few of those, I'd get my stiff arm up and try to bend his neck back through its socket. We'd hit the ground and he'd zing me with a black motherfucker or black "the 'N' word." We'd lock up in one of our football fights.

Football fights, if you're lucky, are quickies. You defend yourself, nobody gets hurt, and the guys pull you apart quickly. After that you had to act as though you were so pissed you wanted to fight some more. Most guys are too damn tired to waste energy fighting, but not this guy. He'd have fought until he dropped or dropped the other person. He thrived on establishing that he was the baddest-ass on the freshman field.

Being a walk-on, and to some "the 'N' word" walk-on, it was important for me to fight back. I was not going to be intimidated. If I didn't fight back, I'd have been a daily whipping boy. Football is as much a head game as it is a physical game. I couldn't let anyone stop me from doing my job.

In one of our first fights, I was so mad I pulled my helmet off. After we were pulled apart, one of the coaches slid over to me and quietly told me to keep my helmet on in a fight. "Less likely to get hurt," he told me.

I felt pretty good about my chances of getting to play. I was up against four scholarship receivers and five walk-ons. I quickly figured out the walk-on receivers would not be a problem. I had speed and they didn't. So that pitted me against the scholarship guys.

The play that earned me a jersey and locker room number occurred on a day I was lined up in the new wishbone offense as a scout team running back. The scout team was made up of freshmen whose job was to give the varsity first-team defense a look at the deceptive wishbone offense. The wishbone, with its multiple fakes by different runners into the line, could give the defense problems if they reacted late and couldn't find the ball. The play could go for a big gain. Our defense was trying to learn their assignments.

The freshman quarterback faked down the line and pitched the ball to me. I hit a crease and sprinted through it. Somebody was either blocked or missed their assignment. I didn't hang around to find out what had gone wrong. I went the distance for a long touchdown run. I hit the end zone feeling great! I'd scored against the first-team defense. I expected congratulations as I jogged back to the team.

Coach Paul Davis, the defensive coordinator, came running up to his defense. He was furious with them and they were furious with me. Coach Davis barked, "Run the play again."

Uh Oh!

I didn't have a chance. I had embarrassed the first-team defense. We ran the play and this time the defense was waiting for me in the hole I was supposed to run into. The first guy hit me hard. I tried to get down but he wouldn't let me. He held me up so several other guys could get good shots at me. Somebody buried his helmet into my ribs. They taught me a lesson about a scout team walk-on making them look bad.

The sore ribs were worth it; I impressed somebody. After practice, I was moved out of "the ghetto" locker room and into the main locker room. I also got a number.

---

After a month of football practice, the fall school year started. I'd underestimated the daily price of walking-on. The intense level of physical play and the mental concentration needed to make the team left me drained for everything else. It would put an extra burden on my freshman studies.

Once school started, I developed my routine. I would attend classes in the mornings and practice in the afternoons. After practice ended around 5:30, I walked the half-mile back to my apartment in Windsor Hall. The scholarship athletes went to the dorm for all-you-could-eat steak, chicken, and veggies. Dog-tired, I would fry a hot dog, and warm up some beans on my hot plate. After my meal, I would study, reviewing my class notes before doing it again the next day. Walking-on was like having a job. It dominated my life.

I took Introduction to Spanish, English, History, and Biology. I would pass everything, but I faced obstacles other students didn't have.

The biology course especially stands out in my mind. I was hustling to make my first ever class at 7:00 a.m. in Funchis Hall, at the farthest end of campus. I'd gotten myself together, put on a freshly ironed shirt and left the apartment at dark. I was tired, sleepy, and sore; football practice was taking its toll, but I was not going to be late for my first class. Huffing and puffing, I barely made it on time.

I walked into the classroom and stepped back into time.

As I entered the classroom of 150 people, everything stopped. A sea of white faces turned to me. I'm sure the dead silence seemed longer than it actually was, but I'd never experienced anything like it. Their looks seemed to say, "What are you doing here?"

I had a more important question. Where in the heck am I going to sit?

I'd faced this situation once before at ACIPCO Medical Clinic. The waiting areas for workers and their families were designated "White" and "Colored"; blacks to the left, whites to the right.

After legal integration, the signs were taken down, but the white patients still sat on their side and the black patients sat on theirs.

That day, I stepped into the waiting room and found no seats on the colored side. There were plenty on the white side, though. I thought of my dad and his job, our livelihood. I didn't want to cause any trouble for my dad. But, I took a deep breath and took the long walk across the room to one of the white seats. I kept my distance from the white patients. I didn't look at them.

The black folks, primarily older spouses and a few workers still in their dirty work overalls and black stained t-shirts, noticed right away. Some averted their eyes, lest they be accused of somehow being in collusion with me, a troublemaker. Others looked on with admiration.

The nurses (there was one black nurse's assistant) stopped and stared. The moment passed. That day in the ACIPCO Medical Center waiting room, a social barrier was crossed. There would be no going back.

Now, here I was, standing in the cold empty Funchis lecture hall.

This feeling was different from the ACIPCO waiting room. Acceptance meant more to me here. It was my first class at Auburn. My future. I wanted to be accepted here.

I started moving toward several empty desks. I recognized a couple of football players from the freshman team. Great! I moved in their direction, but they dropped their heads and averted their eyes. They were pretending they didn't see me. They did not want me sitting with them. Embarrassed, I took the first seat I came to.

---

For the first time, I was cut off from home and my world. I didn't have a car or any money and long-distance phone calls were expensive. My mom and Aunt Clara kept the letters coming. I'd write them back. I would not let on about incidents like the biology class and the fights on the field. Those were my problems. Sometimes, my mom's letters would include a little cash. More often than not, she and I would debate some social issue. We wrote long philosophical letters the entire time I was at college.

---

"Gossom. Gossom," Coach Jones called and I shoved my way through the gathering of players around the coach. "Get in there." I was in the game! All my hard work was paying off.

We were playing the Georgia Bulldogs. Bucky Phillipi, the Auburn quarterback, repeated the play in the huddle. Twenty eyes were all riveted on Bucky. He commanded, "Break." Twenty-two hands clapped simultaneously. Twenty feet lumbered toward the line of scrimmage; I think I floated.

I hustled out to my position. I set myself halfway between the offensive tackle and the sideline. "Hut. Hut," Bucky barked. The ball was snapped. The two lines collided. I ran the defensive back off, then headed to block the safety. Before I could get there, he hurled "the 'N' word" at me. "Black ass 'N' word, " he said. I laughed, hard. He must have thought I was crazy. I'd heard "the 'N' word" so much from my own guys; it was funny to hear it from an opposing player. It was like, "Oh! Is that all you got?" Nothing could spoil the joy of playing my first game. We got in each other's faces and a striped-shirted referee stepped between us.

Back in the huddle I felt a tap. Mike Gates was in for me. "Got you," he said.

I ran off the field, disappointed. Coach Jones was waiting for me. "Good job," he said. I murmured, "Thanks, coach" and walked to the bench. "Keep hustling," he said. "Keep hustling." I only played that one play.

We finished the season 2-2-1.

Coach Jones sought me out wanting to know if I would be back out for spring ball. Try and make the varsity. Try for a scholarship if possible. He said, "The offensive coaches really like you. You can get the chance to prove yourself."

This time, Auburn wanted me. "Yes," I thought, "I'll be there."

[ 1971 ]

# CHAPTER 6

---

# NIGGER'S CORNER

On January 20, 1971, the day before my nineteenth birthday, George Wallace raised his right hand, for the second time, to be inaugurated as governor of the state of Alabama.

Auburn University's Lee County did not vote to elect Wallace, but much of Auburn reflected the Wallace era. To most students, professors, administrators, and citizens of Auburn, black students didn't exist, other than the few athletes on campus. The blacks in the community were needed for manual labor, to cook, or tend to children. Other than that, black citizens of Auburn were invisible.

In Auburn, the distance between my two worlds became much greater and much more difficult to navigate than it had been at John Carroll. I was shocked at the lack of any type of integrated social support system. There were no attempts to make black students feel welcome. There was no black world on campus and the white world wouldn't let us in. We were in no man's land.

All we had was "Nigger's Corner." The two instances in this chapter where "the 'N' word" is stated will be the only times the word will appear in this book.

The student lounge was a big open space that ran across the bottom floor of Haley Center. Among the comfortable benches, chairs, tables, and vending machines, many students came to chill between classes. It was a cool place to meet friends, study, or just hang out.

The black students congregated in a small corner section. The section was right by the main entrance, so anyone coming or leaving had to take notice. We commandeered that piece of turf. It was all we had on campus.

Someone dubbed it "N's Corner," and both blacks and whites referred to it that way.

I don't know how N's Corner came about, because it was already established in Haley Center when I arrived at Auburn. At first, I'm sure it provided some comfort and security for the black students. We all gravitated to that corner of the lounge. Hanging out together in the lounge provided an oasis for thirty students in the midst of 13,000 other students who ignored us. Being ignored was difficult, but being lonely made it worse. By my second quarter on campus N's Corner started to become a mixed blessing.

All of us had grown up in the South, thus we'd all come from segregated communities, but we were used to being around black people of our own choosing. There weren't enough of us at Auburn to be choosy. We were thrown together because we were black, not because we were all alike.

Local commuter students came to N's Corner to see, be seen, and to be heard. N's Corner started as a quiet place to study, read, and converse in each other's company, but it quickly became a space to vent. For many, it was the only social atmosphere on campus. Once in the lounge, some students never made it to class. They'd play cards, talk, laugh.

A long conference table doubled as a card table. Constant calls of "four low," would be shouted during a spirited Bid Whist card game. N's Corner transitioned from a quiet, tranquil gathering place, to a lounge and a social club.

The card games were wild and raucous. Loud laughter and cussing interrupted others trying to study or converse. "We don't need you white folks" was the message. It was a show of bravado, but in some ways, we were assisting the mainstream by segregating ourselves.

N's Corner could also be a prison. If you didn't hang out there, you were "not black enough." If you hung out and didn't "act black" or stopped to talk to white friends, you were "acting white."

Unspoken was the underlying friction between the local black commuter students and the black students who lived on campus. There were more black commuters and local students than black residential students. Commuters and locals were the most vocal; the "blackest." Black students living on campus compromised their blackness. Living among whites brought our black credentials into question.

The separation was magnified among the precious few black female students. Commuter and local females made it their hangout between classes. Few of the on-campus females hung out in N's Corner. They wanted to be perceived differently. Many were "good girls" who had come to Auburn to study and not cause problems. They chose to be involved on campus. They tried out for cheerleader, wrote for the school paper, got involved in student government, and pushed the administration to truly integrate the university.

A lot of the noise in N's Corner was voicing a fear of not fitting in. For commuters, it was their first time traveling to the Auburn University side of the tracks. In truth, we were all just trying to fit in, to belong to the university.

But N's Corner didn't promote fitting in. If a white friend from John Carroll or my apartment complex wandered into N's Corner, they were not welcome. Period. Very seldom would anyone say anything, but sarcastic looks at my friend, or me, would say, "Why is the white boy here?"

Once, an unsuspecting white girl was run out of N's Corner. She wandered within the unofficial boundary, took a seat, and pulled out her book and notebook. A couple of guys started loudly talking. None of it was aimed at the girl, but the purpose was obvious. They were claiming their turf. One of them took a seat close to her. Before long, she was so uncomfortable she was twitching. She gathered up her books and left. Their rationale was that N's Corner was all they had.

The sad thing is they were right. We weren't welcome in plenty of other places. I've heard the early days of integration described as "living behind enemy lines." We knew where in town not to go. We knew not to go to the Auburn Supper Club, where many Auburn players and students went. James Owens was invited to join some ballplayers there one night and the wait staff refused to serve them. They would serve the white guys, but not as long as they had James with them. The other ballplayers were shocked. They didn't know, but we did.

We knew where to hang out, and where not to. We knew what stores to enter. We knew what professors not to sign up for. No study groups included us. Last year's test wasn't floating around for any of us.

The segregation at Auburn rolled through many of my acquaintances from John Carroll. I soon discovered they were not as friendly as they had been in high school. Whereas John Carroll was inclusive, Auburn was not. What had once been thriving friendships became passing "nice to see you, how you doing, see you later," relationships. This was especially true of the females. They could not have more than a "hi" and "bye" conversation. Some frat guy or white football player they liked might see them talking to you.

Kathy, a blonde former cheerleader from John Carroll, found the situation as awkward as I did. Our occasional run-ins on campus went from big "hellos" and hugs to, "hi" and "bye, it was good to see you." It took me a while to get it. We'd always been friendly, kidding friendly, but one day I saw the awkwardness in her eyes. She just wanted to get away from me. She'd never had to balance the two worlds before and it was too difficult for her.

As black athletes, the unspoken barriers were tripled for us. Everyone knew our faces. We were reported for doing routine college student activities or socializing. One Sunday, James, Henry, Virgil, and I went to the pizza joint in Auburn. It was a place run by "long hairs." The people were nice, welcoming. We'd all chip in on a pizza and Cokes. We went back to the dorm after a pleasant and uneventful evening.

Within a couple of days, Coach Brownie Flournoy, the dorm coach, had a talk with us about "that place." Brownie told us it was rumored that marijuana was being sold there. "Be careful, men." How did he know we were there? We were shocked and disappointed to realize we were being monitored so closely. We'd finally found a place outside the athletic dorm where we could relax, and now that was taken away.

Still, as athletes, we were treated differently; even from the other black students. We were hybrids. People were curious, even asking to feel my hair. I was told by one of my white teammates, "You're not like the rest of them, Gossom."

Because we were athletes, our world wasn't relegated only to N's Corner. We could slide between the worlds better than a "normal" black student. We had teammates, so we could befriend whites. Even the commuter students lit up with the opportunity to meet football stars.

Henry, James, and Virgil accepted me as a teammate and a friend. I was still a walk-on, but I'd proven myself. I didn't hang out at the athletic dormitory, since I was not on scholarship. But, the coaches kept tabs on me. They wanted me out for spring ball.

My world of friendships expanded in another important way. Between classes, students would all hang out on the concourse by Haley Center. On beautiful spring days, the grass around the concourse was full of students lounging, throwing Frisbees and footballs, or just hanging out.

I befriended a local black freshman named Joe Nathan Allen. We had a couple of classes together. Joe was the only black in my class's freshman year. We started hanging out on the concourse with a small group of integrated friends. It was a new alternative to N's Corner. Many of the blacks who came in subsequent years never bothered to gravitate to N's Corner. It didn't fit their tastes.

Joe became my best friend. We hung fast and tight for four years. Joe lived across the tracks. His dad worked in one of the cafeterias on campus. Joe and I were different in a lot of ways. I was an athlete. Joe was in ROTC. I was "cool," Joe couldn't care less. Joe pledged Omega Psi Phi, I was none phi none. I was broke, Joe received an ROTC scholarship, and he worked. When things got tight, he'd lend me money. We were alike in several critical ways, though. We were both serious about school, we both loved to laugh; we liked to make up our own minds. Neither of us liked anyone telling us what we could or could not do. We were both intrigued by being pioneers in a new environment. Neither of us was afraid of white people.

As I said, we loved to laugh.

One beautiful spring day in downtown Auburn, Joe and I pulled to a stop at a red light in his blue Volkswagen bug. We pulled alongside two elderly white women. Both cars had their windows down. Our music was loud. We were rocking to War's "The World Is a Ghetto." The elderly white women looked over at us. Two loud black boys with big afros and loud music made them uncomfortable. The red light would not change fast enough. An idea hit Joe and me at the same time. We reached up and locked our doors.

---

One sign of those times was a single word. "What's up, 'N' word?" Henry Ford would say loudly. "The 'N' word" was used daily by both blacks and whites. Those of us from the city who had been in integrated settings used the word sparingly, but those who had grown up in all black settings were pretty loose with it.

"I didn't know any better," Ford says today. "Hey, that's what we said. I would say it and the white folks would look at me funny. Once I got it, I stopped saying it. Hell, I didn't want them saying it."

But they did say it, most of the time as part of their normal conversation. It was what whites called blacks. "The 'N' word" could be used many different ways. You could ride "'N' word," be a "'N' word," or act like a "'N' word." Guys I was friendly with on the football team would tell a "'N' word" joke with me standing right there. It was not meant to disparage, me. "It's what we've always said," would be the response. Others would catch themselves if any black guys were standing around. Someone might even say, "Sorry."

On the field, my teammates would call blacks on other teams "the 'N' word." Once, in the middle of a heated argument on the bench, Bobby Lee Farrior admitted to Coach Morris, "Coach, I can't block the big 'N' word'." He then turned to me and said, "Excuse me, Gossom" before turning back to the coach and repeating that the big "'N' word" was too much to handle.

The hostile use of "the 'N' word" commonly happened in drive-bys. Someone would drive by and shout out "the 'N' word" at you, but they were afraid to stop. One of the few times someone actually got in our faces with "the 'N' word" came while James and I were at Burger King. We had a couple of extra bucks and rather than eat in the dorm that night, we opted for a Whopper and fries. Inside the restaurant, this guy became obsessed with us. He got loud, calling us "the 'N' word" as he spit the word out with venom.

He challenged us to fight and although we wanted to, we knew better. He was trying to bait us. He shouted loudly, "Come on 'N' word's," Instead, we packed up our food and left.

---

One beautiful sunny day, we joined in a march on the president's office to, "demand change at Auburn University." Resentment had been simmering for a while. Several black students had met with the administration in May of 1970 and demands were laid out asking for reforms the university should consider undertaking. There hadn't been any feedback to that group. If silence was supposed to be an answer, the students were not going to accept it. They wanted to be heard and responded to.

We marched through the middle of campus to the president's office. Actually it wasn't much of a march with only twenty of us. There were no signs, singing, or disturbance of any kind. We didn't attract or demand any attention. We were invisible, just like always.

The university had agreed in 1970 "to study the situation." In truth, I found out later, they were doing just that. A President's Advisory Committee on Educational Programs for the Disadvantaged at Auburn University 1970-1971 had been formed. That committee had made the following recommendations to President Philpott:

1. To present efforts to identify, recruit, and admit qualified black students to Auburn. To hire a black person to assist in this effort.

2. To present efforts to recruit and employ black faculty at Auburn.

3. To seek funds from federal and/or private agencies to support disadvantaged students and programs.

4. To continue to admit qualified disadvantaged students and to recruit from a wider area.

We marched into Presidents Philpott's office to give our demands. They were:

1. For Auburn to hire black academic and staff personnel.

2. Curriculum revisions be made to include blacks in subject matter.

3. Black students to be recruited on a statewide basis.

4. For positions in student government to be guaranteed to a black student organization or at least a voice in student government.

The only problem was that President Philpott was not around. He wasn't even in town. At least that's what Dr. H. Floyd Vallery, assistant to the president, told us. For some reason we did not believe him.

Instead, we took over the office. We announced we wouldn't leave until Dr. Philpott talked with us. At first we sat around nice, polite, and quiet, whispering. But as time went on, some got bolder and bolder. Someone broke out a deck of cards and the language of Bid Whist rang out all over Presidents Philpott's office.

What we were doing seemed natural within the context of the times. Dr. Vallery would stick his head into the room occasionally and tell us President Philpott was still out. We had a feeling he was around somewhere. "We will wait," we responded.

Yet we were uneasy too. We were already out on a limb. All of us had parents and communities back home counting on us. Would seeing Dr. Philpott be worth getting kicked out of school? We would disappoint our parents and the elders in our neighborhoods. Somehow, we knew that we would be okay. What we were doing was a part of the times.

I've been asked many times, "Well, why didn't you leave, Auburn?" The simple answer is that we were on a mission. We believed we could make a difference.

Percy Ross, one of the black graduates from the 70s told a story that symbolizes the way we felt: "When I went home to Fairfield, Alabama, on weekends they would take up a special collection for me at church. The minister would have me stand. He'd tell everyone I was going to be one of the first blacks to graduate from Auburn. They would take a special collection for me. Pass around the collection plate. They'd give me the money to take back to school. I represented a community. Man, there was no way I could quit or get kicked out."

James and I knew we would have another problem. We knew we would come under a different scrutiny. The coaches would get involved. James could be punished and I could be dropped off the team before I'd ever really gotten on. Still, we decided to participate. We were already isolated. Why turn our backs on the few friends we had?

Finally, Dr. Philpott arrived. He flashed a nervous smile. He was a nice man and he was prepared to talk. As an educator, I believe he empathized with our dilemma, but as a realist, he knew that there was little he could do.

His look hung a little longer on James and me. He knew who we were. I knew the coaches would know shortly. He listened. He made notes. We made our case. I think he understood. He promised to make efforts to satisfy us.

What was taking place behind the scenes was a different story.

In an oral history interview recorded in 1990 and 1991, Dr. Philpott spoke about the recruitment of black faculty members and staff.

"It was difficult to recruit them to a small community like Auburn. It was critical, but your local community was not a professional community, generally speaking. Those that we had, lived in Tuskegee in large part rather than Auburn because they had more professional blacks there... who had a community interest that they would not find in Auburn. While the prejudice was not overt and demonstrable here, I don't think they felt quite at home in the white community either."

According to Dean Foy, "We tried to bend over backwards to do the right thing. We tried to recruit black students. President Philpott, he was fair. He felt that blacks had suffered enough."

After our march, the university hired Dee Cee Madison in the student services office. He became our black administrator at Auburn University. Before I graduated, black literature and history courses had been added to the curriculum. Later in Dr. Philpott's tenure, the university sought out and hired other black faculty.

Our protest didn't make news beyond the campus. In the school newspaper, *The Plainsman*, an article appeared under the heading "Black Students Confront Philpott with Demands." We also received mention in the alternative newspaper, *Praxis*. But that was it.

James and I were right about the march and being reported to the coaches. Even though I wasn't on scholarship, I was summoned to meet with James and Coach Davis at the coliseum. Coach Davis was the assistant head coach and defensive coordinator. I would come to confide in him on a couple of occasions.

In our meeting, Coach Davis sympathized with us; he said he understood and I believe he did. He knew we were caught between two worlds. Yet, he reminded us, we were Auburn University athletes. What we did reflected on the university.

I respectfully reminded him we were also black students and what we did reflected on black people. He had an answer to that. He told us we had to represent black people AND Auburn and that the best way to do that was by doing well on the football field. Our blessing was also our burden.

Considering that the coach had included me in the meeting with James, I felt good about my chances going into spring training. I was obviously on their radar.

Still, I chose not to go out for winter workout. I'd heard the stories of guys working out in a room filled with steam pipes, guys puking in buckets. Passing out, waking up, and made to continue the drills. If I didn't have to, why do it? I played intramural basketball and focused on academics.

---

Without football there was more time for some socializing and fun. On March 8, 1971, five of us rode forty miles to the Columbus, Georgia coliseum for the closed circuit viewing of the "Fight of the Century," between Muhammad Ali and Joe Frazier. Dwight Drinkard, from Birmingham, had a car and was the only one rooting for Frazier.

We rode him unmercifully. "Ali is the man." "He beat the federal government." "He came back from exile to beat Jerry Quarry, then Oscar Bonavena." "He is 'The Champ' of the people." "He will whip little ugly Joe Frazier, no doubt."

When Ali went down in the fifteenth round, his legs in the air, tassels flying, his jaw swelling, the Madison Square Garden crowd was hysterical; we knew it was over. So did most of the whites in the Columbus Coliseum. They jumped up and screamed at the top of their lungs. They hollered for Joe Frazier, a black man, to "kill that black son of a bitch." It was a good night for Ali haters. The loud-mouthed "'N' word" who wouldn't go to Vietnam was getting his.

We were silent, stunned. Muhammad was the loud, brash, free brother we all wanted to be. He 'shook up the world.' How could he lose? Muhammad represented the future, Joe Frazier the past. Drinkard wasn't unhappy. He rode us unmercifully, all the way back home.

That spring, female companionship would also come my way at a party thrown by some of the older guys who'd been around a couple of years. As always there were more guys than girls, and hardly any of them were from the university. Most of the girls were from Auburn and Opelika. The local girls were more enamored with us because we were university students.

We partied in the "blue light" of the room. There were black light posters around the room. Several were of well-endowed women in seductive outfits. Everyone's favorite was the zodiac poster with a couple engaged in different sexual positions for each of the signs.

In front of the zodiac poster was where I met Jean. "What's your sign?" I asked. I hated that line, but hey, she was standing in front of the poster. She smiled. "Gemini," she responded. "What's yours?" she asked. In the dark I could see Jean's gold tooth, shining.

As Percy Sledge wailed, "When a Man Loves a Woman," we danced close, Jean sinking deeper into my chest. She moved closer into me and wouldn't let go. It was on.

I hadn't dated since I'd been at Auburn. Who was I going to date? I'd continued my relationship with a girl, now in her senior year of high school, in Birmingham. By that time, I'd been up and down Highway 280 between Auburn and Birmingham many a weekend.

Jean and I danced again and again. After the Delfonics sang, "Didn't I Blow Your Mind, This Time" we headed out the door. My apartment was in the complex. I don't remember saying much beyond I was a football player at Auburn.

# CHAPTER 7

---

# COACH RALPH "SHUG" JORDAN

If Hollywood was casting a sports movie and needed a model 1960s Southern football coach, Coach Ralph "Shug" Jordan would be the perfect fit.

Born in Selma, Alabama, in 1910, he was nicknamed "Shug" because of his love for sugarcane. A 1932 graduate of Auburn, he lettered in football, baseball, and basketball. After graduation he became Auburn's head basketball coach and an assistant football coach. He compiled a record of 95-77 in ten seasons.

In 1942, he left Auburn to serve in the Army during WWII. A lieutenant, he took part in the D-Day invasion of Normandy, caught shrapnel in his shoulder, and received the Purple Heart.

Jordan was thirty-five when he returned from the war in 1945 and took a football coaching position at Auburn. A year later, he left to coach professional football, before settling in as a member of the coaching staff at Georgia.

He returned to Auburn in 1951 to coach football for the next twenty-five seasons, compiling a record of 175-83. He coached a national championship team, twelve bowl teams, twenty All-Americans, and a Heisman Trophy winner. He was elected into the College Football Hall of Fame.

Beyond all the statistics, he brought his school fame, dignity, respect, and honor. He taught life lessons to the young men under his tutelage. "Football would not be worth the sacrifice if it did not teach lessons about life," he said.

"When I was being recruited by Auburn," recalled Heisman Trophy winner Pat Sullivan, "Coach Jordan and one of his friends invited me to go to a professional football exhibition game with them at Birmingham's Legion Field. We were stuck in traffic about two or three blocks from the stadium and the car ran hot. Coach Jordan and I got out and walked the last two or three blocks to the stadium. All of a sudden sirens were going off. Motorcycle cops sped by. The traffic parted. A caravan of cars zoomed by. I asked Coach what was going on. He said, 'Boy, that's Coach (Bear) Bryant.' He knew that Alabama was recruiting me too. As I looked at him he said, 'You can either ride with him or walk with me.'"

Ken Bernich, an Auburn linebacker from 1972-1974, recalls, "Every one of Coach's players learned his seven D's of success: discipline, desire to excel, determination, dedication, dependability, desperation, and damn it anyway."

Discipline was the D most Auburn players became familiar with early in their careers.

"My first day of practice, I was so excited," James Owens recalled. "I was pumped. I would finally get to prove myself, get some respect. I figured when we got on the field all that first black football player stuff wouldn't mean a whole lot. Hell, we'd just play football.

"I ran onto the field. I wasn't out there one minute when Coach Jordan signaled me over to him. I jogged over, figured he was going to welcome me. He pointed at my shoes. I'd worn white shoes ever since I started playing football. I wore them when they were recruiting me; they were my calling card. Coach said to me, 'We don't wear those down here, son.' Right then, I had to go back in and take them off."

In a *Sports Illustrated* story for the upcoming 1971 season, Coach Jordan was featured in an article entitled, "First Class Section of Coaches." The article highlighted the top coaches of the era: Ara

Parseghian, Notre Dame; Bear Bryant, Alabama; Darryl Royal, Texas; Woody Hayes, Ohio State; John McKay, Southern California; Frank Broyles, Arkansas; Bob Devaney, Nebraska; and Coach Jordan, Auburn. Coach Jordan's teams were described by saying, "Shug's teams don't quit."

In an article in *The Plainsman*, Coach Jordan said simply, "We just ask our players to pay the price necessary to play good football."

I didn't know Coach Jordan, but I was ready to pay the price. I had five weeks to prove myself.

---

On the first day of spring practice in 1971, I felt frisky, excited. I ran onto the varsity practice field in my white jersey. The offense wore white in practice, the defense blue. My opportunity had arrived.

A hundred players crowded the field, along with thirty coaches; graduate assistant coaches, managers, and trainers. Spring training, for most players, would be the chance to prove ourselves. Some players would compete for a starting job. Others, like quarterback Pat Sullivan and receiver Terry Beasley, would work on refining their game. This would be a senior-led team, so many of the senior starters would get less repetitions in practice so the younger guys could work out and compete for playing time. For walk-ons like Bill Newton, Roger Mitchell, John Mardis, Johnny Sumner, and me it was the opportunity to compete for a spot on the squad and maybe a scholarship. Individually, the coaches had encouraged each of us that we would get a shot at the varsity but they had made no promises.

The four blacks out for the squad were James, Virgil, John, and me. James and Virgil were scholarship, John and I were not. It was the largest number of black players ever on the Auburn varsity practice fields.

As we lined up for calisthenics, I got in one of the lines near the back of the team, away from the coaches. Coach Jordan rode by in his golf cart. He was "The Man." Everyone called him that, players and coaches. The younger guys felt a respect coupled with fear. In the almost nine months since I'd walked on, I'd never had a conversation with Coach Jordan. I wouldn't have known what to say to him. He didn't initiate any conversation with me.

Coach drove to the end of the practice field and leaned against the goal posts to watch practice.

He had on his traditional garb; khaki pants, a fisherman's hat, a jacket zipped at the bottom over a coach's shirt, and coach's shoes. There was no Nike or Under Armor gear then. If there had been, he wouldn't have worn it; he resisted the commercialization of the game. He hated Astro Turf, and because of that, so did we.

We went through the traditional drills. There was one difference for us walk-ons. We were no longer treated as second class. We all worked out together, as a team. This time there wasn't as much dummy holding. This time, if I caught a warm up pass from Pat Sullivan, I was doing it as a tryout for the varsity.

In my third or fourth practice that spring, I ran out for a deep ball and snagged it. As I headed back to the end of the line, I saw Coach Jordan walking toward me. I pretended I didn't see him coming. He made me nervous. Every good head coach inspires some fear in his players, especially the freshmen. It's part of a coach's mystique. He has your future in his hands.

The head coach establishes, early on, that a football team is not a democracy. There's only one vote and he's got it. He leads, you follow.

Coach Jordan stopped next to me. I acted surprised to see him. He said to me, "We'll be watching you," and he walked off.

I was determined to put on a show. I started out on the fourth team. In one scrimmage, I went out for a curl route. I was supposed to go down about twelve yards and hook back to the quarterback. I went down twelve yards, planted, and cut back toward the quarterback. He let the ball go. It sailed too high and I had to jump. I jumped and I kept going up, up. The ball stuck between my fingers. I caught it! Coming down, the defenders tattooed me pretty hard; flipped me to the ground. But I held onto the ball. The other players watching gasped. I heard Coach Lorendo holler, "Damn it, that's what I'm talking about. Go and get the damn ball." When I went back to the huddle, everyone congratulated me with pats on the ass and my helmet. It was the play of the day's scrimmage. At the end of practice, we gathered on one knee around Coach Jordan to get his summation of our day. I felt a pat on my head. It was Coach Lorendo.

The next day I was on the second team.

I was making an impression. I was put at defensive back for one scrimmage. It was a defense made up of a group of scrubs against the first-team offense. When the offense broke the huddle, Beasley the other half of the Sullivan-Beasley duo, split out to my side. Pat saw me and signaled to Beasley. I knew he was coming after me. The ball was snapped. Beasley took off like lighting. I turned and ran with him. Pat let it go. Forty yards down the field, I intercepted the ball.

On a rare occasion, I was inserted into a scrimmage with the first-team offense against the first-team defense. Pat stepped into the huddle and called my number. He guaranteed, "This one is going to be a touchdown." In full flight, I got behind both the safety and the defensive back. The ball sailed perfectly into my hands. Touchdown. I'd scored on the biggest play of the day. Pat gave me a grin. I sheepishly grinned back.

I also had my not-so-good days. One time, when I was playing safety, a massive hole opened in our defensive line and guess who came rumbling through. James was ripping and snorting like a bull. He wore a horse collar. It made him look bigger, nastier. He was looking to bring some pain on whoever had the nerve to get in front of him. I rushed up before James could pick up too much steam. He must have felt sorry for me, because he didn't flatten me totally. Still, it was a collision. Afterward, I checked to make sure everything was still working: my arms and legs; I still had all my teeth.

I fought for a job every day, but "the 'N' word" fights ended. There were fewer "'N' word's" slung around on the varsity fields.

To get a scholarship, I knew I'd have to keep my grades up to maintain eligibility. There could be no let down in the classroom. I'd learned from the scholarship guys that Coach Shot Senn, the academic coach, assisted them in planning their schedules. Coach Senn's job, as the academic coach, was to make sure the guys stayed eligible to play by passing enough classes. That didn't necessarily mean they would be on a graduation track. I bypassed Coach Senn and plotted my course with my academic advisor.

I felt good about being able to handle my academic load. I was still taking the mandatory English and History. I was in my third quarter of Spanish and had a B average. I was still the only black in most of my classes, other than Joe Nathan in English. But I'd adjusted since the biology class.

I took my first film course, Modes of Film, with Jay Sanders. Professor Sanders had a reputation for being willing to "work with the football players" in terms of passing a needed class. He never gave me anything, but he wasn't a hard ass either.

One film we watched in class hit close to home; *The Birth of a Nation* by D. W. Griffith. *The Birth of a Nation* is one of the landmarks in the history of American cinema and a landmark in American racism. The Birth of a Nation was based on two historical novels, *The Clansman*, a historical Romance of the Klu Klux Klan (1905) and *The Leopard's Spots: A Romance of the White Man's Burden, 1865-1900.* In other words, it depicted white Southerners, reacting to the newly freed slaves, finally being rescued by the gallant, hooded riders of the Klu Klux Klan.

In our classroom discussion, the film was praised and "the 'N' word" was used repeatedly as a part of the discussion. Some in the class were "considerate enough" to use "the 'N' word's" close cousin, Nigra. I remember Professor Sanders looked at me when the words were used, but he never said anything. I felt alone, under attack. The class was required for my major, but I didn't participate in any of the discussion.

[ 90 ]

Those experiences proved to be as tough as anything on the football field.

In fact, the football field was proving easier. As spring training progressed, so did I. Coach Jordan believed in wind sprints at the end of practice, when we were tired and dead-legged. The sprints were considered another test of manhood, who wanted it the most. We had to sprint fifty yards, ten to fifteen times, back and forth. I ran with the young receivers and generally would win the heat. For the final sprint, Coach Lorendo barked to the others lined up with me. "Don't you scholarship boys let that damn walk-on beat you! We'll start taking your meals and feeding the walk-ons." The pep talk didn't take. I led from start to finish.

After that practice, we gathered on one knee for Coach Jordan's end of the day talk. A heavy hand rested on my shoulder. I didn't look up. I didn't have to. Coach Lorendo stood over me with his freshly lit pipe sending smoke signals into the sky. That day, I was invited to eat in the athletic dorm. Every day from then on I got to eat lunch and dinner. No more hot plate dinners. I'd moved up a notch.

When spring practice was over, I sat across from my position coach, Tim Christian, in the athletic dormitory lounge. "We are impressed with your ability," Coach Christian told me. "You had a helluva spring. You picked up everything real well. We want you back next year. You haven't planned on going anywhere else, have you?"

I was waiting for him to tell me more and I said, "No, I don't want to, but I've got to try to get a scholarship somewhere."

Coach Lorendo walked in on cue, his trusty pipe clenched between his teeth. He lowered himself to the couch in front of me, exhaled a white stream of smoke.

He cut straight to the chase. "We've always had the tradition of walk-on's making it here," he told me. "You probably had one of the best springs of any walk-on we've had around here for quite a while. We have two or three scholarships we plan on giving before next season starts. We are going to have to go back and review the film. We'll be in touch."

I'd already received word that my grant and loan had been renewed for another year, but I didn't share that with the coaches. With or without an athletic scholarship, I would be back at Auburn in the fall.

Other than "We'll be watching you," I never had a conversation with Coach Jordan about my future. I knew Coach Lorendo would not be considering me for a scholarship if Coach Jordan did not approve. I wanted his approval. I was willing to earn it.

# CHAPTER 8

# SOMETHING FOR THE ENTIRE FAMILY!

I heard nothing from the coaches that summer. Every time I'd get a letter from the athletic department, I'd rip it open only to find another one of the impersonal, impossible "volunteer" workouts they periodically sent.

At home, I had no other contact with Auburn. Little in the Heights reminded me of Auburn, no one in my neighborhood went to Auburn, and no one from campus was coming to visit me. I didn't know of anyone I'd go visit, certainly not any of the new teammates I'd met. Several of the white players lived in Birmingham, but we didn't exchange phone numbers.

I was back with my buddies in our all-black world. All of them had gotten "good plant jobs." Cool worked for U.S. Pipe, Bubba for Chicago Bridge and Iron, and Duck for the railroad. Cool also went to Lawson State Community College. They'd all bought big cars, nice clothes, and they could flash wads of cash. As the college boy, home for the summer, I was always broke. The money got to me, but the differences went further than that. I was back in my old world and I didn't totally fit anymore.

My dad understood. "You'll get yours," he would say. "Get your education and you will make a living where you won't be at the mercy of the steel plants. You don't want to work outside in the rain, or have to clean people's offices, or crawl under people's houses." He didn't think that type of work was beneath him or me. He just wanted things to be better for me than they'd been for him.

Daddy was right about the offices and steel plants. The "good plant jobs" were starting to disappear. Guys would get laid off and hired back two or three months later. It was the beginning of the decline of the steel industry in Birmingham.

When I wasn't working out or working, I was with the guys. I didn't talk about college much. It was part of my other world. My friends had never been to Auburn and didn't know anyone there. We all knew it was a good opportunity for me, but leaving the neighborhood to go off to college made me different. I would talk a little about football, but I didn't talk about my potential scholarship. I knew the guys supported me, but I didn't want to mention anything more until I was sure it was going to happen.

Still, being home was a relief for me, a great mental break. I could relax. I wasn't under constant scrutiny. No one called me "the 'N' word."

I worked out as hard as I ever had. Each week, I would join a couple of guys at John Carroll's field and then I'd work out with the students at the all-black Hayes High School. The coach there, Melvin Scurlock, an old-school black coach, worked his boys hard. Tales of his rants are legendary, but Coach Scurlock was a good community man who touched a lot of lives. He was proud of me for what I was doing at Auburn and he always greeted me with a handshake and a smile. He told me I could use their facilities anytime.

Before I left Auburn, the coaches had given several of us the name of a man to call in Birmingham about a summer job. When I called him, I was told to report to the employment office at U.S. Steel in Fairfield, Alabama. I showed up and was given a job in the rail mill. I was handed a huge iron tool and put on the assembly line for steel rails sliding down a track and into a conveyor. It was man's work and if you didn't know what you were doing or were careless, you could get seriously hurt.

I recognized a number of the Auburn football players there. Somehow, they'd all gotten cushy jobs. I was the only one doing such heavy work. None of them were on the assembly line; none of them had to lug around huge steel tools. They walked around with a wheelbarrow, brooms and shovels, doing clean up detail.

Within the first week, I asked one of the guys how they'd gotten such "gravy train" jobs. They told me they had just spoken with the guy in the office, the same guy I'd talked to. For some reason he'd given me the hard work in the rail mail. I'd heard of these summer jobs before I left school; they were not "gimmes." It was explained that you had to work, but it was also understood that you wouldn't be put in an area where you might get hurt and jeopardize your football career.

I went to the supervisor and told him I needed to be on the work detail with the other football players. I dropped Coach Jordan's name: "Coach Jordan told me not to get hurt." He regarded me with disgust, but I didn't care. I was moved to the clean-up detail. Of course I didn't work with the other guys. I was given clean-up duties in another area, working alone.

I made good money at the steel plant. I saved about half of it for school, planning to use it for spending money for the year if I got a scholarship. If not, I'd need it for rent and other incidentals at school.

Only once that summer did we sit down as a family to discuss the potential scholarship. I explained I'd done well, but that didn't mean I was guaranteed a scholarship. Also, I explained that if I did get a scholarship, it might not be until the second or third year; it might not be this year. Daddy and Mama made it clear that school and getting a degree was their primary concern. If football worked out, fine. If not, I needed to make sure I concentrated on school. I assured them I would focus on my studies and focus on my schooling regardless of what happened with football.

Still, the idea of receiving a scholarship was never far from any of our minds. My sisters monitored the mail while Mom prayed diligently and Daddy continued to learn about football. We didn't talk about what could happen, but it quietly dominated our household.

One night I overheard Mama and Daddy, "I just hope he gets it," she said. Daddy countered, "He'll be okay. He's strong. Can't control what white folks gon' do. White folks gon' be white folks. He got to learn how to handle them."

By the time August rolled around, I quit my job to prepare to go back to school. We still hadn't heard from the Auburn athletic department, but the grant and loan would pay my tuition, fees, and rent; and I'd saved $500 to pay for my books. I was hoping that I'd get to eat in the athletic dorm from time to time.

The reporting date for football summer camp was August 13. On August 3, the phone rang and my mom answered. I watched as her round face lit up like the man in the moon. "Nice to meet you too," she said, beaming as she handed the phone to me.

"Hello," I answered.

"Thomas. How you doing, son?" It was Coach Lorendo!

"Oh. Okay Coach, how are you? " I asked.

"Doing fine, Thomas," he responded. As usual he cut to the chase.

"I am in Birmingham doing some recruiting. You been working out?"

"Yeah, Coach," I answered. "Just got back this morning from running."

"You and your folks going to be home today? " he asked.

"My dad is working," I answered. "But my mom will be here."

"What time does your dad get home?"

"He should be here about three," I answered.

"You think your mom and dad would mind if I stopped by?" he asked.

"Well, no. I guess not," I answered.

Then he dropped the bomb. "I've got something for the entire family!"

The phone line went dead. I hung up.

"What did he say?" my sister, Kim, asked. My mom, Donna, and Kim listened while I told them he said he "had something for the entire family." Mom made the sign of the cross and Dad soon made it home. We told him about the call and he decided he would go to the second job a little late.

About 3:30 in the afternoon, a long, blue Ford LTD pulled into our driveway and Coach Lorendo, bigger and whiter than I remembered, rose from the car. When another white man emerged from the passenger side. I knew our neighbors would be coming over later that day, asking my mom why two white men were at our house. Even before the men's shoes hit our driveway, our neighbors were all on their porches, trying to get a look at our visitors

Nervously, I stepped out to greet the coach. He seemed bigger than ever. When Dad invited him inside, he filled up our living room. "Well," Coach Lorendo said, "we're very impressed with your boy here. We've been watching his progress and think he will make a fine player for our team." Dad got very quiet as he listened to the coach tell him about the opportunities for a young man on his team. When the coach was done, he pulled out some papers from his case and offered me a full four-year athletic scholarship to Auburn University.

I couldn't breathe. This was it! A chance to play ball at Auburn. I looked at my mom. Her eyes were brimming as she nodded at me. I knew that this was beyond her wildest hopes for me. She had made it clear that school was supposed to be my main goal, but I also wanted to play ball for Auburn. I had written it down that New Year's Eve. What Mom wanted for me was to get a great education and this man was offering us both our dreams on one piece of paper.

I took the paper and signed it.

Thom Gossom "sparring" with Muhammad Ali, 1973

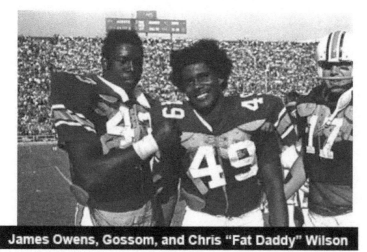

James Owens, Gossom, and Chris "Fat Daddy" Wilson

Gossom, 1974

Gossom, 1971, before changing his number to 49

Gossom going up for the catch in the 1974 game against Georgia

Taking a breather on the sidelines

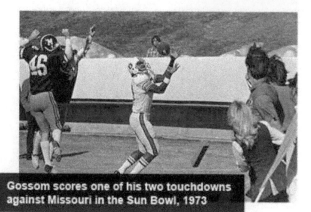

Gossom scores one of his two touchdowns against Missouri in the Sun Bowl, 1973

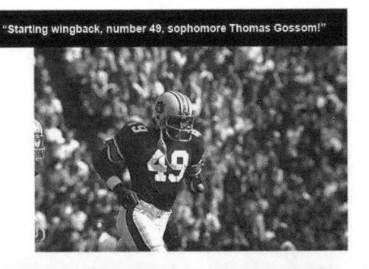

"Starting wingback, number 49, sophomore Thomas Gossom!"

Coach Ralph "Shug" Jordan patrolling the sideline

Coach Jordan counsels young quarterback Chris Vacarella

Defensive Coordinator Paul Davis and Coach Jordan watching a play unfold, 1974. Line Coach Pap Morris stands with arms crossed in the background.

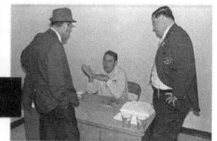

Coach Jordan in the locker room with bowl scouts

Governor George Wallace receives the game ball following the homecoming game of 1974

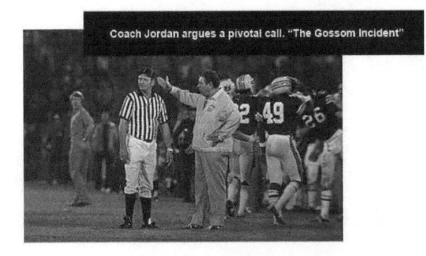

Coach Jordan argues a pivotal call. "The Gossom Incident"

Gossom and offensive tackle Chuck Fletcher's (74) blocks spring Scedrick McIntyre (44) for a touchdown run

Auburn University football team, 1971. Heisman Trophy winner Pat Sullivan in front row (7); James Owens in fourth row (43); Thom Gossom in sixth row (82)

Tom "Doc" Gossom. Thom's father was on the picket line in class action lawsuit against a local employer.

Thom's mother, Catherine "Cat" Gossom, was the inspiration for his drive to get an education

James Owens scores a touchdown against University of Florida in Gainesville - the first TD scored by a black player for Auburn University, 1971

It takes two Tennessee Volunteers to knock Gossom out of bounds

# CHAPTER 9

## RED SHIRT

The phone rang every two minutes. "Did you see Tommy in the newspaper?" an excited neighbor, relative, or friend would shout from the other end of the phone. I'd made *The Birmingham Post Herald*; Bill Lumpkin's column, "Another Walk-On Makes It," was on the front page of the sports section. Other articles appeared in the local Auburn paper and *The Plainsman*.

Coach Lorendo was quoted in one of the articles. "When a walk-on impresses the coaches the first day, the coaches wonder why the player didn't get a scholarship somewhere. Thomas was impressive right away. He played ball at John Carroll in Birmingham, but we had never heard of him. Even our players from Birmingham had never heard of him. He had the size and the build to be a good player and he had good speed. We just wondered where he had been."

While my name in the newspaper was exhilarating for me, it was a pain for my dad. "I didn't tell anyone that didn't need to know that you were at Auburn," Dad said. "I just didn't say anything, and when the men in the neighborhood found out you were there, they told me my boy couldn't play at Auburn. That they were the best of the best." Daddy went on, "They caused me to have doubts, and I was scared something might happen to you down there."

The articles in the paper let my dad's secret out. One afternoon Dad came home and told me he had been called into his bosses' office. Dad told me the story, "My supervisor at work came out to the loading yard to get me. He told me the plant superintendent wanted to see me. I'd never had a conversation with the superintendent and I went, trying to figure out what I'd done. I knew I hadn't done anything, but I also knew that they could just fire me if they wanted to. They could just make up a reason. When I grew up, a black man couldn't be uppity. Hell man, your boy want to go to college, they could fire you."

He laughed at this point in his story, before going on. Years of trying to stay one step ahead of what the white man was thinking on his mind. "I walked in the office and the superintendent had the newspaper article in his hand. He asked me if that was my boy in the paper. I told him yes. He congratulated me and shook my hand. I just stood there. It felt good when everybody all over the plant started asking about your playing. I couldn't go anywhere without somebody asking how you were doing." My dad paused. "Things change."

Yes, they change. For me, they changed drastically. I moved into the athletic dormitory and roomed with Virgil. I no longer had the stress of being just a walk-on with the long hours, cooking my meals on the hotplate, and scraping up enough money to buy books. I'd arrived. I was a scholarship football player at Auburn University.

My first visitor was the dorm Coach, Brownie Flourney. He welcomed me in his nice gentle manner, which was different from the coaches on the field. He gave me the rules of the dorm; and then, he told me to get a haircut.

I wore my hair in the afro style of the day. My mom was always on me about getting it cut. I was proud of it. I kept it neat, but I wasn't going to make a fuss with Brownie about it.

James took me through the ritual of getting a haircut from the only black barber in Auburn. The barber doubled as the school bus driver and cut hair between bus trips. If we timed it out right we could catch him right after lunch. At times, when I couldn't make the schedule work, I'd wash my hair and "pack it down" so that it didn't stick up as high as when dry. The coaches didn't know any better. They'd glance over and compliment me on the nice haircut.

The athletic dorm, Sewell Hall, was raucous and wild. It was a three-story, red brick building across the parking lot from the coliseum and football offices. In every suite, there were four rooms with a common bathroom that had a couple of toilets and two showers. This meant not a lot of privacy and eight guys to one bathroom.

Outsiders called the athletic dorm "the zoo." Apt name; there was plenty of testosterone. Fist fights, food bombs thrown from the top floor, cars screeching in and out of the parking lot, gun-toting hunters in camouflage gear, and co-eds being sneaked out of the dorm after curfew were all normal daily activities.

Days began with a 6:30 wake-up call and ended with a 10:30 curfew. In between were mandatory breakfast, classes, lunch, football meetings, practices, more meetings, dinner, and a couple hours of studying. We had time for little else but football and school.

One huge benefit of being on scholarship was the books at the University bookstore were free. Some of the guys would take their books for classes and immediately sell them to the off-campus bookstores for half price. It may have been good pocket money, but I would keep mine.

Mama was a voracious reader and I followed in her footsteps. During the time I was on scholarship, I read many of the socially relevant books of the era. *The Autobiography of Malcolm X* by Malcolm X and Alex Haley; *Native Son* by Richard Wright; *Invisible Man* by Ralph Ellison; *Before the Mayflower* and *The History of the Negro in America* by Lerone Bennett, Jr.; and every book I could find by James Baldwin. I became a huge fan of Langston Hughes and the Harlem Renaissance writers. I devoured the fiction of Robert Ludlum, Leon Uris, and *Catch 22* by Joseph Heller. For the next four years I would read anything and everything I could.

---

The rest of the country forged ahead with the civil rights agenda of the 1960s and Auburn started to loosen up. Attorney General Bill Baxley ruled that college students could register to vote in their college towns. Before then, Auburn students could not vote in Lee County elections. Massive student registration followed, but I continued to vote in Birmingham. An Auburn chapter of NORML (National Organization for the Reform of Marijuana Laws) organized and an Auburn University-specific chapter of ACLU opened in September. On October 16,1971, Coretta King came to Auburn and spoke to the Southeast Alabama Self-Help Association on campus.

Astronaut Ken Mattingly, an Auburn grad and former SGA president, was the pilot for the command module for *Apollo 16*. He literally put Auburn on the moon. NASA officials contacted President Harry Philpott to see if Auburn would be willing to design and construct ten flags. Auburn did, and Mattingly took the flags to the moon. Mattingly became part of a pipeline of Auburn aviation students that would someday be at NASA.

That fall on campus, I saw the Ike and Tina Turner Revue. Several of us football players were sitting on the front row for Ike and Tina and we went crazy when Tina and the dancers shimmied all over the stage in short, short skirts singing, "Proud Mary."

That was also the year *Shaft* hit movie screens. *Shaft* was the first black movie that I saw at the all-black Carver Theater. As detective John Shaft crossed a busy Manhattan street in his all black leather outfit, Isaac Hayes crooned the *Shaft* theme song to a racing guitar beat. "Who's the black private dick that's a sex machine to all the chicks?" The background singers sang, "*Shaft*," and Ike confirmed it, "You damn right."

After a lifetime supply of John Wayne, Tarzan, and Elvis, blacks couldn't wait to see John Shaft go head up with crooked white cops and bad white gangsters. *Shaft* was the first of the so-called Blaxploitation movies; a movie for blacks, about blacks, and by blacks. Supposedly *Shaft*, and the black themed movies that followed, exploited black people. But black writers wrote the movies, black directors directed them, and black actors and crews worked them.

---

The previous spring's protest at Dr. Philpott's office netted a black administrator, Dee Cee Madison as a "black recruiter." Madison was appointed in August and served in the office of High School and Junior College Relations and as a specialist in Student Development Services.

I, like most of the black students, got to know Madison. He made a point to get to know us. He pushed for funds for black students' activities. Dee Cee didn't solve all our problems, but at least with Dee Cee we felt we had a voice.

Archie Deevers, a blind, 300 pound plus, black student was awarded the special position of "Mr. Spirit." He had tried out for cheerleader and didn't make it, but he was so enthusiastic that the position of "Mr. Spirit," an unofficial cheerleader, was created for him. Archie's appointment caused some resentment among some of the black students, male and female, who tried out for cheerleader and never made it. Archie could not do any of the tumbles or jumps the regular cheerleaders did. His blindness, blackness, and size, in some minds, made him more a spectacle or a mascot. Other black students with cheerleading experience, who were more deserving and could actually do the cheers, were discarded; there was no special position created for them.

Archie could be seen with the cheerleaders on the sidelines of home games. The first away game, no provisions were made for Archie to attend. He hitchhiked to Knoxville for the Auburn game against Tennessee. After he arrived, he couldn't get into the game because he didn't have a ticket. One of the cheerleaders had to be called to vouch for him. After the Tennessee game, the Tau Kappa Epsilon fraternity vowed to see that Archie was driven to every game.

―――――――――――

I now had a full-time job, playing college football. It provided my books, food, and education. Getting a scholarship was just the beginning of a whole new way of life at Auburn. Coach Lorendo rode me harder than ever in summer camp. "Damnit, Gossom, the next ball you catch will be the first one," he'd say. If a ball went through my hands, he'd say, "You must have played the cymbals in high school." He'd tell my position coach, Tim Christian, "Get him out of there, Coach. He don't want to play today." They'd given me a scholarship and now I had to earn it every minute of every practice.

In truth, I was playing quite a bit. Beasley didn't practice that much so I got a lot of his practice time. In a simulated game scrimmage with officials, I went out for a pass over the middle of the field. David Langner arrived before the ball. BAM! He drilled his helmet deeply into my back. The ball slipped from my grasp and fell harmlessly to the ground. I kicked at Langner from the ground. "Interference," I shouted to the official. "Let me call the game, son," the official said. I huffed off mumbling "chicken shit" under my breath. The ref heard me and said, "Hey, you... you're out of the game."

I realized I'd screwed up. I'd been kicked out of the last big scrimmage before the season started. I flung my helmet to the ground and took a seat on the bench.

I then heard, "Thomas." It was Coach Jordan wheeling up in his gold cart.

"Yes, Coach," I answered.

Never leaving the cart, he told me, "Everything that happened out there today is part of football. You had a legitimate interference call, but you didn't get it. Now you're out of the game. What good does that do us?"

I pawed at the ground with my foot. "None, Coach," I answered.

"Okay," he said as he drove off.

The pre-season magazine hype was full of Auburn and pre-season All-Americans Pat Sullivan and Terry Beasley. Auburn was ranked ninth in the nation. *Gridiron* put Pat Sullivan on the cover and asked, "Can Pat Sullivan Lose the Heisman Trophy?" *Football Roundup* picked Auburn to finish as high as second.

The first game of 1971 was a mismatch, Auburn versus Chattanooga. Forty-five thousand Auburn fans jumped to their feet screaming as we ran out of the tunnel and into the painted orange and blue end zone in front of the Auburn student section. The players were bursting with excitement. We jumped, punched, butted heads, and released months of pent-up energy.

There I was, in the middle of it all. After all the games I'd listened to on the radio, after all my secret plans, I stood in the center of the stadium and I took it all in; the crowd, the teams warming up, footballs flying through the air and landing into the soft hands of receivers. The marching band, full of energy, belted out song after song. This was where I was supposed to be.

My parents and sisters were in the stands. Daddy had been promoted to supervisor on the night job. He was making extra money for the weekend trips to Auburn.

I found my parents in the stands. I shot my dad the secret signal, a little quick wave we'd devised, so he'd know I saw them. He got it. Dad had become a football enthusiast. I knew he'd be watching my every move.

The cheerleaders were jumping and cheering. Drunken students joined in the Auburn cheers.

"Two Bits!

Four Bits!

Six Bits!

A Dollar!

All for Auburn Stand up and holler!"

The entire stadium stood as one. "War Eagle" roars rolled through the stands.

I was one of ten sophomores dressing for the first game. The rest were to be red-shirted. A red-shirt player is a part of the team, but is withheld from competition for a year. The player can practice with the team and even dress out but if that athlete doesn't play during the year he retains that year of eligibility. In essence, he had five years to play four. In theory, the extra year gives the player another year to get bigger, stronger. It also gives the player an extra year to get his degree or a graduate degree.

There was talk of red-shirting me, but I didn't want to be. I wanted to play on this team with Pat Sullivan. "We're still not sure," Coach Lorendo told me. "We may need you."

We whipped Chattanooga 60-7. Langner had an eighty-eight-yard interception return for a touchdown. With the score 53-6, I found Coach Lorendo on the sideline. "Can I go in?" I asked. He smiled. "We'll decide next week," he said. Next week would be Tennessee.

The receiver ranks were thin. If someone went down with an injury, I'd play. If we made it through the Tennessee game without serious injury to any of the receivers, I'd be red-shirted for the year.

I was included on the traveling squad, so I would be on the sideline, dressed and available for every game. I just wouldn't play. It was an honor of sorts. James kidded me that they brought me along so he'd have a roommate. There may have been some truth to that.

Auburn was ranked seventh, Tennessee eighth. Auburn had thumped them the year before 36-23, Tennessee's only loss of the season. The loss took them out of the hunt for the national championship and Tennessee wanted revenge.

Two things were working against us. The game was on ABC and Auburn had not won a televised regular season game since 1965. Also, Tennessee's stadium was carpeted with artificial turf. Coach Jordan hated it. We hated it. It became a psychological obstacle for us. The players would wrap arms, legs, everywhere with gauze tape to keep from getting painful turf burns. When you slid on that turf, it would literally burn the skin off your arms and legs. We would become so preoccupied with it we didn't play well.

The game was not only my first road trip, it was my first ever plane ride. On the plane, I sat next to James. I was scared out of my mind. After gaining max speed, the plane made its ascent into the sky. I had a death grip on my seat handle. My face showed calm but my insides were all fluttering. James, now a veteran of plane rides, looked down at my hands locked in mortal fear. He smiled and let it go at that.

The rabid Tennessee students did their part for their team. Throughout the night, the students drove through the hotel parking lot, blowing horns, making noise. They figured the less sleep we had, the less energy we would have for the next day's game.

In the 1970s, there wasn't a prettier place to play a college football game than Knoxville, Tennessee. The fall leaves were highlighted with yellows and reds. The stadium rose alongside the Tennessee River. Tailgating boats floated down the river to dock outside the stadium. Crowds of orange clad fans swept into the massive concrete structure.

During the first half, we were locked in a tight defensive struggle and went into the locker room at halftime trailing 6-0. Coach Jordan told us, "You got the whip hand." He meant that we were right where we wanted to be. We were locked in a tight game on the road. You want to keep the game close on the road against a good opponent.

At the end of a long third quarter drive, we had the ball on Tennessee's two-yard line. Coach called James into the game; it was a crucial situation, but that's why they paid our tuition. I pushed my way to the front of the sideline for a better look.

The play call was a straight dive. Pat handed the ball to James but the ball rolled down James' leg and into the end zone. Tennessee recovered.

James was devastated. I met him on the sideline and tried to cheer him up. He felt he'd let everyone down. There was some discussion about the handoff and, "Did he get it?" Regardless, James' mistake came at a critical point in a big game. It also came at a critical time in his career. James got the reputation of being a fumbler. James says, "Coaches lost confidence in me."

We had to rally to win. I became a cheerleader. I went to Sullivan at the water cooler. There was a favorite DJ in Birmingham with a particular catchphrase that I liked. I turned to Pat and said, "You know you can do it, cause you so used to it." A confident smile creased Pat's face and I gave him some skin.

We got the ball back. Sullivan hit Dick Schmalz for twenty-three yards. He hit him again for twenty-two yards. He hit Beasley. He hit Schmalz. Before long we were on the two-yard line again. This time, Harry Unger took it in. We won 10-9. When Pat came off the field, I had a big smile waiting for him. We slapped hands again. The next week we moved up to number five in the polls.

The next week, Coach Lorendo informed me I would be red-shirted. I wouldn't play one down all year, but I would dress and remain on the travel squad for every game. As a consolation, I'd get a close-up look at the media circus surrounding Pat Sullivan's quest for the Heisman trophy.

I was getting an invaluable football education, traveling and learning with a top-five team and studying a guy who was in line to win the Heisman as the country's best player. It was fantastic to watch it all unfold.

Pat Sullivan, at various times during the season, led the nation in completion percentage (62.8), passing, and he was ranked fifth in total offense. We all knew that if he did well against Georgia, he would have a great chance at the Heisman Trophy.

Auburn-Georgia is the "Deep South's oldest rivalry." There are always many boys from the state of Georgia on Auburn's team. Georgia's head coach, Vince Dooley, went to school at Auburn. Coach Lorendo had gone to Georgia.

This year, we would play in their stadium, "between the hedges." We were both undefeated, Auburn ranked sixth, Georgia seventh. To that point in my life, I'd never been in an atmosphere quite like the Georgia game. Pat Sullivan remembered, "The Georgia game was not on television. The atmosphere was like nothing else. It was the only time both teams were undefeated." Scalpers were getting $150 for a pair of $14 tickets. The Georgia athletic department announced that it would sell 400 tickets to the general public for rights to stand on a train trestle at one end of Sanford Stadium and 400 tickets to a crosswalk at the other end.

Electricity crackled in the air. The Georgia fans were unruly. "On the way into town, the students met our bus thirty miles outside of town," said Sullivan. They paraded us into town, horns blowing, calling us names. Like Tennessee fans, the Georgia fans worked to keep us tired for the ballgame. They drove around our hotel all night, blowing their horns and running up to knock on our doors.

Coach Jordan called the game "the biggest game Auburn's been associated with since I've been here." The Georgia students in the stands rolled out a big bed sheet. The message it carried was, "Piss On Pat."

Michael O told me, "I drove over there without a ticket and tried to sneak in, but the security guards caught me and put me out. I went into a nearby building and crawled through the air conditioning vents to the roof and watched the game from the rooftop."

Sullivan was magnificent in the game that would earn him the award as the best college player in the country. He threw four touchdowns, completed 14 out of 24 passes, for 248 yards. We won 35-20. It was beautiful to watch. Pat Sullivan recalls, "After the game, you could hear a pin drop, it was so quiet."

As was the custom, we players got a piece of the hedges that surround the field. We would tear off a piece of the hedge and parade around with the torn bush to irritate the Georgia fans.

But, custom and tradition could go to hell as far as Georgia fans were concerned. They were disappointed and angry. At Georgia, losing to Auburn cuts deep. They didn't appreciate us tearing at the hedge.

The coaches hustled us to the buses. We ran a gauntlet to get there. "Keep your helmets on," Coach Lorendo told us. We ran through the Georgia fans up the hill to the bus. We moved away from the bus windows. They threw whatever they could get their hands on, beer cans, whiskey bottles; it didn't matter. They busted windows in the bus and tore the bubble off of the state trooper's car. As soon as we were all on the bus, we hauled out of town.

On Thanksgiving Day, 1971, Pat Sullivan was announced as the winner of college football's Heisman Trophy. He was officially the best football player in the country. He finished his career with 7,553 yards passing, and fifty-six touchdowns. His achievements came in an era when coaches, and certainly Coach Jordan, did not believe in passing the football.

Beyond the sheer numbers, Pat Sullivan was an inspirational leader, one of the last college field generals. He believed, so you believed. If he asked the line for an extra second of protection, they gave it to him. If he called on Schmalz to go over the middle, make a catch, and take a big hit to give us a first down. Dick did it. It was an opportunity of a lifetime for me to have been included on that team.

Unfortunately, the season went downhill from there. Archrival Alabama ran the wishbone down our throats. They beat us 31-7. It took some of the luster off of the Heisman. I didn't dress for the game. I sat in the stands wishing I could be out there.

In the Sugar Bowl at Tulane Stadium in New Orleans, before a record crowd of 84,031, Oklahoma creamed us and it wasn't pretty. We were embarrassed by a score of 40-22. From the sideline, the game wasn't that close. Arguably, Oklahoma was one of the two best teams in the country. I got to see why. It was 31-0 at halftime. Oklahoma rushed for 439 yards. They only threw four passes. Auburn rushed for a total of 40 yards. Pat Sullivan was harassed and hounded all day

In a film review session of the game, I overheard Coach Lorendo tell another coach, "We couldn't have beat them sons of bitches if we'd had machetes."

After the Oklahoma game, as had been the pattern since I joined the team, the white teammates went their way and left us to go ours. We never knew where they went. No one ever talked about the parties and dinners when we were around.

We would sing the school fight song, "War Eagle fly down the field…" We'd all get the analysis from the coaches, meet with the press, introduce each other to our parents and girlfriends, but after a game, our teammates would be gone. We never knew where. We weren't invited.

The black players from Oklahoma rescued James and me by inviting us to go to a party with them. We took them up on their invitation, went, and had a good time with the guys who, earlier that day, had beaten our socks off.

[ 1972 ]

# CHAPTER 10

# THE BUILDING OF A TEAM

The year 1972 started with an edict from the athletic department. Getting your butt kicked by Oklahoma can do that. The memorandum tacked onto locker room billboards and in the lobby of the athletic dormitory was clear,

"In the interest of total appearance and pride of the Athletic Department at Auburn University no excess growth or wad of hair is permitted on the back of one's head. (1) Sideburns will be limited to approximately the middle of the ear. (2) The ears will be clearly visible and the length of the hair will not touch the shirt or coat collar. (3) The length of the hair in front will not hang in bangs over ones' eyes. (4) No mustaches or beards will be permitted."

The school newspaper, *The Plainsman*, gave full coverage to the story on the front page. It quoted the athletic director, G. W. "Jeff" Beard; "The main reason for the rules is that a well groomed team is needed for a well disciplined team."

The ruling caused a stir on campus. Several letters to the editor appeared in the February 17 edition of *The Plainsman*. Most were not complimentary of the athletic department. Athletes who disagreed with the new regulation were quoted anonymously. "Most players feel the rule is wrong. I can see wanting to kept the hair out of player's eyes, but I can't see how letting one's sideburn's reach the bottom of his ear can affect his field performance."

It wasn't a coincidence the new rules coincided with the departure of the Auburn stars, Pat Sullivan and Terry Beasley. They'd worn their hair in the clean cut but somewhat longer styles of the seventies. It also wasn't a coincidence that we had just lost to Oklahoma. The team knew that our losing had something to do with it. Several football players were overheard sarcastically discussing the new policy. "The reason we lost the game was long hair, lack of discipline, and lack of pride on the part of the players."

Beard tried to play it down. "There have been no resignations because of the rule and no disciplinary action has been taken. The only people who have argued about the rules are marginal athletes; they are also marginal students and marginal people."

Luckily, I wasn't asked for a quote. I didn't consider myself marginal and I had certainly been one of the ones to complain. My hair had been a problem for the athletic department since I came on scholarship. I had a lot of a hair. For me it was a form of self-expression. As a walk-on nobody minded much. But now that I was on scholarship, I'd been often reminded that my afro was too long.

When we absolutely had to, James and I would make the trek "across the tracks" to get haircuts. I never got much hair cut, just enough to get by with the coaches.

The crackdown on long hair was just the beginning. The real trouble was that the super stars of Auburn football for the last four years were gone to football heaven, the NFL and the coaches were under pressure. Even with the best player in the country, we'd lost our last two games of the 1971 season. More importantly, we'd lost badly to rival Alabama. Some sports writers dropped hints that Auburn had been "out coached."

Going into 1972, there was something to prove. Our offense, the Auburn scoring-machine, without Sullivan would have very little experience. Half the offense would be first-time starters. There was no one close to Sullivan at the quarterback position now. Reporters and competitors whispered under their collective breath, "Let's see if they can coach without Pat Sullivan around to make them look good." The coaches did what they'd always done; they decided to go back to the future.

"Voluntary" winter workout was what it was called. I'd skipped it the year before as a walk-on.

This year, I had to go. I psyched myself up. How bad could it be? Everyone else had made it through. I could handle it.

I was wrong. I'd never been through anything like that before. I haven't been through anything like it since. It was hell on earth.

We were assigned to groups and scheduled afternoon times. The workout started with running. Running wasn't bad. As an athlete, running is what you do. A receiver runs maybe five miles a practice. I could handle the running.

The room with the hot steam pipes was a different story. The room was a mini-hell. For an hour and a half, under the direction of Coach Lorendo and Coach Tim Christian, we were in continuous motion in the heat of the steam room.

We started with agility drills. Endless agility drills. We'd go back and forth, back and forth, then back and forth some more. It was torture, mental and physical.

Buckets were scattered around the room for those needing to vomit. If a guy was bent over a bucket losing his lunch, we continued the workout. You could not stop to help a guy or see if he was okay. Wasting time throwing up didn't help you. When you finished throwing up, you still had to finish the drill.

Thick pads on the floor sapped my leg strength. My legs became rubbery. I stumbled around like a drunk. I wasn't going to lose my lunch, but I felt like I was done. Lightheaded, I knew that there was nothing left in my tank. But we weren't done; now we had to wrestle.

The whistle blew. Two players flopped all over the mat. The action was physical; elbows flying, grunts, bodies hitting the concrete floor covered by the mat. It was supposed to be wrestling. The other players, all in a circle along the edge of the mat screamed catcalls. "Git him." "Who is man enough?" "Yeah." The two players in the circle went at it like pit bulls until finally coach blew the whistle to stop. One of the guys rushed to one of the throw-up buckets.

Coach Lorendo called out, "Gossom." My name startled me. The whole thing had me nervous. I wasn't a wrestler. I wasn't strong at all in my upper body. I'd just started to lift weights. At John Carroll, we didn't have much of a weight program. Most high schools didn't back then.

I scrambled to the middle of the circle, pretended I was eager to flop around in a hot room with no air.

"Lanier," I heard coach call. I hesitated. There must be a mistake. Gaines Lanier, a defensive tackle weighed 235 pounds to my 185. Coach Lorendo gave me a wicked smile. Gaines Lanier lumbered into the middle of the circle.

The coaches were pitting offense against defense. We had returning, proven guys on defense. The offense in the coming year would be green. The coaches had decided that the offense wouldn't be pretty or fancy, so the players had better be tough. I'd better show Coach Lorendo I was willing to fight this big defensive tackle.

Gaines and I went down on all fours. Hands around each other's necks, faces close to each other. The whistle blew. Whap! Gaines flipped me over on my back in what had to be record time. The big guy was all over me. I squirmed underneath him.

Coach Lorendo said in that deep voice, "You better get up, Gossom." As I lay underneath this big ogre, I managed to cut a look at Coach. I thought, "Is he kidding? Get this monster off me." But I was faster, quicker, and I managed to wiggle free. I slipped behind Gaines, got him in a neck hold. That lasted about ten seconds. Whap. I was on my back again. Coach Lorendo called, "Time."

I looked back at Coach. I'd shown him I would fight. A little grin tugged at his lips.

The next thing I remember is sitting naked on the floor in the shower, the water pouring down on my head. I couldn't move. I tried but

I couldn't get up. My muscles ached. I was light headed. I sat in the shower with the water cascading down my head. I didn't care if I didn't get up. I didn't care if I didn't eat. I didn't care about anything. My body was as lifeless as a wet noodle. I tried standing to shower. I couldn't. My legs would not cooperate. I showered sitting. Winter workout had knocked me flat.

By the time I made it back to the locker room, almost everyone was gone. It was close to six o'clock, time for dinner. I gathered the strength to walk the quarter mile to the dorm. I made it to my room and fell into my bed. I slept until the next morning.

If winter workout was our foundation, we built our house in spring training. Pap Morris saw to that.

The first day we met Pap Morris, he told us, "I'm the new line coach. Coach Jordan hired me to teach ya'll to block like Oklahoma." He stood on the back of a seven-man sled. "We're going to hit this sled and push it all the way down the field and back, 100 yards down, 100 yards back, seven guys at a time." We did, all of us, linemen, backs, receivers, even quarterbacks and kickers.

It is still said to be the roughest winter and spring workouts in Auburn football history. We had marathon practices; two and a half to three hours of constant hitting. Everybody blocked and tackled in savage drills. There were everyday scrimmages. First-team offense against the first-team defense. Injured guys were dragged off the field.

Sherman Moon, a wingback on the 1972 team said, "We went back to a World War II coaching mentality. You had to prove your manhood every day. Sell out your body every day. They broke you down and remade you."

Discipline was our first D. We had to have our helmets on, with chinstrap fastened, the entire practice. No exceptions. There was one water break per practice. There was no Gatorade or buckets of water. There was that same outdoor faucet, a foot off the ground.

Defense was the second D. We would have a good defense for the upcoming year. We had several starters back and several who had gotten considerable playing time. The offense would consist of young guys, vying for a starting role. The coaches challenged us to an offense versus defense daily competition. Fights broke out almost every day. Many guys just walked off, called it quits.

"I quit twice," Ken Bernich tells me. "That spring was the most brutal thing I'd ever been through." A linebacker, Ken would become a starter on the '72 team and an All-American on the '74 team. "I packed up a suitcase and walked to the little bus station in town. Coach Davis pulled up in his car, 'You're not leaving,' he told me. I got in and came back."

Most scrimmages, we never threw a pass. It was just one run after another. The same play over and over. When guys bristled, the coaches didn't back down. Henley says, "One day, Coach Lorendo tried to run me to death. I ran the ball like twenty-something times in a row. He was testing me. I knew it. I wanted to prove to him I could stand what he could dish out. I fumbled the ball a couple of times, a big no-no. He grabbed me. Spun me around. I balled up my fist. He got close to me and whispered 'I know you want to hit me but if you do, I'm going to kill you.'" Henley laughed, "That sort of took the edge off my wanting to hit him."

Near the end of a rough two and a half hour practice with very little left in our tanks, we would do goal-line drills. We'd start at the ten-yard line, first and goal. Full speed, first-team offense against first-team defense. We had four downs to score.

We offensive guys would break the huddle, run to the line of scrimmage. The defense awaited us. The quarterback, Dave Lyons, would bark signals. Coach Lorendo would step between the offense and defense.

"Point to that son of a bitch you're going to block," he'd command us. We knew the drill. We would point to the defender we were going to block. "Tell him you're going to block him." As the wingback, my assignment was to double-team the defensive end with the offensive tackle. "We're going to block you." We pointed to Danny Sanspree. Danny would make All-Conference. Coach Lorendo would take it further, "Tell them who's getting the ball." We would turn and point to Henley. "Henley's getting the ball," we'd say. "Tell them the play," Coach Lorendo would demand. "Twenty-Seven Slant," we'd say. "Point to the hole he's running in." We would point to the hole off the outside of the right tackle. Coach Lorendo had one more thing he wanted us to tell the defense "Tell them the snap count." We'd tell them, "The snap count is two." Coach Lorendo would then back out of the way. Before leaving he'd tell the offense, "You better score."

Sometimes we did. Most of the time, the defense was waiting in the hole. When we didn't score, we started over from the ten. As we grew as an offense that summer, we could tell them the play and score anyway. Not every time, not even often, but enough to gain confidence and respect.

Several of us were vying for the starting wingback slot. The wingback in our offense would block, catch passes, and run the occasional reverse play. I was alternating with Mike Fuller for the starting spot.

Dave Lyons was starting at quarterback. He had a good arm and was a damn good athlete. I liked playing with him. He could get me the ball. Whenever we got through this hell of spring training we had plans for each other.

The third week of the five-week spring training, I got a twisted reprieve. It happened on a sweep play. I'd thrown a body block into defensive end, Danny Sanspree. You couldn't hold a player back then like you can now. Your hands could not be extended in any way. You had to engage him with your body in a cross-body block. We practiced throwing our bodies at the opposing player.

After throwing the block at Sanspree, I put my hand down on the ground to get up. Mike Neel, our rover linebacker, pursuing the play, stepped right onto my left hand. His steel-toed cleats cracked the bones in the back of my hand like toothpicks. Crack! Pain shot through my body. I couldn't move my fingers. I could feel at least two bones were broken. Kenny Howard, the trainer, came over. He fingered my hand and announced, "It's broken. Go on in and shower. We'll have to get it set and put it in a cast." I was done for the spring. I almost kissed him.

It had taken a broken hand to get me out of that living hell. I continued to attend practice and the meetings, but there were no workouts for me.

I'd proven myself for three weeks. I thought my position was safe. The two broken fingers, winter workout, and the monster spring training proved that I could and would do what it would take to play. It may sound weird, but I was satisfied. Happy.

Two other significant events during the '72 spring would determine the team's destiny. James was moved to fullback. The fullback in the '72 team's offense would block, block, and block some more. The offense was predicated on the success of the fullback position, but James would do very little running of the football.

James wanted to play and he was a team guy. "The coaches told me I was the best one to do the blocking." The coaches reasoned that James was the bigger, stronger guy. He could block for Henley, not vice versa. James was not happy about it. "Going out and blocking every day on almost every play is pretty tough. I really haven't experienced any great problems so far except my neck seems to stay sore. I've just got to have the attitude that I'm going to block every play. I just want to play."

During the last brutal scrimmage of the spring, the worst imaginable tragedy happened for our offense. Dave Lyons went down to a devastating knee injury. That spring, we were looking for an offensive identity and Dave Lyons had provided it. He was a good athlete, had good speed, could run the option, and more importantly for me, he could pass. We would have been great together.

Now we would have to search for a quarterback all over again in August. For Dave Lyons, not only was spring over, his career as an Auburn starting quarterback was done.

Not playing, I tended to other business. I'd met a girl. Actually I'd met her the summer before. She lived in Birmingham, still a senior in high school. I fell hard, like a rock.

Debra was a pretty cocoa brown girl with an absolutely beautiful smile. While home over the last summer and holidays we'd gotten tight. We thought we were in love. But there was no doubt, we had great sex, great car sex, in the back seat of my folk's 1965 Chevy.

When we were apart, we would spend long, long, hours on the telephone, longing for more car sex. She would come down to Auburn periodically. Mainly, I would jet up to Birmingham when I had the opportunity.

The trips to Birmingham ended on a rainy Saturday on Highway 280. Over the summer before his senior year, James had gotten a car, a four-door 1966 Falcon. True to his open nature, James would let anyone borrow it. He rarely used it himself since he had nowhere to go. Oftentimes, the few black coeds on campus would walk from their dormitory to ours and borrow James' car for grocery shopping. He always left the keys in it.

Still, I had to ask to go all the way to Birmingham.

After a Saturday practice, the coaches set curfew for 1:30 a.m. Generally, there was no room check. If a guy had something better to do, he'd spend the night out.

Within thirty minutes of practice ending on this Saturday, I was on my way to Birmingham. About thirty miles into the 125-mile trip it started to rain. I didn't care. I pushed the little Falcon for all it was worth. It rained harder. Isaac Hayes crooned on the eight-track tape deck. I could taste Debra's lips already.

In Goodwater, Alabama, I rounded a curve. The Falcon started to skid. The back end of the car went one way, the front another. The steering wheel spun like the steering wheel in a carnival bumper car.

I was traveling at sixty-five miles an hour, but I felt like I was moving in slow motion. The car headed into a hill alongside the road. I frantically turned the wheel, first this way, then that. I continued on toward the hill. Crash! Crash!

The front end of James' Falcon hit the hill, listed like a ship, and then turned over on its top; it's tires spinning in the air. The glass in the windshield crumpled like plastic. Isaac Hayes wound to a halt.

The front seat of the Falcon lay on my head. I was upside down. I thought the car might explode and I tried to get out but I couldn't. Panicking, I was able to roll the window up into its door. I crawled out onto the highway. The rain was pouring down. Cars I'd previously gone by passed me back. I felt funny, standing there, rain pounding, people pointing at me as they passed me by.

Then I remembered. It was James' car! Shit! What would I do? I gathered James' eight-track tapes. The Falcon was bent in a grotesque shape from the front left fender to the back door. I thought it was totaled.

A gray, state trooper's car pulled over on the side of the road. We talked, and then I got in the car with him. He gave me a ride to the state trooper post. He had the mangled car towed.

I carried eight of James' eight-track tapes in my hands. The trooper let me use the phone to call James. I called Virgil instead. I told him what had happened. He said he would go and get James.

James and Virgil picked me up in Virgil's car. I said weakly to James, "I managed to salvage your tapes." James Owens' temperature never rose above cool. He didn't say much. He reminded me he'd told me before that the love thing was going to get me in trouble. Now it had.

We packed up the tapes and drove back to Auburn. We left the Falcon at the trooper post. Neither one of us looked back.

I got off light. I paid a $50 deductible and James' insurance company took care of the rest. That was it. I scrounged up the $50 to give to James. Neither of our parents found out. Nor did the coaches.

Before long, Debra and I stopped seeing each other.

---

I continued to breeze along in my classes. I enjoyed my specialization courses in radio and television and journalism. My grade-point average rose to 2.0 out of 3.0. I followed a pattern that I'd followed most of my school years. I excelled in what I liked and got by in what I wasn't interested in.

Official university records say that in 1972, there were 211 black students on campus out of a total of 14, 528. Again, I didn't see 211 black students, but it was evident things were getting better.

Dr. Philpott approved a request for colonization by the first black fraternity, Omega Psi Phi, on Auburn's campus. It was a major social step for many of the black students on campus. Many of my friends were in the charter group.

George Smith was an original member. "Dee Cee (Madison) was an Omega from Tuskegee. He took the idea to Dr. Philpott. Dr. Philpott agreed and things were put into motion. The original guys were handpicked. The fraternity gave us a sense of belonging. It was something worldwide, bigger than Auburn."

Another social development would play a major role in my time at Auburn. I took my first hit of marijuana. The "evil weed" was new for me. Even though I was a city boy, I'd never seen it in high school or my neighborhood. The first time I smelled marijuana, I was a freshman and Bill Vance, a friend from John Carroll, came to visit me at my tiny apartment in Auburn. Bill, a great guy, was a "longhair." His parents approved of our friendship and in high school I was often at their home.

Bill was on his way to an Alice Cooper concert in Montgomery when he showed up at my door. I was washing dishes, my back to him. I smelled something foul. I turned around, and Bill, a self-described hippie, was toking away. I lost it. I made him go outside and do it.

Later, at card games at Windsor Hall, the guys would toke. The group was all black and everybody trusted each other. They had to. In Auburn, possession of several joints could get you busted with jail time and dismissed from school. The joint would be passed around, but I wasn't ready to smoke. Not yet anyway.

After our brutal spring practices, many of the guys would take the hour or so left before dinner and go to a little shack called The Tiger for ice-cold beer. There were no chairs, but throughout the evening half the team would go through there. Guys would split off and go for a ride in the beautiful countryside within a half-mile of campus. Farmland dotted the landscape. It was beautiful and relaxing. A joint would appear. Guys would hit it. I tried it. Inhaled. Liked it.

Not that I was atoning for my sins, but I continued going to church. I had ever since I'd been in Auburn, but I didn't like it. I walked from the athletic dorm every Sunday to a Catholic church past downtown Auburn. I'd been in Catholic churches all my life, but this one was different. The church was filled with many students, people from the university community, and families with children. Yet, I was the only black. I was never welcomed, just ignored. I never met the priest or any of the parishioners. Finally after two and a half years, I stopped going. Called my mom up and told her, "I'm done with that church."

All around us, the old was giving way to the new. Roe vs. Wade was decided in 1972. Black congresswoman Shirley Chisholm became the first woman to make a serious run at the presidency. Her campaign slogan was "Unbought and Unbossed."

But still, in the Deep South, change moved in confusing and ironic patterns. In an on-campus poll of students in the student newspaper, Richard Nixon was the Republican choice for president for eighty-two percent of the students. George Wallace was the leading

Democratic choice with thirty-three percent of the students supporting him. Sixty-nine percent of the students were against the legalization of marijuana. And while only fifty-nine percent of the students approved of premarital sex, eighty-two percent believed in legalizing abortion.

The biggest news in the state of Alabama happened on May 15. Arthur Bremer shot George Wallace as he was campaigning for president. Bremer walked up on Wallace in a crowd and fired away. The bullet that hit Wallace lodged in his spine. He was left paralyzed in his legs for the rest of his life.

Kenny Howard came running out onto the stadium field as we were nearing the end of a scrimmage. The second team was on the field. James and I rested on the bench. Kenny headed straight to Coach Jordan. They talked. Coach Jordan looked worried. What was up?

Offensive guard Bobby Lee Farrior overheard and ran off the field, headed straight to me. He blurted out, "Gossom, the governor's been shot, and one of your people did it."

"Shit," I thought. I turned to James, "We'd better see if we can go in early."

# CHAPTER 11

# FAT DADDY & THE ZOO

"Do you still see 'Fat Daddy'?" If I see a black Auburn alumnus from my era, the question is inevitable. After catching up with a few, "How you been's?" "How are the kids?" I wait for it to come. "Hey, what happened to 'Fat Daddy'? You still see him?"

"Yes," is the answer. We live about eight miles from each other. An island and a bridge separate us. Not much separated us at Auburn.

"Fat Daddy" is white. He became a suite mate to James and me in the athletic dorm. He was our freshman. Before 1972, freshmen were ineligible for varsity competition and the tradition of varsity athletes hazing freshman athletes was big. Some freshmen in the dormitory were made to do simple things, pick up pizza. Others were taken out in the country and dropped off in their underwear. They had to make it back to the dorm without getting caught. The hazing could be fun, but sometimes it got nasty, oftentimes erupting in cowboy fights, knuckles on flesh resulting in bloody, swollen faces.

James and I didn't participate much. We didn't feel comfortable telling a white freshman what to do. It wasn't worth any trouble it might cause.

We hadn't counted on Chris "Fat Daddy" Wilson.

"When the son of a bitch kicks field goals and extra points, they have to go and get the ball in the parking lot. He kicks it out of the stadium." It was Coach Lorendo bragging on the new kicker Auburn had signed from Gainesville, Florida. I thought, "This guy must be good."

Kickers generally didn't get scholarships. Coaches tried to persuade kickers to walk on.

"Coach Jim Hilyer recruited me," Wilson recalls. "Auburn signed forty-four guys that year. At the end of four years, eight of us finished out of that class of forty-four."

Wilson also made history of a sort. "I was the last of the straight ahead kickers, the end of an era. I was also one of three freshmen to make the varsity in '72 and play. We were the first freshmen to play at Auburn in the modern era of college football."

Why Auburn?

"When I visited Auburn, the people were so friendly. It just felt right. Everybody was nice. Good manners. Once I walked through campus, one time, I knew.

"Still, I was different from most of the guys on the team. Many of them were from little small towns in Alabama. They had certain viewpoints. There were things I just didn't agree with. Guys like me were thought of as worldly. There was a divide between the worldly guys and the guys from the small towns in Alabama."

James named him Fat Daddy. He had a gut as a freshman unlike most kickers who were generally small guys. Wilson was more like a small defensive tackle at about six foot one and weighed over 200 pounds.

"Since we were suitemates, I would tell the other guys I was you guy's freshman. They didn't like it, but they couldn't bother me. All you and James ever made me do was go to the Goal Post (a grill) and pick up hamburgers and fries."

We laugh at the memories.

"Whenever you guys went to the Goal Post, I went with you," he says. "Because Mary and Ernie would give you guys extra helpings of food."

Ernie and Mary were black. Mary was the cashier and waitress and Ernie the short order cook. They were proud of us and yes, they gave us much more than we ever paid for. It was a perk we got from Auburn's black community.

Fat Daddy loved to eat, then and now. "Ernie would lift the fry rack out of the hot grease and reach that big old hand in there and get a huge hand full of hot fries and dump them on the plate. If you guys ordered one hamburger, he would give you guys an extra one. I said, 'Hey, I'm hanging with the brothers.'"

There were other attractions to hanging with the brothers. Wilson also got to use James' car for his dates. One of my first memories of Wilson was him bringing a date to his room, which was against the rules. He and the girl had gotten carried away and they lost track of time. At the 10:30 curfew, Brownie would check rooms. You had to be in your room with the lights out ready for bed. Brownie would open the door with his master key and stick his head in.

By now, like many of the guys, I considered Brownie a snitch, not to be trusted. If he caught you doing something, he would promise you he'd keep it confidential. "This is just between you and me, men," he would say. The confidentiality lasted until the next morning when he would hustle over to the coach's offices and spill the beans. I guess it was his job.

We heard him checking two doors away from Wilson's room. Wilson and the girl were stuck. They were going to get caught. Less than two months on campus and already he was heading for the doghouse, maybe even home. Wilson, out of breath, ran into our room. "What do I do?" he blurted out. "Help, guys."

There wasn't much time. As mentioned, the dorm consisted of four room quadrants, with a common bathroom. Brownie was one door away from Wilson's room, so we shuffled the girl through the bathroom and into our room. Wilson ran back into his room, shut the door, got into bed, and turned out the light.

The poor girl was terrified as she stood in our room. James and I lay on our beds shirtless. I wondered whether she was more afraid of Brownie, or of James and me.

After Brownie checked Fat Daddy's room we shuffled the girl back through the bathroom into Wilson's room. Brownie made his way around to our room. We turned out the light as requested. When Brownie left, James and I helped Wilson and the girl sneak through the woods next to the dorm.

Wilson and I would become tight friends. He credits his family's many geographic moves with shaping his views on prejudice. "Man, I moved something like thirteen times growing up, all over the South. I was different from a lot of the guys in the dorm. I probably was prejudiced and maybe would have been more so if I'd stayed in one spot. We moved from Virginia to Vicksburg, Mississippi, then to Birmingham, twice. I always had to make new friends. People wouldn't treat you nice. There were cliques that wouldn't let you in.

"In the eighth grade, we moved to Key West and this black guy befriended me. For a while he was my only friend. I decided then I'd judge people by who they were."

Wilson quickly became our friend. He hung in our room between practice and meetings. He didn't care what others thought.

He did his best to keep us laughing and his exploits are legendary. At one point, he decided he wanted to experience a prostitute. Someone told him he could have such an experience in Montgomery, Alabama. He borrowed a car. He went to some shady hotel in downtown Montgomery. The older woman and a room came as a package deal. I think the highlight for him was being able to come back and tell us all the little details.

He loved to be naked. He loved walking into our room for a game of cards buck-naked. He'd sit down and deal a hand of cards. We'd laugh; tease him about his lack of an ass or not much of a pecker. It didn't matter if females were present, he'd sit naked, as though he were normal, which all of us realized by now, he was not.

One night, I asked him, "You want to go see *Superfly?* " James, Mitzi, Joe Nathan, Ford, and I were going. "Sure," came his reply. *Superfly*, released the year after *Shaft*, is the story of a black dope dealer who has to fight the bad guys, including the cops, to get out of the business and go straight. Everyone thought it a big deal that Wilson went to the movies with us. I didn't. He was my friend, so I asked him if he wanted to go to a movie.

Word spread among the blacks students that Fat Daddy was cool. His freshman year, Wilson and I spent a lot of time together. We played cards together, hung out with girls together, both black, and white. We even dated a couple of the same girls. Blacks didn't object when I brought Fat Daddy around. That's why so many remember him today. He was one of a kind in Auburn. We weren't inseparable and we both had other friends, but the uniqueness of our situation made us an item.

Over the years, I went home with him and he with me. Our parents got along. But even with Fat Daddy, the social pressure of fitting in at Auburn would send him through changes. He'd spend hours in front of the mirror trying to straighten his curly hair. We'd tease him about it. "Quit trying to look like a white boy." He'd burn up several hot combs trying to get that hair straight.

We became like brothers, with James as our dad. "You guys took care of me," he says. James was like our daddy. I went to him for counseling. You wrote my papers for me."

I did. I'd write his English composition papers. The first time he asked me for help, I agreed, but when he asked again, I realized it would be faster if I just wrote it for him. He was okay with that. He started to come back again and again. Before long I'd charge him money.

Soon, I had a little business in the dorm. Guys would come ask me to write their papers. I'd charge $10 or $20. I'd do well enough to get them a C. In fact, Wilson asked me once if he could get an A, and I told him no because they would know he didn't write it.

Was it cheating? Yes. But, there was much more serious cheating on campus than my writing papers. Many of the fraternities had the professors' tests. In some classes, the passing around of test booklets was blatant. I saw writing the papers as a way to make spending money. The university paid for my tuition, books, and fees, and paid me $15 a month for laundry money. My dad could afford to send me $10 a month. The money I made writing papers came in handy.

James was my roommate because Virgil had gotten fed up and transferred to Jacksonville State University. As roommates and teammates my first year in the dorm, Virgil and I got to be friends. We played the same position. We liked each other.

Coach Lorendo had predicted that Virgil would be the next great Auburn receiver. He liked Virgil's ability, but Virgil wasn't the type to take the constant criticism, cussing, and put downs of Coach Lorendo and Coach Christian. Virgil figured if he missed a pass, he would catch the next one. He'd catch far more than he would ever miss. Coach Lorendo rode him hard. After all, he was the second black signee. He had to work out.

At night in our room, Virgil would let me know he'd just about had enough. One practice he reached his tipping point. He packed up that evening and left.

I hated to see Virgil go. We were close. But Virgil had choices. He did not have to take the abuse like most of us did. I always felt that since Virgil and I played the same position, he was expendable. They exchanged one black athlete for another.

That sophomore year, I adjusted to "the zoo." There were far more advantages to living there than disadvantages. But it was awkward at first.

A macho, infantile culture ruled the dorm. Bragging, whether about a play on the field or a female conquest, was the conversation norm.

Football ruled. There was little time for most anything else. Serious girlfriends or too many friends outside the athletic department were discouraged. They could take away from a player's concentration on football.

We were being bred to play football.

There were several cliques and cultures that dominated the dorm. Stereotypically, they fell along the following lines.

The first type, the "Johnny Jock" guys, were the closest thing we had to frat guys. Some in fact belonged to frats. They had access to money, a nice car, and new clothes. They dressed up to go to class, pants riding up high on their waist, not a hair on their head out of place. They liked themselves almost as much as they liked girls, maybe more.

The Fellowship of Christian Athletes (FCA), was another clique. They hung together off the field. They held Bible study sessions in the dorm. Most were good guys, born again, but they could be judgmental. James read his Bible every night, but I never remember him being invited to one of their studies. On one occasion, a guy came to our room to witness to us and was surprised when we knew more about the Bible than he did. He never came back.

The Florida and big city guys came from Atlanta, Miami, cities in Florida, or the rare guy from "up north or out west." They had different views on life than the guys from small towns in Alabama and Georgia. The "Florida boys" were derisively called "Beach Boys," an insinuation that they were not tough enough.

Another group consisted of scholar athletes. Among the student body, being called a "jock" had a very negative connotation. Jocks were considered dumb, one-dimensional airheads. The smart guys were serious about college. They had a plan for their lives after football. These guys didn't delude themselves into thinking they would play professional football. They stayed on track to graduate.

We also had some outcasts. These guys might have had a legal problem or two, problems with their eligibility. Yet, they were really good athletes, or kids who made a mistake and were thought to be worth the trouble of keeping them in school.

We had a few hardcore racists. I avoided these guys. At best we were teammates.

Most of the guy's prejudices were the result of ignorance and their sheltered upbringing. These guys had never played with a black guy, never socialized with black people. Didn't know any black people. One example was Harry Ward who hailed from a small town in Alabama. Harry wore his hair in the 1960s country boy flattop style. Harry didn't bother anyone. He kept to himself. Yet, if a black guy sat next to Harry at the dinner table, he would get up and move. When I was told that, I didn't believe it. I went over and sat down next to him. Harry got up, without a word, and moved.

Harry came a long way during his four years at Auburn. We never became tight friends; but we became friendly. We shared a friendship based on being teammates who trusted and believed in each other. That became the basis for a relationship based on respect. I saw him at our reunion. I like him. I respect him. He had a long journey to travel. He came a long way.

Finally, James and I were in our own unique category. We were black. But we were not as invisible as the other black students on campus. We were black football players.

As a general rule, I hung with some of the outcasts and the Florida, or big city, guys. There was mutual admiration between the smart guys and me. We shared a common purpose, a life after football.

The unspoken racial barrier held for most of our teammates. Fat Daddy, Mike Flynn, Rett Davis, and a couple of others were the only white guys I developed a full relationship with. Others I settled for. We didn't go out together. We didn't hang at parties together. We were friendly because we were teammates, not because we were friends. Half of the guys, I never developed any relationship with. Some of these guys I played with two, three, four years. They weren't interested and neither was I. I also came to realize that even the good guys on the team were not going to risk being ostracized by befriending me or any other black student at Auburn.

Living in the dorm, the scholarship, and the football team had given me celebrity status. My name appeared in the newspapers, usually with my picture. I was interviewed on television and radio. Everyone on campus and in the town knew me. People all over Birmingham knew me. My relatives all over the country were proud of me.

There were other perks. Registration for school was easier. We were given priority admit status for classes. Smart guys in class offered help if needed. Smart girls too.

We were big men on campus and we knew it. People liked and admired us. Walking into a classroom was different now than in my freshman biology class. Now when I walked into a class, I could hear the whispers, "That's Thomas Gossom." I was somebody. Yeah, it felt good.

With this group of guys, we were ready to begin the 1972 season. Both the players and the coaches felt we had great team chemistry. That didn't mean that everyone got along or even liked each other. However, the coaches had worked us to the point where our individual differences were irrelevant when we hit the field. We shared a common belief. Through hard word and subjugating our individual preferences and life styles, we realized that collectively we were better than we were individually. We wanted to win. I wanted to win.

# CHAPTER 12

# "WE'RE JUST NOT GOING TO HAVE IT ANY OTHER WAY"

The fire burned in my gut. The clock slowly moved toward 7:00 pm. Hurry! Hurry! I wanted to shout at it.

I sat dressed and ready in my white road uniform in the visitor's locker room in Jackson, Mississippi. The 49 on my jersey, in honor of Bobby Mitchell, spread across my back and chest. I was "getting my mind right" to go out and play my first game. The opponent was Mississippi State.

The locker room was full of false bravado and jangled nerves. Most of the guys sat with their game faces on. The game face was a coach's tradition where a player was instructed to look mean and intent as the player "got his mind right," for the upcoming game.

Mixed emotions raced throughout my body. I thought of all the days of practice, hot sun, sweat, the fights, coaches in my face, and my broken hand. I felt relief that the moment had finally arrived. That morning I'd checked my old New Year's resolution. I smiled as I opened the well-folded and worn piece of paper. I reread the words I'd scribbled over two years ago. I safely tucked it back into my wallet.

Coach Jordan gave us the pep talk. "For some of you it will be the biggest test of your young lives." He paced the concrete floor. I noticed his limp was becoming more pronounced. He had health concerns. He'd undergone two serious operations. Physically, it was starting to show. He stood slightly hunched over. He had a paunch below his waistline.

As usual, he wore his gray hat, matching jacket, khaki pants, and black coaching shoes. This would be his twenty-second football team at Auburn University. He had coached his first Auburn team in 1951, the year before I was born. He made eye contact with each of us as he went around the room. Our eyes held onto each other's for a few precious seconds. I was one of Shug's boys.

Coach talked about our youthfulness on offense. He reminded us not to beat ourselves by making mistakes. "We're going to go out there tonight and beat Mississippi State with five plays. Five plays. That's it." He looked at each of us to make sure we understood. We did.

It wouldn't be fancy. It would be an old-fashioned, man-on-man fight for sixty minutes. The last man standing would win.

We were underdogs, but unlike our practices, the Mississippi State guys didn't know our plays. They didn't know what to expect. If we executed the five plays as we'd done in practice, over and over again until the opposition tired, we'd win. Coach Jordan often told us, "Fatigue will make a coward out of a man."

Coach Jordan ended his talk with one of my favorite sayings of his. In tight games, with all things being close to equal, Coach believed the game could be won on willpower. "We're just not going to have it any other way."

Johnny Simmons, our starting safety, asked Coach if he could speak to the team. Johnny lit a fire under the players. "I was emotional, crying," Simmons related. "I stood up and said I'd been an Auburn fan all my life, and that Auburn teams weren't supposed to be underdogs to Mississippi State, and that I'd be damned if I was going to be on an Auburn team that lost to Mississippi State."

Many of the guys were crying, screaming. They calmed down enough to kneel and say the Lord's Prayer. I never prayed for us to win. I figured God didn't much care if we beat Mississippi State. I figured He loved them just like He loved us. I prayed that no one was seriously injured.

"All right," Coach Jordan raised his left fist into the air and dropped it into his right hand. "Let's go." The reverberating cry bounced throughout the locker room. We stumbled over each other as we filed out onto the concrete runway.

"Let's go, damnit," someone shouted. "1 and 0 tonight," another cried. "Let's kick their ass."

Forty-seven thousand partisan fans waited restlessly for the announcer to introduce the Mississippi State starting lineup. But first he was making his way through the Auburn lineup.

We stood in the players' tunnel. The announcer continued, "At starting halfback, number twenty-three, Terry Henley." His name blared over the loudspeaker. There was sparse applause from the few thousand Auburn fans. "At fullback number forty-three, James Owens." I patted James on his butt. "Let's go baby," he said to me. We slapped skin.

Then...

"The starting wingback, number forty-nine, Sophomore Thomas Gossom."

If there was any applause I was oblivious to it. I felt someone slap me on the head. The adrenalin flowed. I adjusted my socks and sweatbands. I untied and retied my shoes. Rubbed any sweat from my hands.

On the sideline, the national anthem began. The U.S. flag surged in the black skyline. Players from both teams lined the sidelines, helmets held waist high in our hands. Some covered their hearts with padded hands.

We won the toss and elected to receive. I limbered up with sophomore quarterback, Randy Walls. He had been given the quarterback nod once we resumed practice from summer break. With Dave Lyons out, the coaches decided Randy had the best chance of leading us on the field.

From Brundidge, Randy was a typical Auburn football player from small town Alabama. He'd grown up listening to Auburn on the radio. Now all of Brundidge was proud of their native son, the starting quarterback for Auburn University.

Randy leaned over and asked me if I was nervous. I knew he was. He'd already had to go back into the locker room complaining his jersey was too tight. He said it was choking him. Someone finally noticed that he had it on backward. We got a laugh out of that. It lightened up our mood, but not Randy's.

"I'm scared shitless," he told me. He studied for a final time the eight plays on his wristband. We were only going to run five.

The game was not televised. In the pre-ESPN era, only one national game and one regional game would be televised per Saturday. That year, I believe two or three of our games were televised. People followed their teams by radio.

After the kickoff, it was first and ten, Auburn's ball. As would become my custom, I would sprint out on the field, the first of our players to reach the spot where we would huddle. I was excited, ready to go. In the huddle, our moment was at hand. We'd heard all the talk about being underdogs. We'd heard the talk about no one believing in us. None of that mattered anymore. The time for talking was done. "Let's play ball," I said to James. He nodded.

Senior Mac Lorendo, Coach Lorendo's son and our captain, extended his hand into the middle of the huddle. We put our hands together. Eleven hands met. Mac told us, "We know what we got to do, let's do it." The hands broke.

Randy, in his nervous voice called out, "Wing right twenty-seven slant on two... Okay ... Ready. " Eleven voices in chorus resounded, "Break."

I lined up on the right side behind the offensive tackle. The play would come off of my butt. My job was to double-team the defensive tackle with our offensive tackle. We would have to bury him. James would lead Henley through the hole and block the defensive end. With the hole cleared, Henley would hurl his body through it. We'd done the same play thousands of times since last January.

"Hike." The ball was snapped. The tackle, Caldwell, and I slammed into the Mississippi State tackle. We eliminated him from the play. James rammed the defensive end to his knees. The end groaned as he went down. Henley said later, James had blacktopped the guy.

I thought about my dad listening to the game on the hi-fi radio in our living room. He would be hunched over, paying particularly close attention every time the radio announcer would say, "Gossom is at wing right" or "Gossom is split left." I didn't think my mom was listening. She and Kim would monitor the game through Daddy. Donna was now a freshman at Auburn.

My family would make all the home games. Auburn was a day trip for them. The away games would have required hotels and added expense. It was never even a point of discussion.

On that first drive, Henley scored on a three-yard run. On that run, we found our bread and butter for the year in the left side of our offensive line. Seniors Mac and Jay cleared out their right defensive side. James crushed the end, pushing him down the field unmercifully.

James also scored on a rare run, a beautiful sixteen-yard rumble through the middle of the Mississippi State line. He took a quick-hitting hand-off, sidestepped a block, and broke a tackle. James ran into Mississippi State's defensive back Frank Downsing (Mississippi State's first black football player) at the five-yard line. Downsing must have felt what I felt that day in practice when James bore down on me and I had to tackle him in the open field. James hit Downsing, ran over him, and then stepped over him and into the end zone. The offense mobbed James.

Henley ran for 136 yards. Walls completed five passes for forty-one yards. I caught one pass for nine yards and had one run for nine yards.

We won the game 14-3. We manhandled them. We had the ball for thirty-nine of the sixty minutes. We knew our defenders were the foundation that would carry the team until the young guys on offense could grow up. That night our defense played with a vengeance, holding Mississippi State to ninety-eight yards rushing on forty carries.

Mississippi State had a black quarterback, Melvin Barkum, who alternated with the other quarterback. Barkum was the first black quarterback we played against in the SEC. He didn't fare well against us. Our defense would turn it up a notch when we played against black quarterbacks. It gave those guys an adrenaline rush.

After the game, many of us younger guys were too excited to sleep. Several of the guys met on a little hillside near the parking lot of the motel we stayed in overnight. We talked and laughed. For most of us it was our first game. We relived it. One of the guys brought along a joint. I don't remember who it was. The joint was passed around.

The guys in the hillside group were all starters and guys who received a lot of playing time. It was a secretive group out of necessity. We all had a lot to lose.

We were 1-0, but the coaches made sure to keep us levelheaded. The next week's practice was as brutal as spring training and summer camp. The mental and physical pounding started to take its toll. We were a tired team. We were favored in our next game against Chattanooga, but we barely survived. Recognizing we could be taken, Chattanooga got after us. We were playing our first game at home. We wanted it easy. We wanted them to fold. They wouldn't cooperate. In the end, we pulled it out. Henley broke a thirty-seven-yard run to seal the victory. Bernich ended the day by intercepting a pass and we ran out the clock. We finally beat them, 14-7.

I had two rushing attempts for minus one yard. My designated play was a wingback reverse, back through the center of the line. I hated that play. We never gained any yards on it because the play required the linemen to hold their blocks too long. I wanted the ball out in space where I could make somebody miss. But I did what I was asked. We were a team. We won as a unit. The individual stuff didn't matter.

Those were good days for the Gossom's. Daddy would not work on those weekends. They would load up the car with goodies and drive down for the day's game. I would pace back and forth waiting for them to come. James's family and my family got along well. Our mothers would prepare baskets of our favorite foods.

After the games, both families would gather in our room at the dorm and we'd all celebrate. There would be much food, love, and laughter. Fat Daddy would come by and speak to my parents. The games became our social events. It gave our parents and families an affordable social outing to look forward to. It was satisfying to watch our parents, who had never before been on a college campus, enjoy themselves. Because Donna was now on campus and could get student tickets, Mama and Daddy could also bring along an uncle or aunt.

After our parents left Auburn, reality would set in. We had nowhere to go. After everyone had left, I'd get dressed to go out. On most Saturday nights, the few blacks on campus would try to have a party in someone's apartment. On other Saturdays, I'd join James in the dark of the TV room in the dorm. We'd watch television the rest of the night, that day's game a distant memory.

We were 2-0. We were starting to get noticed by sports reporters and newspapers, but not much credit. A headline in *The Birmingham News* said what most people seemed to feel, "JURY STILL OUT ON THE TIGERS." The article concluded, "The real verdict on the Tigers' season will be returned Saturday afternoon by a Tennessee jury."

Tennessee was undefeated, ranked number four in the nation. They had two All-American linebackers, the nation's number one defense, and a multi-talented black quarterback in Condredge Holloway from Huntsville, Alabama. A gifted athlete, the Yankees drafted Holloway to play professional baseball. Neither Auburn nor Alabama tried to recruit Holloway as a quarterback.

Our defense would have its first major challenge. Could we stop their high-powered offense? On offense, James would be the key. Could he block the Tennessee linebackers?

We were three touchdown underdogs.

Coach Jordan called us all together in the dining room before boarding the bus to Birmingham, where we would play Tennessee. Henley recalls, "He told us that he didn't want a single person to get on the bus that didn't think we could beat Tennessee. He said that if only eight people got on the bus, we would find a way to win with those eight."

In our offensive meeting with Coach Lorendo, we were quiet but intense. Coach Lorendo was somber. This would be our first big test. It would be against the best defense in the country. "Go out there and score twice," Coach Lorendo said. "And I guarantee we win the game. Give me two touchdowns or a touchdown and a field goal, and we win. The defense is not going to let them score more than once. I promise you."

Neither James nor I slept much the night before the game. James spent a good part of the night getting into his stance and charging into the wall. He was pumped, getting ready for his clashes with the All-American linebackers. It was the biggest game either of us had ever played.

The atmosphere was charged in Birmingham's sold-out Legion Field. I was home. My folks were in the stands. Coach Jordan told us to go out there and get after them. We did.

Tennessee could only muster ten first downs. Langner had an interception. The defense gave us a fumble that led to a field goal. Our defense chased and harassed Holloway all day

Henry Ford recalled how the fans reacted to the black quarterback. "As a walk-on, I was sitting with the freshman team in the stands. After the opening sack of Holloway, some of the fans started to chant, 'Kill that "N" word,' kill that "N" word,'" he said.

"Because many of the black students refused to go to the games, there were times when I would be the only black person in the stadium besides our two players on the field and the building and grounds guys who sat in the special bleachers set aside for them. If the other team had a black player, it was hard on him, especially a black quarterback."

On offense, we ran right at the two All-Americans. Henley right. Henley left. James led the way. The clashes were brutal and fierce. We threw only four passes and completed one. We all blocked like we never had before. It was a sixty-minute dogfight.

On our touchdown-scoring drive we ran the same running play, 21-power, right up the middle, ten straight times until Henley dove over the pile for the score. We won, 10-6. Coach Lorendo had asked us to give him two scores. We gave him two scores, a touchdown and a field goal.

*The Birmingham News* answered any questions that anyone still had about the '72 Auburn Tigers and inadvertently gave us a nickname.

"One could see as well as feel the intensity of the Auburn team as they took the field. Auburn was spoiling for a fight.

"...The jury is now in on the Tigers and the rest of the conference had better beware. The Tigers are for real. The 10-6 score of Saturday's game does not reflect the whipping Tennessee took. From the opening play, when Holloway was slammed to the turf for a ten-yard loss, the Tigers dominated the game. The lone Tennessee score came with 1:36 left in the ball game and proved too little too late. For its sparse talent, truly this Auburn team is amazing."

"The Amazins." The name would stick. We were now ranked number seventeen in the country.

In the huddle against Ole Miss, Randy called, "A-right drop back pass X takeoff, on two." We broke to the line. Randy hunched over the behind of center Steve Taylor. He barked, "Hut Hut" The ball was snapped. I shot out of my stance like a rocket. The defender never had a chance. He was beaten by five yards as Randy let it go, a beautiful spiral. I can still see it now, floating down toward my hands. My first, touchdown!

On the 1972 highlight tape, I catch the touchdown, slide into the end zone and jump up and down, pogo stick style, in celebration until I hand the ball to the ref. The first person I see running to greet me is James.

Randy Walls had proven himself. He threw for that touchdown and ran for another against Ole Miss. Sportswriters had dubbed him "the ugly duckling." But so far, he was undefeated. We were now ranked number nine.

Our next opponent, LSU was number eight. We were playing in Baton Rogue, the roughest college stadium in the country.

The night started out wrong. We broke from our dressing room to find Mike the Tiger, LSU's live Tiger mascot, waiting for us outside the dressing room. He roared and we stopped in our tracks. All of us piled into each other like Keystone cops. We slowly took wide turns to get around the tiger. Then, we ran to the wrong end of the field to warm up. Their rabid fans mocked us.

The game snowballed on us. It was as though we were in slow motion while everything around us was on fast forward. "They kicked our brains in," says Mac Lorendo. Bert Jones, the LSU quarterback, threw three touchdowns and ran for another score. When it was over, they'd beaten us 35-7. I had a good game, got us in position to score by catching two passes for forty-one yards. But there was no joy.

We were despondent. We had not thought about going undefeated, but we'd also not imagined losing. Again, we could not sleep. The game ate at us. The hillside gang of guys decided to get together. We met behind a church and replayed the plays of the game over and over. Someone brought some marijuana again, but there were no rolling papers. Someone came up with the idea of rolling it in the yellow pages from the phone book. Somehow it stayed together. We laughed at the idea of smoking the yellow pages. The silly laughter lessened our pain.

# WALK-ON

---

We became celebrities on campus. I began to hang around outside Haley Center between classes, chatting up girls. James even made his way to class from time to time. He'd go on Thursdays "to get a *Plainsman* and see if my picture is in it."

Posters of individual team members hung all over campus and in downtown stores. A new deck of cards with the players' pictures on them was sold in the local bookstores. Each card sported a photo of your favorite Auburn Tiger. I was the eight of hearts. James was the ace of diamonds. Coach Jordan, the ace of spades.

The adulation spread to Birmingham. My mom and dad had always kept an unlisted phone number, but, somehow or other, people would get their number anyway and call "about that boy of yours at Auburn."

The girls certainly paid me more attention. Our phone in the dorm rang often. There were a few new black women on campus and that fall I dated a couple of freshman roommates. We'd do movies; go to the few black parties on campus. The community girls competed with the campus girls for our attention. Sometimes we would make runs to Tuskegee.

I began seeing a white girl from Childersburg, Alabama. We had a class together and our looks lingered. After one class, we made polite talk and I asked her for her phone number. We started seeing each other. We never went out on a date, never went anywhere in public. We mostly stayed at her apartment. Her roommate did not like me being there and she would not socialize with us. She would go into her bedroom and lock the door.

Still, we got along fine within the confines of the situation. Neither of us wanted to publicly challenge the social taboos of Auburn. I didn't want to risk the wrath of the athletic department. We were not serious enough about each other for that.

I learned to manage this complexity from Henry. Henry had a white girlfriend when I met him. He kept her "undercover," no movies, dinners, or anything public. She came to his games, and we all knew her. He'd bring her around the brothers. Maybe a couple of the white guys knew; maybe a couple of her friends, but that was it. Henry knew the score: "It's Auburn." To put the complicated dating situation in perspective, it would remain illegal for blacks and whites to marry in Alabama until 1999.

A slow cultural thaw was beginning on campus as Dr. Philpott's administration reacted to black students' previous demands and needs.

On September 1, 1972, Dean E. H. Hobbs, of the School of Arts and Sciences, appointed Dr. Robert Reid as professor of history. Reid was the first black faculty member to serve in the capacity of full professor. Dr. Reid, originally from Selma, had a distinguished career but did not consider himself "any kind of pioneer." I never knew him.

Still, Dr. Reid's hiring was not enough. The "Focus" section of the October 5, 1972, *Plainsman* was dedicated to the Black Student at Auburn. In an un-credited piece titled, "Black Students Want Areas of Improvement," several black students voiced their frustrations. "Race relations haven't changed in the three years I've been at Auburn." "I believe that relations at Auburn are possibly worse that the rest of the South." "Students here are trying to uphold an image of segregation."

While *The Plainsman* took as progressive a view as any organization on campus, Dean Foy, the administrator responsible for the student paper, told me that there were many times he did not agree with points of view expressed in the student newspaper, but, "I never censored the paper. I never asked to read any piece before it was published."

In that edition of *The Plainsman*, Roy Summerford's story titled, "Black Athletes Have Broken Race Barrier," includes a quote from me.

"Tom Gossom, sophomore wingback, observed that even though Auburn is trying to recruit more blacks, it is not doing so in proportion to whites. 'More effort could be made,' Gossom said. 'It might help to have blacks recruiting for Auburn. The problem is that more black players in the state favor Alabama, where there is more social life.'"

That fall our numbers grew to six black athletes in the athlete dormitory. In addition to James, Mitzi Jackson, and me, three black basketball players signed with Auburn. Gary Redding, a prized recruit from Atlanta, chose Auburn over fifty other schools.

After the LSU loss, the coaches surprised us. They never showed us the game film. They never talked about it to us. It had happened and it was over. It was brilliant coaching. We could play better and we knew it. There would be nothing to gain from punishing or pushing us any harder.

The Auburn-Georgia Tech matchup was a rivalry game. The Georgia Tech Yellow Jackets had dropped out of the Southeastern Conference, but Auburn continued to play them every year. There was an annual "Wreck Tech" parade. We did a lot more than that. We took the LSU loss out on Georgia Tech. We fell behind 14-0 but righted the ship and rolled over them for twenty-four straight points. We won 24-14. With Henley injured, Chris Linderman, a fine runner, rushed for ninety-nine yards. I had two runs for three yards. I also had two catches for twenty-four yards and a touchdown. My touchdown catch sealed the victory. We were 5-1. Wilson recalls, "After the Georgia Tech game, my dad told me 'you will never play on a team this good again.'"

We rolled on. We beat Florida State on ABC television. Henley rushed for 105 yards and scored three touchdowns. I had a big game, hauling in two big receptions for sixty yards and one touchdown. After my touchdown catch, I coolly flipped the ball to the official in the back of the end zone. Remember, we were on television. When I turned to go back to our sideline, Mac Lorendo came running up. He lifted me up in a bear hug. My other teammates came and congratulated me. I tried to get down, but Mac continued to hold me. Finally, I said, "Mac let me down." He responded, "We're on television. You just scored, so we're both on television." We laughed.

James and I got in trouble with Brownie after that game. We were invited to a party at Tuskegee Institute, and we were excited to go. It was something to do. We had a fun time dancing and hanging out. We didn't do much drinking. We never drank a lot. We made it back to the dorm by 2:30 a.m. Curfew the night after a game was 1:30 a.m., but the coaches never enforced it. It was a guideline more than anything.

We pulled into the dorm parking lot and there was Brownie. Shit. He met us at the steps. We told him where we'd been. We told him we were not drunk and it was the only time we'd ever been late. Brownie assured us the incident would be, "just between us, men." We felt it was behind us and went to bed.

We had a loosening-up session at 7 a.m. on Sunday mornings after a game. The session helped us to work out the soreness from the previous day's game. The injured guys received treatment.

That morning, to our surprise, Coach Jordan was waiting for us. He'd "heard" we'd been late for curfew. We had to run extra for being late. We accepted the punishment.

Several days later, Coach Davis called us into his office after lunch. He counseled us about being late, about being so far away from campus. He said he understood our situation but we needed to be careful. He continued questioning us, and then James went off. It was the only time I ever saw James get upset. It was the only time Coach Davis had ever seen him upset. James demanded to know, "So what are we supposed to do Coach? There's nothing to do here. Hell, the guys don't want to be with us. There aren't any black women here on campus." He was trying to be respectful. Still, anger crept into his voice. Finally he was letting go of four years of frustration. James never cussed, but he asked, "Damn. What do we do?"

I never said a word. Coach Davis didn't say much more. He mumbled something about being careful. He had grabbed a hold of a tiger and he quickly turned loose. We were dismissed. It was probably the best airing-out session we'd ever had.

In the meantime, we moved up to number eleven in the polls.

We rolled past the Florida Gators, 26-20. Henley rushed for eighty yards in the first half. He sprained his knee and sat out the second half. We beat Georgia, 27-10, with second-team tailback Chris Linderman again, subbing for Henley. Linderman rushed for 149 yards. David Langner had two interceptions.

Georgia was our last home game of the year. Besides the winning and the actual games, I have two clear memories of our home games. At the end of the third quarter, the crowd would rise from their seats. The game would be stopped. The players and the fans would stand at attention. The band would play "Dixie" as the confederate flag, flying over the stadium with the U.S. flag, was lowered. Most of the fans stood with a hand over their heart. It was a moment right out of the Old South. Once the flag was lowered, the place erupted in cheers.

Whenever we got to this moment in the game, I became terribly uncomfortable, if not pissed. Maybe it was one of my first acting jobs because I did not let anyone know what I felt. I never made a deal out of it to anyone, but I would not, could not, honor the tradition. I would not put my hand over my heart. I would not look up at that flag. I kept my eyes trained on the ground.

There's another vivid memory of home games. Makeshift, temporary wooden bleachers were assembled in the corner of the end zone nearest the player's entrance to the field. That was seating for B&G. B&G stood for building and grounds. The Auburn University janitors, maintenance, and grounds attendants, who were all black, did not sit in the stands with everyone else. They sat on the rickety bleachers in the corner of the far end zone away from the rest of the crowd. We would pass the B&G men as we ran to the field from the locker room. The men's eyes were always riveted on James and me. Many of the men reminded me of my dad and the men from my neighborhood. Not only were we getting an opportunity they'd never had, they had to sit and watch us on bleachers that were the equivalent of them sitting in the back of the bus. James and I represented their opportunity. Many times, I felt I carried the weight of their dreams on my shoulders.

We were now 8-1 and ranked ninth in the nation. The athletic department administration had already accepted an invitation to the Gator Bowl where we would play Colorado.

The only game left in the season was the only game that mattered to most folks in Auburn: Auburn vs. The University of Alabama. This year looked like a marquee match up.

Alabama was undefeated, 10-0. They were ranked second in the nation behind Southern Cal. They'd already agreed to go to the Cotton Bowl to play Texas. They ran an awesome wishbone offense that averaged thirty-eight points and 425 yards per game.

This would be our biggest test yet. Could The Amazins pull off a miraculous end to a miraculous season? The bookies didn't think so. They made us sixteen-point underdogs.

# CHAPTER 13

---

# 17-16

During the first nine years of my life, the "Iron Bowl," the big annual game between Auburn University and the University of Alabama, in Birmingham's Legion Field, was a major pain for my family. My dad hated that Saturday.

When I was a child, we lived near Legion Field. On the day of the game, if my mom wanted to shop for groceries, she had to leave home as soon as the store opened. She had better return home before mid-morning. If my dad had to get repairs done on the car, he had better have them done early.

By midday on that Saturday, thousands of white folks would descend like ants on our neighborhood, going to the game. I would sit on our tiny front porch and watch the mayhem of traffic moving along the city streets. It was out of control. It was as if our neighborhood was under attack. The white folks came with full glasses, blood shot eyes, and loud shrill voices hollering "War Eagle" and "Roll Tide." They never said so much as "Hi" to us. We were just a part of the scenery on the way to the game.

My dad complained to me about the traffic, noise, and drunken white people. "I hate that game," he would say. The huge crowd blew their horns, cussed loudly, and paraded through our neighborhood like they owned it. They commandeered our neighborhood for a day.

Legion Field in Birmingham, like many city-owned stadiums, is located in the middle of a black neighborhood. Black folks didn't play in the games or go to them unless they were selling Cokes in the stands. The best you could hope for was to park a white fan's car in your yard for a few bucks. You may as well get the few bucks because they would park in your yard anyway. It didn't pay to harass the people going to the game. In a dispute, the police would favor the game patron. They represented commerce for the city. If your protested too much, you could get your head cracked.

On December 2, 1972, the thirty-seventh annual game between Auburn University and the University of Alabama would be played again in Legion Field. Only, this time, my dad and my uncle, Bobby Tankersley, were among the 72,386 crazed fans crammed into the stands. Daddy didn't seem to mind the traffic that day. The first Iron Bowl he would see would be the first one I played in.

The entire state of Alabama was buzzing. The atmosphere was crazy. The annual Iron Bowl was the social event of the year in the state. It was the center of the state's sports universe. Could The Amazins slow down their juggernaut archrival, The University of Alabama?

Both teams bussed to Birmingham. The stadium was half orange and blue, half red and white. For fans, it was about bragging rights. For us players, it was the biggest game of the year.

Alabama Coach Bear Bryant had upped the stakes by calling Auburn "a cow college." When asked about the Cotton Bowl game and Alabama's chances for a national championship, Bryant replied he'd rather beat the "cow college" than Texas any day. Many Auburn fans were outraged. Alabama fans didn't see the slight as giving us any more incentive. They figured we didn't have a chance either way. As a team, we remained focused on our mission. It didn't take an opponent's words to get you up for this game.

We entered the game ranked number nine, but not many believed we could win. Mike Tankersley in the *Montgomery Advertiser* summed up what many people thought: "Alabama appeared invincible. Auburn was the little engine that could."

In *The Plainsman*, I predicted a victory. My prediction seemed far-fetched; even my dad had his doubts. He told me, "You know I don't know as much about football, but I don't believe you all are going to be able to beat them with just good defense and kicking." He warned, "You're going to have to try and hit a big pass or something."

I knew what he was saying. He thought I could help the team more if they would throw to me more. I agreed. I'd caught eight passes all year, and I was second on the team in receptions. I'd averaged twenty-one yards a catch, with three touchdowns. Every ball I caught went either for a first down or a touchdown. But I didn't call the plays. In the Southeastern Conference of the early seventies, the coaches' philosophy on passing was simple. Either one of three things could happen when you passed, a completion, an interception, or an incompletion, and two of them were bad. Besides, we were winning. We were a team. We were all for one, one for all.

For Alabama, we would do what we'd done all year. Remain conservative on offense. Try and score a few points. Then keep them backed up by winning the field position battle. The coaches stressed our being physical with them on both offense and defense. "Deliver the first blow."

To a man we thought we could win the game. That feeling was not based on comparable statistics, rankings, or wins. The feeling was based on what we'd been through, how much confidence we had in each other. It was based on believing we were not going to have it any other way. As Coach Jordan often told us, "It's Americana boys. Country boy goes to town and accomplishes something he's not supposed to."

We would depend on our defense. But could our defense save us against their wishbone offense? The year before was the first time our defense had ever seen the wishbone. We were too passive. We tried to read and react. This year the coaches had decided to attack their offense, break the plays down before they could get going.

David Langner recalls his last minute instructions from Coach Sam Mitchell. "We had a real aggressive defense all year under Coach Paul Davis. The very first play of the game, Coach Mitchell told me to get a running start and when they snapped the ball, to try and take out

(Wayne) Wheeler (the Alabama wide receiver). They were running the wishbone and he was the only one split out. He and I got in a fight the first play of the game. That kind of got the game started. It wasn't any big deal to get into a fight during a ballgame back then. It kept us fired up."

Our defense hung in there like a rusty nail. Alabama would manage only 251 yards for the game. Our best offensive weapon was our punter, David Beverly. He punted eight times for an average of forty-three yards. He boomed one punt fifty-seven yards. Our captain, Mac Lorendo, remembers, "We struggled offensively. Everything was off. It wasn't so much what they did, but we failed to execute."

I disagree with Mac. Their defense knew exactly what we were doing. They'd studied a year's worth of film on us. We didn't do anything different. Our man-on-man blocking didn't work because they were stuffing the holes. They had no fear of us passing.

We had a chance to score early. Langner intercepted a ball deep in Alabama territory, giving us first and goal on their four-yard line. Excited, I raced onto the field. On, first down, Henley slammed into the line. Nothing. Second down, nothing. Third down, nothing. They swarmed fast to the hole, clogging everything up. We were forced to try a field goal. On the field goal try, the snap from center sailed over our holder Dave Beck's head, and Alabama recovered. We walked away empty.

Coaches say little plays make big victories. A little play in the first half of the game would prove decisive in the game's outcome. Alabama scored to take a 6-0 lead but Roger Mitchell, my walk-on friend, blocked the extra point.

On offense, we were thoroughly throttled. We tried a pass. Alabama intercepted it. They kicked a field goal, making it 9-0. In the third quarter, Alabama's big wishbone drove seventy-eight yards. Although every yard was vigorously contested, Alabama was not number two in the country for nothing. They scored to go up 16-0. Luckily, they would later miss a field goal to extend their lead.

Finally, near the end of the third quarter, our toughness paid off. We'd gotten a tongue lashing from Coach Lorendo. We had to produce. Again, we were not going to trick them, or run around them. We would have to run through them. We'd come so far. Did we believe we could do it one more time?

We mounted our only drive of the game for fifty-six yards. On third down, faced with ending the best drive we'd had all day, Coach Lorendo called a pass. Randy fired the ball and I caught it for a fourteen-yard gain. We had another first down. New life.

We bogged down on the Alabama twenty-four-yard line. Faced with fourth and eight with 9:15 left in the game, down 16-0, Coach Jordan had to face the question: Do we go for the first down? To have any possibility of winning the game, we would need three scores.

Excitement buzzed through the Auburn stands. Other than the early scoring opportunity, this was our best chance of the day. The feeling in the stands was surely Coach Jordan would go for it with so little time left.

On the sideline, Coach Jordan grabbed our place kicker, Gardner Jett. "Can you kick it?" Coach Jordan wanted to know. Gardner replied, "I think I can." Coach Jordan hollered, "This is a helluva time to be thinking about it."

When we lined up for the kick, I heard something I'd never heard at an Auburn game. The Auburn fans booed. They wanted us to go for it. They thought we were giving up by not going for it. As it turns out it wasn't just Auburn people booing. The Alabama fans were booing too. The field goal would mess up the betting spread of sixteen points.

Gardner kicked his longest kick ever, forty-two yards. The ball hit the left upright, glanced off, and fell through. Good! The score was now 16-3.

Then the miracle happened.

Alabama picked up three first downs following the kickoff, but their drive stalled at midfield. Greg Gantt came on to punt for Alabama. Auburn put ten men on the line of scrimmage. We were going after the punt.

In what would become a famous recording for Gary Sanders, the Auburn play-by-play announcer that day, he described what happened next.

"Greg Gantt is in to punt. Johnny Simmons is going back as a single safety... Mitchell and Langner are on the line of scrimmage coming from either side, to try to block the kick... Auburn trying to go after it... Here's the snap. They got it! Blocked kick! Ball's back to the twenty-five, picked up on the bounce on the twenty-five yard line and in for a touchdown is David Langner."

At the snap of the ball, former walk-on Bill Newton charged between the Alabama guard and tackle untouched, dived, and blocked the punt at the Alabama forty. The ball miraculously bounced into Langner's hands at the twenty-five-yard line. Langner caught it on the dead run. Touchdown! Jett kicked the extra point.

We were down 16-10 with 5:30 left in the game. Coach Jordan's decision to kick the field goal didn't seem so bad now.

Alabama drove the ball to their forty-two-yard line, the drive stalled again. Defensive captain Mike Neel broke through to sack the quarterback on third down. Alabama lined up to punt again and Coach Lorendo gathered the offense on the bench. The crowd was going crazy. We would get the ball again. We had a chance. Coach Lorendo didn't fuss or cuss. He pleaded. We'd gained eighty yards of offense all day. "Come on, guys." On the field, the Auburn defense was going after the punt block again.

Legendary Auburn coach Pat Dye was on the Alabama sideline that day as an assistant to Alabama coach Bear Bryant.

He said, "Coach Bryant made the decision to move the punter up two yards, figuring he'd get the punt off faster."

Coach Lorendo was making his final plea to us when I heard a thud, then a fierce roar from the crowd. Half the guys broke from the bench, leaving Coach Lorendo standing there. I jumped onto the bench, in time to see David Langner running across the goal line with the ball.

Once again, Gary Sanders' recording tells it best: "Langner will be on the far right... Roger Mitchell on the left and Auburn is again going after the kick, as you might imagine... Greg Gantt standing on his own thirty Auburn will try to block it... Auburn's going after it... Here's a good snap... It is blocked! It is blocked! It's caught on the run. It's caught on the run! He's gonna score. David Langner. David Langner has scored... and Auburn has tied the game.

Pandemonium broke out on the Auburn sideline. We were flagged for a delay of game penalty. Luckily, it would be enforced on the kickoff. The Alabama side of the stadium went deathly silent, stunned in disbelief.

Bill Newton had blocked the second kick just like the first. In what looked like instant replay, Bill blocked it and David Langer scooped the ball up on the dead run and scored again. The score was 16-16.

In the confusion, we offensive guys had to regain our composure. We had to kick the extra point. Gardner Jett, our place kicker remembers the day as though it were yesterday. "I didn't have time to think about anything," Jett said. "I was standing around when the second block happened and then I started looking for my tee. I couldn't find it because Joe Tanory (another kicker) had it. He was looking at me and holding the tee saying, 'Do you want to be a hero? What's it worth to you?' I had to wrestle the tee from him, and I didn't have time to think about anything."

In the huddle for the extra point, guard Jay Casey worked over Gardner Jett. "Damnit Gardner, you better make it. We have been working our ass off all day. You don't make it, I'll kick your little ass." Henley and I backed Jay off. "Leave him alone Jay." Everyone in the huddle let Gardner deal with his thoughts while we dealt with our own.

Alabama was coming after the extra point. They needed to block it. In the huddle, Dave Beck called, "Extra point on two."

We broke to the line of scrimmage. We would go to the line and point to the guy we would block, just like in spring practice. I lined up on the right side as the wingback. My job was not to let anybody rush the gap between our offensive tackle and myself. Make them go around me or through me. But not inside for what could be a direct line to the kicker.

Alabama lined up Ernest Odum and Leroy Washington over me. I knew them both from Birmingham. Both black, they were outstanding athletes, fast. Both guys were attending Alabama on basketball scholarships. I got in position. The ball was hiked.

Bodies collided. I spread my body, Ernest ran into me. I held him off. Leroy tried going around. I leg whipped him. From the pile of bodies, I looked up. The ball twirled its way through the goal posts. Good!

We were up 17-16 with 1:34 left in the game. Alabama received the ball, but their attitude had changed. Doubt had crept into their minds. The unthinkable was happening. They were no longer the confident, superior team of the first three and a half quarters. We tightened the screws.

"Hut." The Alabama quarterback dropped back, looked downfield, and threw. The ball sailed over the intended receiver's head. Fittingly, the ball settled into the arms of David Langner.

At the end, they had tried to change from the wishbone attack to a passing attack. They had come unglued before our eyes. The clock ticked down to 0:00. The scoreboard read Auburn 17, Alabama 16. We'd done it!

We ran toward the locker room like we'd stolen something. We had. Both sides of the stands were still full and would be full an hour later when we remerged from the locker room. No one had ever witnessed anything like what they had just seen. The Auburn people cheered. The Alabama people sat, stunned.

My dad was waiting at the fence leading from the field to the locker room. He was ecstatic. My uncle Bobby was with him. He'd won good money betting on us.

We pushed our way through the bodies to the locker room. I got into a pushing fight with an unhappy Alabama fan. He pushed and cussed me as we ran through the gauntlet of fans. My dad pushed me into the locker room. Fights broke out throughout the stands.

In the locker room, the celebration and long-awaited accolades began. It started with Coach Jordan. "In twenty-two years, I've always hesitated to put one of my teams ahead of another. Today I'm putting this team at the top of the list."

The game proved to be a moment in history that will never be duplicated, according to the *Montgomery Advertiser*. "...Fate intervened for a group of Tigers who fought so hard and so long, who refused to bow to defeat with such determination that they picked up the nickname, The Amazins. They scored seventeen unanswered points in the most bizarre way possible to pull off what – to this day – remains the greatest victory in the history of Auburn athletics."

The 17-16 "Punt Bama Punt" game is Alabama folklore. It's become one of those events that, if you were living in Alabama, you remember where you were when the two kicks were blocked. There is a great photo of Shug and Bear post-game at midfield. Face to face, they stand. Shug has his left hand behind Bear's neck, his sly as a fox grin says, "I got you."

Coach Jordan would be named Southeastern Conference Coach of the Year. He had been coaching forty years. He was the Dean of Southeastern Conference Head Coaches. This was his twenty-second season at Auburn. He had now won 154 games, gone to nine bowl games, won a national championship, produced twenty All-Americans and a Heisman trophy winner. He'd put his '72 team, us, at the top of that list. We were his favorite.

We would finish number five nationally. In the Gator Bowl, we beat Colorado like a drum, 24-3.

But for us, the greater honor was to be at the top of Coach Jordan's list. James says, "Coach told us at the beginning of the season, that everyone had counted us out and didn't give us a chance; but he said he would take us and play anyone, anywhere, anytime. We believed him."

[ 1973 ]

# CHAPTER 14

# THE INTOXICATIONS OF LIFE

Muhammad Ali stood five rows in front of me. "The Champ"! I couldn't believe it!

The occasion was an afternoon press conference with Muhammad Ali on Auburn's campus where he would make a speech that night. My journalism and reporting class had been given the assignment of covering The Champ's press conference. Those of us students in the reporting class knew we'd gotten lucky. With the press and media, we crowded into a first floor auditorium in Haley Center. The place was buzzing.

We waited anxiously as Ali started talking. We wanted one of his poems. A pronouncement of "I am the Greatest." Surprisingly, The Champ was subdued, thoughtful. He had reason to be. After losing to Joe Frazier two years earlier, he'd lost to Ken Norton. He had his jaw broken in the first round of the fight but fought the rest of the way in hopes of pulling out a decision.

None of us had ever seen The Champ like this. Quiet. We all wondered, "When is he going to put on the show?" He never did.

After he finished, I rushed outside to get in good position to see The Champ when he came out. Luckily, I ended up next to Les King, the university photographer. Mr. King shot all of the football games. He'd get great dramatic black and white action shots that he'd give us for our families.

Ali exited the auditorium. An athlete in fine condition, he bounced as he walked. A line of starry-eyed people waited. Many shook his hand, wished him well.

There was still no sign of the old flashy Ali, the jokester.

Mr. King leaned over to me. "Get close to him," he said. "I'll get your picture."

He didn't have to repeat himself. I slid over behind The Champ. When he turned, I stuck my hand out. "Mr. Muhammad," I said.

He went into the routine everyone had come to see. In a serious boxing crouch, his left fist balled and cocked slightly in front of his cocked right fist, he announced to everyone, "Joe Frazier. Joe Frazier." He squared off against me, ready to take me on. The show everyone had come to see was now on. "Joe Frazier," he called me again.

I leaned back, my fists half balled, half cocked. I was grinning a big, huge grin. It was funny, but I also wanted him to know that I was no threat. I made sure I was out of the way of his lighting-fast fists.

Mr. King got the shot. The photo is of Ali, a prime-cut athlete, with a dead serious look on his face squared off against me, grinning, with spectators in the background. It's still on my office wall, a life highlight.

That night before a massive audience, The Champ spoke on "The Intoxications of Life." For a minute or two he gave us some of the silly, fun Ali. "For a prize fighter, I'm pretty good looking," he told us.

Then he turned serious. He told us that his losses in the ring were due to his immersion into "life's intoxications." He'd become distracted from his life's spiritual mission by forgetting what had made him a champion in the first place. Life's intoxications, too much money, too many women, long nights, not enough training, and not enough godly living had led to his downfall.

I was mesmerized by The Champ's talk. Instead of a loud-talking, brash jokester, we listened to a man who felt he'd betrayed his God and his faith. I held on to the idea of life's intoxications.

Would we become intoxicated with our previous season's success, the miracle victory over Alabama? Would we be able to carry over our success to the next year? Based on the '72 season's success, we had begun to live large.

In the athletic dormitory, a solitary congratulatory telegram graced the lobby bulletin board. It bore the signature of Governor George C. Wallace. New clothes flashed around the dorm. I netted a new three-piece suit. The team's stars were popular. Newton and Langner were in demand. Everyone wanted a piece of them. The seniors who'd finished their eligibility prospered by speaking to Auburn Clubs around the state.

For some guys, their schoolwork suffered. A history professor stopped me after class to remind me that two of my teammates, Ken Bernich and Dan Nugent, were in his class. I told him I didn't know that since I'd never seen them. He said, "That's the problem. I'm going to pass them but I need them to come sometime." I replied, "Then I must be getting an A since I've been to every class and passed all the tests." He didn't respond. I reminded Bernich and Nugent they had a history class. I got an A.

Several coaches sported shiny new cars. So did several players, myself included; although my 1965 Chevrolet was neither new nor shiny. I'd bought it from my dad with my earnings the previous summer. I also paid the insurance, bought the gas, took care of all the maintenance, and added some rims. "If you are going to have a car," he said. "You have to be responsible for it."

The entire team would be introduced and individually presented certificates of merit by the student government president at a concert by the pop group, The Fifth Dimension. It would become another life moment for me.

Inside the packed coliseum, beautiful lead singer Marilyn McCoo walked into the audience in the middle of a song and held out her hand to me. She led me to the stage to the crowd's applause. As the group sang, Ms. McCoo and I danced. She pretended she liked me while her husband, singer Billy Davis, "protested" and feigned anger. The photo of "Tom dances with the Fifth Dimension," would make the next day's newspaper.

The adulation spread to Birmingham and my parents. Our last name, Gossom, now attracted attention, mostly uncomfortable, for my parents. Visitors showed up at their house to ask, "Is it your son that plays at Auburn?" Daddy told me, "This white lady at the medical center asked me if I was related to you. I told her 'Yeah.' She hugged me." My dad had never been hugged or even touched by anyone white.

My mom, proud but shy, didn't want any attention. It was enough for her that I had the opportunity to exercise the talents and ideas we'd always shared, the promise she never got to put into practice out in the world. I felt proud for my mom.

Yet, my parents' and sisters' support remained focused on the pride of achievement, and getting an education rather than football. Football was making us popular. The achievement of mastering college and negotiating a way in the newly opened society, made us all proud. For the time being though, I would bask in football glory.

Coach Mel Rosen, the track coach, asked if I was interested in running track. I could run the sixty-yard sprint and help on the relay team. "Yes," was my answer. I'd lettered in track in high school and done well. I could outrun everyone on Auburn's football team. I could run forty yards in 4.4 seconds. My best time in the hundred-yard dash had been 9.8 seconds.

I had no illusions of becoming a great sprint champion. I was not a track guy. I was a football player, with good size, who could run. Besides, I could work on my quickness, stamina, and lose weight. I weighed close to 195 now. If I could learn some technique to get a jump out of the starting blocks, I could be pretty good. Either way, track beat the hell out of wrestling some big defensive lineman in the football winter workout program.

Coach Lorendo reluctantly gave me permission to run track. He accused me of wanting to get out of the winter training program and he was right. I was excused from the winter program but not spring training. That meant I could run the indoor season but not the outdoor season in the spring.

As it turned out, track was a bore compared to football. Practice rarely lasted more than an hour and a half. It did however give me time to live a somewhat normal student life.

I approached the office of *The Plainsman* to inquire about writing for the school paper. I knew several writers from *The Plainsman* from my journalism classes. Pulitzer Prize winning editorial columnist Cynthia Tucker, and award-winning syndicated columnist Rheta Grimsley, were two of my classmates. The sports editor was excited to meet me. We talked for thirty minutes, mainly about my football exploits. I told him of my high school experience and he gave me an assignment!

I was to write a feature on Clifford Outlin, a world-class sprinter from Birmingham. That was easy. I had access and I knew track. I jumped on it.

Clifford had already caused a stir in his short time on campus. He became the surprise indoor sprinter in the nation by tying the world's record for sixty meters in a dual meet with the Russians. He capped off his first season by winning the National Indoor sixty-yard dash in Detroit. He lost by close margins to world record holder, Herb Washington, twice. He won the LSU Invitational in the early outdoor season.

I captured all this in my story in *The Plainsman*. The headline read: "Outlin Expects Outdoor Season to be Tougher Track Test, by Thomas Gossom, *Plainsman* Sports Writer."

"Before you leave here, we are going to find out you got all kinds of talent," Coach Lorendo commented. "What do you mean, Coach?" I asked. He responded, "The article you wrote in the paper was good." I hadn't seen the article yet. "Coach Jordan likes it too," he said.

Coach Jordan had read my article. He never mentioned it.

It would be the first of many articles I would write. I had access to the athletes that others didn't. I could relate, ask questions that would get honest answers. They trusted me. Classmates, instructors, and coaches commended me on my blossoming journalistic talents. It was satisfying to have a campus reputation in addition to football. It was equally satisfying to have the coaches commend me on my talents off the football field.

As for track, I flamed out pretty fast. In my first meet in the coliseum, I tore a hamstring. The football coaches were not happy. To make matters worse, halfway through my rehab, they rushed me back out on the track. They figured I was loafing. I didn't want to rush myself. I knew my body. They overruled Coach Rosen and me and forced me to run again too soon. I promptly tore it again. It took me a while to recover. During that time, I was no good to either the track team or the football team. With the few weeks left in the winter quarter, Buddy Davidson, the sports information director, arranged for me to become the track announcer for the remainder of the indoor meets. The announcer job became part of my practicum for my broadcasting class. I was getting a grade and gaining practical experience for talking about something I loved.

I was occupying my time, keeping myself out of trouble. Then…

Rett Davis, Chris Wilson, and I decided to take a trip to New Orleans for Mardi Gras. Going to the Mardi Gras was an annual event for many Auburn football players. Tales of the debauchery of New Orleans were legendary around the dorm.

We would need a good excuse to miss two days of winter training. We put our plan into action a week before we went to New Orleans. We decided that each of us would come up with a good story to tell our position coach explaining why we would not be at winter workout the following Monday and Tuesday. I told Coach Christian a story about needing to go to Birmingham for something with my parents. I wasn't worried about the coaches calling them. Other than Coach Lorendo, they'd never had a single conversation with my parents and didn't even know what they looked like. Rett's dad was the assistant head coach. I don't know what Rett told him. Wilson told his mother in Gainesville, but not his position coach. I talked Joe Nathan into going and Mike Flynn also joined us.

We left Auburn on the Saturday before Fat Tuesday. Rett drove, so did Joe Nathan. We figured we'd find a place to stay after we got there.

Once on the road, we counted up our assets. Rett had $15. Flynn and I had $25 each. Wilson, the freshman, had $40. Joe, the capitalist among us, had $100. Joe was our insurance.

In 1973, our little money could go a long way. Gas was still less than fifty cents a gallon. An ice-cold six-pack of beer was less than $2.25. Cheap wine cost less than $2. You could get a rib-eye steak, salad, baked potato, and bread at the Bonanza Sirloin Pit for $1.49. A "Deluxe Hamburger" at famous Auburn Landmark, the Sani-Freeze, went for twenty cents.

We rolled into New Orleans looking for adventure. Rett fancied himself our leader. Steve McQueen, he called himself. I was John Shaft, the black super hero detective. We called the shots. Wilson wanted a nickname, but we told him Fat Daddy was it.

We had a ball for three days. We roamed all over town. At Tulane, their athletes welcomed us. We showered in their athletic dormitory. One night, we slept in the car. Another night, we crashed on cots at an Auburn wrestler's home in New Orleans.

We paraded up and down Bourbon Street. We drank cheap wine from pouches slung around our necks.

We were picked up by a pimp in a long Cadillac, demanding that we sell him drugs we didn't have. It was freezing cold. We were walking a couple of miles back to our car. The pimp guy, as we called him, pulled over and told us to get in. We were excited to have a ride. He was black, so Rett and Wilson figured I knew the guy. I didn't, but they jumped into the back seat anyway. There were two guys in the front seat. All of us crowded into the back. A little white, fluffy dog jumped from back seat to front seat. The dog climbed all over us, over and over. The pimp guy said to me, "Go ahead, I'm cool." I didn't know what he was talking about. He said it again, "Go ahead, I'm cool." Wilson pinched me to say something. I mumbled something to the effect of "Uh-huh, we were just trying to get a ride to our car." The pimp guy eyed me in the rearview mirror. He pointed to the other guy in the front seat and said, "This guy said you all had drugs." "We don't have any drugs," I said. "I don't even know that guy."

Pimp guy's Cadillac screeched to a halt. He puts us all out in the cold, including the guy from the front seat, who he didn't know either. We begged him to take us to our car, but he sped off, flinging the little dog up against the back seat.

We celebrated Fat Tuesday at the Mardi Gras parade. When we ran out of money, we headed back to Auburn.

When we returned the coaches were waiting for us. Since Wilson hadn't told his position coach why he would not be at winter workout, the coaches had called his mother. She unknowingly told on all of us: "Oh, he's in New Orleans with Thomas, Flynn, and Rett."

That's why Wilson didn't rate a nickname other than Fat Daddy.

Wilson and Rett had to run the coliseum steps, all of them. It was brutal. Wilson puked. Since I couldn't run, the coaches made me do fifty-yard rolls. I lay on the cold concrete floor in the coliseum and rolled down the concourse fifty yards, then fifty yards back. Was Mardi Gras worth it? We would go again the next year.

It took a trip to Atlanta to finally slow us down.

Rett, Wilson, James, Steve "Smitty" Smith, and I decided to take a Saturday day trip to Atlanta, planning to be back sometime that night.

We struck out in the afternoon for the two and a half hour drive. It was good to get away. We played silly games in the car on the way over. We listened to the eight-track tape player and sang along loudly to "For the Love of Money," by the O Jays, "Living for the City" by Stevie Wonder, and "Let's Get it On," by Marvin Gaye. We played the musical instruments along with the Allman Brothers on "Whipping Post."

We rolled into Atlanta. We headed for the strip, then a stretch of downtown Peachtree Street with clubs, strip joints, and seedy bars.

The most significant aspect about this trip was that it marked the first time James and I ever bought any marijuana. I had continued to dabble but never bought any. James didn't even bother to dabble much. Looking back, I guess we did it out of boredom more than anything.

We'd gotten our laundry money check for the month, $15. We both took $7.50 and one of the guys in the dorm sold us a bag. The guy was on the team so we didn't worry about him telling.

In Atlanta, we took off down Peachtree Street. At a seedy bar, a big biker-looking bouncer stood in the door. He took a close look at James, then me, and said we couldn't go in. The bouncer had big biker chains around his neck and one in his hand. Other bikers joined him. They made their stand in the doorway.

We decided to move on, cruise, smoke a joint. Smitty drove since he was from Atlanta. We were driving through a nice neighborhood when a car started following us. We were sure he was following us because we turned around in the middle of the block and he turned around as well. He followed us down one street, then another. It was a neighborhood security guard.

"I'm on probation," Smitty announced as he kept trying to lose the guy. "Probation?" I asked. "What are you talking about?" "Probation with the law," he snapped. "I can't go back to jail."

We didn't know anything about his troubles with the law. The car got real quiet.

The guy behind us was talking into a car radio microphone, Smitty panicked. He turned into a driveway. Drove up next to the garage. The guy followed us. He blocked the driveway, so we couldn't get out. Rett "Steve McQueen" Davis decided he'd handle it. He and I got out of the car, went up to the front door, and rang the doorbell. The people wouldn't open the door. I don't blame them. We asked for Brenda. Someone through the door said Brenda didn't live there.

We stood on the front porch. The guy sat in the driveway with his engine running.

We went back to the car, told Smitty to back out. He did. The guy let us out. He backed out one way. We shot out the other, but he again got on our tail. "Throw the weed out," Smitty commanded. I knew we had to. Damn! The first time I'd ever bought any of the danged stuff and now I had to throw it away. I didn't care about the weed as much as the money I'd wasted.

"Okay," I said, but I hesitated, hoping the guy would leave us alone. Finally, we rounded a curve. The guy had yet to come around, so he couldn't see us. I opened the car door, leaned out on the curve, and threw the weed into the gutter. We marked the street. It was the corner of Friar Tuck Road and Lionel Lane.

We left the neighborhood and the guy dropped off our tail. We rode back down to the strip, but no one felt like partying any longer. "Let's go back to Auburn," James suggested.

First, we went back to Friar Tuck Road and Lionel Lane. The weed was still there. I was afraid to get out of the car so Smitty pulled close to the curb. With the car running, I opened the door. I leaned out with Rett holding my legs and scooped up the weed. We got the hell out of Atlanta.

With James' eligibility up, he was no longer my teammate or roommate. The coaches allowed him to continue to live in the dorm while he waited for the National Football League draft. He had his own room. He also had a bum knee, needing surgery, but he had no money.

The school did not volunteer to pay for his knee surgery. James would not graduate. His hopes now rested with the NFL.

I was finally having fun in school. I took an Introduction to Theatre class. I enjoyed the classes where I got to meet people from campus I would have never met otherwise. There were several long hairs and hippie girls, even a couple of gay guys in the class. I say "even" because it was not cool to be openly gay in Auburn in 1973. In one of our acting sessions, our professor instructed us to lie on the floor and grow like a tree. I was lying on the floor to grow like a tree when a couple of the football players passed by. They saw me on the floor, growing like a tree, and howled. I knew I would hear about it later at the athletics facilities and I did. I was ridiculed for hanging out with the hippies and "F's" (the negative slur aimed at gays). I didn't take any more theater classes.

For my broadcasting class, I wrote and produced a television show. We filmed it at the educational television studios on campus. The sports show featured a mock interview with Howard Cosell and Muhammad Ali. Joe took the class with me. He got to be Cosell. I, of course, was Ali.

A welcome edition to my Auburn life was my younger sister, Donna. She had followed me to John Carroll High School, and now, to Auburn. "I went to Auburn because you, were there," she says. "Mama and Daddy thought it might be best to follow my older brother." Donna was a better student than me. She always made better grades. We got along well. We were very close at home. All of us. It could have been hard for her to establish her own identity. But Donna said, "It was fine to me. At the time I was so naïve and sheltered, as were many of the other young ladies, anything would have been fine."

My sisters were sheltered. They grew up under the southern double standard. I got to do things my sisters did not. I got to explore things in the world as "a boy." They did not get to explore those same things as "girls." This was also a part of the coming cultural change.

At Auburn, Donna and I would socialize together. We had no choice. When one black person had a party, all the black students went. There was no other outlet. There were now nearly 15,000 students on campus. It still felt as though there were still fewer than 100 blacks.

I asked Donna if it was awkward being there with me. "Yes," she said, "especially since you were a football star. Most people wanted to talk to you. Once, a young kid asked for my autograph, since he could not get yours."

Her funniest story has to be the one about the teacher in Physiology 101. "When the professor called the roll and saw my last name, Gossom, he asked if 'I was married to the football player.' All the other class members were waiting to hear my answer. I said, 'No, he is my brother.' Everyone seemed relieved, especially the girls."

It was awkward when guys in the athletic dorm wanted to date my sister. I knew the attitude in the dorm regarding women. At parties, the guys who liked Donna would feel awkward with me around. Donna would feel awkward. So would I.

We somehow found a peace with it. I let her know that I was there but that she was on her own. She could handle herself. She did well academically. She made friends. We stayed out of each other's business. We didn't take things home to Mom and Dad that didn't need to go there.

As the winter drew to a close, I'd had another good quarter in school. My grades were hovering above a B average. I'd had some fun and managed to avoid life's intoxications, at least up to now.

# CHAPTER 15

---

# "YOU'VE BEEN SMOKING MARIJUANA"

I'd gotten the message at lunch. "Coach wants to see you."

It was the first time I'd ever been in Coach Jordan's office. Photos lined the walls. There was a photo of Coach and his family. Another framed picture of Coach and Governor Wallace. There was even a copy of the celebrated photo of Coach and Bear Bryant after the Punt Bama Punt game.

He sat behind the desk. His jaw was set in stone. He was not happy.

He didn't waste any time. As soon as I sat down, he fired the first barrel. "Thomas, you been smoking marijuana?" It wasn't as much a question as it was an accusation. We both knew the answer.

I wavered. He had me on my heels. I stalled for time. "Sir," I weakly responded.

He didn't look cross, or yell, but he was angry. It was a quiet anger, the most dangerous kind. He fired the second barrel. "You've been smoking marijuana."

I recovered somewhat from the first assault. I didn't cower. I respected him too much to lie to him. Both my father and my coach taught me to be a man and I would be one now. "Yes, Sir," I responded.

"I am going to have to take your scholarship," he shot back. "You're off the team."

Silence. His order was final. His demeanor said there was no recourse. He waited for me to leave his office.

I stood and answered, "It's been an honor to play for you, Coach. Thank you for everything." I stuck out my hand and he extended his. We shook. That was it. All I'd worked for was gone because of a few tokes of a marijuana cigarette.

Jangled emotions rushed through my head. I'd blown it. I knew it. I wished I could talk to him. But Coach and I had never had a conversation beyond a couple of sentences. Now I never would.

I went to James' room and learned he'd been busted, too. With his eligibility gone, he'd been asked to leave the athletic dorm. Where would he live? Where else could he go? He'd known only the dorm since he arrived in Auburn. It was his home.

We talked briefly outside his room. James didn't deserve the stain. He'd given Auburn so much. He wasn't a dope head. None of us were. We never even drank much. But... we were wrong. We didn't make excuses.

I spotted "Fat Daddy" Wilson walking aimlessly through the dorm parking lot. He was dragging, looking pitiful. I knew he was gone too. I shouted down at him, "Fat Daddy, don't worry, I'm gone too." He sprinted to James and me. He didn't want to be alone.

"I was in the Coliseum," Wilson said. "Coach Hilyer told me, 'Coach Jordan wants to see you upstairs.' I went up to see him. Before I could sit down, he said, 'You been smoking marijuana?' I didn't answer. He said again, 'Do you smoke marijuana?' I said yes. I don't remember what he said after that. I just knew I was done. He stood. The meeting was over. I blurted out, 'I still think you're the best coach in the world.' He shook my hand. That was it."

"What are we going to do?" Wilson asked me. He was terrified. Like us, and most of the guys in the dorm, he was the first in his family to go to college. The news would devastate his parents. What would he do?

"My parents and grandmother will be here tomorrow. My grandmother is coming to see me. I can't face them," he explained. His parents knew he smoked pot, but telling them he'd gotten kicked off the team would be too much. "I can't be here. I can't tell them. I can't see my grandmother."

We found out that we three were the only ones to be kicked off. We were not the only ones who smoked, though. A good fourth of the team did. We found out that at least ten others had been questioned. They all lied to Coach Jordan.

I made my way to my room. I closed the blinds and turned out all the lights. I waited and waited.

Finally, I made the call. My mom answered. "How you doing Mama?" I said.

"I'm doing fine," she responded. "Is something wrong?"

"Yes," I answered, "but you had better put Daddy on."

"What is it?" she wanted to know.

"Can you put Daddy on?" I repeated.

She called for my dad to pick up the other phone. There was silence until I heard the click of another phone being lifted.

"Hello," Daddy answered, "How's it going?"

"Uh, not too good," I answered. I got straight to the point. "I got kicked off the team today."

"What for?" My mom nearly shouted.

I answered, "Coach said I was smoking marijuana."

"Were you?" my dad wanted to know.

"Yes," I answered.

My mom responded, "I thought you'd be smarter than that."

I don't remember much more. There wasn't much more to say. Mama started crying first. Hearing that, I couldn't hold my own emotions back. I hated to hurt them. It was faint at first, but then I heard an unfamiliar sob. A sad slow wail I'd never heard before. My dad was crying.

I pleaded, "I'll come home, get a job, and go to school there," I promised. The sobs continued. "I'm sorry," I said. It's all I could say. "I'm sorry." I'd let everyone down.

We agreed I would come home either on the weekend, or once I found out what, if any, options I had. Since my parents had never had as much as a "hi and bye" conversation with Coach Jordan, asking him to relent was not an option.

My dad wanted to come down. "I'll take off work and come down there tomorrow," he offered.

"No, Daddy." It was my mess. I needed to fix it if it could be fixed. We hung up.

Smoking marijuana wasn't a big deal on campus or in the dorm. It was not hard to get. There weren't any addicts on our team. As a matter of fact, marijuana was the only "drug" I ever saw in college. But in Auburn in the 1970s a joint of marijuana could get you jail time.

I lay in the dark. There was a knock on my door. I didn't answer. I didn't want to see anybody. The knock came again. I still didn't answer. Coach Lorendo called out, "Thomas. Thomas, open the door."

I didn't turn the light on. Red-eyed, I opened the door. Coach Lorendo walked in. We did not make eye contact. I didn't want him to

[ 190 ]

see the tears. I was ashamed and he knew it. He didn't reach for the light either. He was a hard ass, but he'd believed in me. I felt a loyalty to him. I wiped my eyes.

"Coach has decided not to take your scholarship," he began. I didn't react. I never looked up. "Coach is going to reconsider and let you boys back on the team. He knows the others lied. He questioned about eleven of you. You guys were the only ones to tell the truth. Don't call your parents."

I didn't say a word. "Did you already call your parents?" he wanted to know. "Yes," I murmured.

So they knew there were more guys than just us. A few of the others included some of their favorite Johnny Jock guys and a couple of FCA guys. It also included Coach Davis's son, my friend Rett. Is that why they reconsidered?

It didn't matter to me. I'd just done the hardest thing I'd ever done in my life. I'd made my parents cry. Sadly, I told Coach Lorendo, " I don't care what happens."

He asked me to hold on. "Don't go anywhere. Don't call anybody else. We're having a meeting tonight. Coach will want to see you at ten in the morning." He left.

I was alone in the dark. I reached for the phone, called my parents.

How had all this happened?

Brownie had keys to all our rooms and our private closets. We all knew that. About a week before, word had spread throughout the dorm that a cop who was friendly to the athletic department would go through the dorm with Brownie to check everyone's room. What prompted the inspection? I don't know. Who originated the rumor? I can't remember. We felt it came from the athletic department. Spreading the word early about the check would give everyone time to "clean up." Well, almost everyone.

Sylvester Davenport, a freshman basketball player from Chattanooga, fancied himself a six-foot-nine Jimi Hendrix. For whatever reason, Sylvester bought a fresh bag of marijuana and left it in his closet while the basketball team went on a road trip to LSU. During their search, the cop and Brownie opened the closet door and found the marijuana sitting in plain view.

Upon his return, Sylvester was taken to the athletic department. They turned the pressure up on him. They had no intention of taking him to jail and told him so. The told him they could work out a compromise if he told on any others using marijuana. He gave up my name, James and Wilson, and at least ten others. No one else confessed.

The next morning, Coach Jordan reconsidered. In a brief meeting, we were reinstated on the team. Our scholarships were restored. He said it was because we told the truth. But Wilson and I were banished to the only other male dorm on campus, Magnolia Hall, for the remainder of the quarter. We were not allowed to sleep or eat in the athletic dorm. We were separated from our teammates. No one else was punished.

It was also up to me to square things away with my parents.

The New Orleans Saints drafted James into the NFL. He soon left Auburn to get ready for camp. Before he did, James and I had a long talk with Coach Lorendo and Coach Davis. They asked all kinds of questions about the marijuana incident. "Where do you get it?" they wanted to know. "All over the campus, all around town," we responded. "Can you get it at the athletic dorm?" they asked. "Yes," we answered. "Does it affect your performance?" We didn't know. We'd never done it while playing. Didn't want to. Didn't need to. They never asked names. They knew we wouldn't snitch.

We also used the rare opportunity to talk about social issues. James talked about how things would need to change to attract more black athletes, and more black students. We talked about how college should be fun as opposed to being as stressful as it was for us. They showed us respect and listened. They didn't object. Again, we did not make excuses for what we had done.

Shortly thereafter, Mike Flynn relayed an incident to us that showed how much the coaches felt they needed to learn about marijuana. Flynn wandered down the halls of the athletic offices only to smell marijuana smoke drifting down the hall. A voice rose from one of the conference rooms. "As you can smell, marijuana has a definite tell-tale scent. You can detect it in a person's clothing or hair. Another sign is their eyes. They may be red or glassy." Flynn got a closer look. All the coaches were attending a marijuana seminar.

Rumors flew around the campus, but not many people outside the athletic department knew what actually had happened. Sylvester was quietly dropped from the basketball team and sent on his way.

I went home that weekend and faced my parents. They were relieved I was back in school, back on the team. We'd always had a rule. If something negative happened, we would sit down and talk it out, as long as I told the truth. I laid it all out for them.

Before I came home Mom had already found a seminar on marijuana. She had a brochure, "Your Kids and Marijuana." She'd read it several times. We talked it out. They were disappointed in my choices, but they seemed assured I wasn't a dope addict. My dad was the most disappointed. Growing up as a sharecropper, he couldn't understand my throwing away an opportunity. It hurt him, deeply.

My parents wanted to know about my subsequent conversation with Coach Jordan. It wasn't much. He simply informed me that I was back on the team and I needed to live in Magnolia Hall for the rest of the quarter.

My scholarship was intact. I was still on schedule to graduate. I promised to stop using marijuana.

My parents were disappointed that they did not hear from any of the coaches. Looking back, some might wonder why they didn't call the coaches themselves. I don't. They didn't know they could. As I've said, they had no relationship with the athletic department.

Wilson had his own view of the issue. "The only reason they took me back was because of you. They wanted you back. Hell, they needed you."

Wilson's parents and grandmother did come to Auburn, the day we were reinstated. Wilson got away with only having to tell his dad. His dad was relieved that we were reinstated. He didn't throw a tantrum, for he knew his son. Before he left he said to me, "He's from a different culture. Take care of him." I told him I would.

The punishment did fragment the team. Wilson and I became pariahs in the athletic department. We couldn't live or eat in the athletic dormitory. We were made to feel like outsiders on the occasional visit. The "good guys" looked on us as dope heads. There was a big divide with the guys who'd lied and left us out to dry. The FCA guys wouldn't have anything to do with us. Rett and Flynn remained friends. But for the most part, without James, it was just Fat Daddy and me.

I often wondered, if we were the only ones to tell the truth, why were we the only ones punished.

But we bounced back. Before long, Fat Daddy and I were kings of Magnolia Hall. The guys in the dorm and the girls in Noble Hall, the adjoining women's dorm, loved us. The word was out on campus that two football players had been moved to Magnolia Hall. Many still did not know why we were being punished. The rumors were we'd done something that warranted punishment. But few knew what our offense was. The first time we went into the dining hall, you could hear the whispers. "There they are."

Chris would tell the Magnolia Hall stories. "I went into one of the guy's room and he asked me, 'Is that Thomas Gossom in that room?' I told him it was. He fell back on his bed and said, 'He's a legend around here.'"

Those guys were good to us. We were gods to them. We were Auburn University football players, starters, living among them. They took us in.

For my part, I enjoyed the freedom of living in Magnolia Hall. I was back among the general student body, where I had started. We could have female visitors. Other than the better meals in the athletic dormitory, I enjoyed life on the outside.

At the beginning of the next quarter, Fat Daddy and I were moved back into the athletic dorm. We moved in together. We didn't give it a second thought. Neither did our parents, who would get to know each other. On weekends, we'd go to Birmingham and stay with my folks or to Gainesville and stay with his.

Fat Daddy finally told me, ten years after our Auburn days about the shit he caught from some of our teammates for rooming with me. "How could you live with that "'N" word,'? " they would ask him. "Here comes 'the "N" word' lover." They liked me as a teammate, but living with me was reprehensible. "Once, when they were riding me pretty hard, I shut them up good," Wilson says. "I told them. ' Well, he's the only one I know in the dorm that gets down on his knees and prays every night.'"

While no one said anything to me, I got signals that maybe I shouldn't live with Wilson. I never took the looks and insinuations seriously.

Fat Daddy and I did well as roommates. We even went out with the same girl for a while. I encouraged him to hit the books. Plus, we didn't solely hang with each other. He still had his friends. I still hung out with Joe Nathan and the brothers.

We tried to get our lives back to normal. I started dating a woman from my journalism classes. She was black and a couple of years younger than me. I enjoyed her company. We would date on and off for the rest of the year. We liked each other, but we ended up better friends than lovers. She was smart. She didn't take any shit, which is why I liked her. We would debate issues. She was headstrong, so was I. We would date for a while, get tired of each other, and move on. But we would remain friends. We were both career driven. We'd both decided individually neither one of us would marry right after school. She would go on to an award-winning career in journalism and we still remain friends.

School was fun for me even with the turmoil. I was stimulated by the intellectual currents around me. For the quarter, I recorded an A, two B's, and two C's.

I came to really enjoy writing for the newspaper. My journalism and speech classes were fascinating. I was offered the opportunity to intern at the Columbus, Georgia newspaper, the *Columbus Enquirer*.

It would have been a great opportunity, but I needed to work in the summers. Living and working for free in Columbus, Georgia, was an adventure I couldn't afford.

On a wider front, Dr. Philpott and the administration were making some progress in their attempts to diversify the university. There were a couple of black classes now. The black literature class was small, lively, fun, and popular with the students, who were mostly white, with the exception of my friends Henry Ford and Joe Nathan. It was a cool hour of poetry, short stories, and study of the modern-day written word. I developed a good relationship with the professor, Dr. Robert Overstreet, who taught oral interpretation and black literature. Dr. Overstreet encouraged thinking and discussion. In class we read poetry and literature, and interpreted the writer's meaning. Everyone's opinion was valued. He selected a few of us from the class to stage an oral dramatization of *The Autobiography of Malcolm X*. Everyone in the class had to attend. For most, it was enjoyable and something they would not have otherwise been exposed to.

For the remainder of the school year, I got into my books and stayed out of everyone's way. I was even more excited about getting back on the field. I rededicated myself in spring practice. During the annual spring game, I caught several passes for close to a hundred yards. I had something to prove.

A newspaper account of the spring game compared me to earlier Auburn greats. "…This athlete might have the distinction of being compared to such greats as Terry Beasley and Connie Frederick during the upcoming season."

Still, for some I carried a stain. I was a druggie. I was shunned by teammates that I had been friendly with. In most cases I didn't care. Those guys weren't friends anyway. But, the growing divisions could hurt us as a team if we fed into them and the coaches played us off against each other.

Looking ahead to the fall, we faced some challenges. Would we be able to put the divisions behind us enough to have a good season? We had a ton of talent on the upcoming team. Could we pull a repeat of 1972?

# CHAPTER 16

---

# THE MISERY OF 6-6

We started the 1973 season ranked number thirteen in the AP poll. National Sportswriters had us at number four.

We were anxious and ready to go. Many of the players on this year's squad had played the previous year, but the leadership from the '72 team had come from the seniors. Some of us would now have to fill that role. The comparisons were inevitable. The '73 team was individually talented. But the '72 team caught lighting in a bottle. It was a team of destiny.

In the last scrimmage before our first game against Oregon State, I caught a forty-seven-yard pass from Randy Walls and capped the drive with a subsequent four-yard touchdown catch. In the article, "Tigers Open New Season with Beavers Saturday," Randy laid out his plan for the year: "He plans to throw the ball more this season and his favorite target will be fleet split-end Tom Gossom, a junior who came to Auburn without a scholarship."

Based on the previous year, and what I'd been able to do in summer camp, I had lofty predictions for myself. As it would turn out, we all had lofty forecasts for ourselves, but those predictions were based on individual skill not team unity.

In the first ever meeting between the two teams, we were picked to beat the Oregon State Beavers by twenty-one points. We beat them, but only 18-9. It was a disappointing performance. We misfired all day. What was supposed to be our big coming out party disintegrated from the start.

The biggest highlight, again, was a nasty fight with Langner at its center. Both benches emptied. We couldn't beat them badly on the scoreboard, so we beat them up.

In the previous signing period, Auburn had signed two black running backs from Montgomery, Secedrick McIntyre and Sullivan Walker. They would contribute right away.

Secedrick scored on a seven-yard run. It was obvious that with both him and Mitzi in the backfield and me at split end, we would have plenty of speed.

But, the win would prove costly. Both Mitzi and Secedrick went down with knee injuries. Mitzi's was the more serious of the two. In what would be a preview of the year, we also lost all three linebackers to injuries.

I had four catches for twenty-eight yards, three runs for another sixteen.

We moved on to Chattanooga. It was an exceptionally bright sunny day. The sun's glare would be a problem for catching passes and kicks. The coaches recommended we wear eye black, the black smudge under a players eyes used to shield the sun's glare. "Are you gonna wear any eye black, Gossom?" It was the locker room joke. I already was. "You can't see the eye black on Gossom." They laughed. I wiped it off my face before the game.

We blitzed Chattanooga 31-0.

Against Tennessee our course for the season became painfully obvious. We learned that we were not the team from a year ago. We were the hunted, rather than the hunters. It was a role we would have trouble adjusting to.

We had beaten Tennessee for the past three years and they wanted revenge. They had a "Beat Auburn Week" in Knoxville before the game. Tennessee's sports information director proclaimed in print, "I think everybody around here is tired of being Auburn's whipping boy."

Coach Jordan warned us that, "It was the first time I could remember a Tennessee team being more fired up for Auburn than for Alabama." They got their revenge. They embarrassed us, 21-0.

What started out as a beautiful sunny day quickly turned into a windy monsoon. The rain came down in stingy, blinding sheets. It became impossible to see across the field, let alone throw the ball. We had four turnovers, two interceptions, and two fumbles. Tennessee jumped ahead 13-0. Then the Tennessee coach embarrassed us.

Once the rain started, Tennessee's Coach Bill Battle refused to play, at least on offense. We would run three plays in the driving rain, fail to get a first down, and then punt to them. Coach Battle, instead of sending his offense on the field, would send his punt team out immediately and on first down, punt the ball back to us. It made some sense. You could barely see for the rain. The ball was slippery wet. They were ahead and didn't want to let us back into the game with turnovers of their own. But it was embarrassing. We were inept on offense and they would punt the ball back to us on first down. I've never seen a team do that before, or since.

After the game ended, the Tennessee fans added insult to injury by throwing bottles at us. Drenched, we hustled into the locker room. It was a long plane ride back to Auburn.

The Ole Miss game was played on a historic day. On October 6, 1973, Cliff Hare Stadium was rededicated as Jordan-Hare stadium. It would become the only stadium in the country to be named for an active coach.

It was a big day on campus. Governor Wallace, as chairman of the board of trustees, offered his congratulations to Coach Jordan in the rededication ceremony. "It is my pleasure to announce that henceforth this stadium shall be called Jordan-Hare Stadium."

We wanted to have a big game for Coach's day. I was feeling frisky before the game. I'd scored my first touchdown on these guys last year.

I never made the game.

In a freak injury, I tore my hamstring in warm-ups. Rett was stretching me, extending my leg backwards to get a good stretch. I was never the most flexible guy on the team and he stretched me too far. My hamstring popped. I knew immediately, I was done. Rett would start for me.

I walked dejectedly into the locker room, and got an ice treatment. I came out and watched the game from the sidelines. The team wanted to win it for Coach, but he and all of us, had to sweat it out. We played a raggedy game. With an ice pack taped to my right leg, I felt responsible that I wasn't out there to help. With little more than a minute left in the game, Rick Neel saved the day for Coach Jordan. He scored the winning touchdown on a thirty-three-yard touchdown run. We sneaked by 14-7.

Although we were 3-1, we couldn't conjure up the magic, chemistry, or fun from the previous season. We tried, but the magic would not come. Every week, someone went down with an injury. Every week, we had to plug new guys into the starting lineup. With tenth ranked LSU coming to town, we'd need everything and every able body we could get.

A record crowd of 63,331 filled up Jordan-Hare. I would miss my second game. It was hard to stand on the sidelines and watch, but I still couldn't run at full speed. Maybe, with the rest and treatment, I'd be back next week. LSU rocked us 20-6.

Our offense had started to stink, but there was nothing I could do to help. It was very frustrating. The coaches started to give me those, "How much longer?" looks. I was about a week away from playing. I didn't want to rush myself but I knew they needed me.

Being 3-2 was a much different feeling than the previous year when we were 5-0. That two game swing in the won/lost column caused us to doubt ourselves. We lost our team swagger, team chemistry, the good communication between the coaches and players, and knowing how to win. Winning breeds winning and losing breeds losing.

After the LSU game, Coach Jordan lit into the team, called us a bunch of "fat-headed athletes wanting to live off last year's reputation." He accused us of being content to sit around and read our press clippings. He shot a "You need to get well!" look at me.

I started to get more looks and snide remarks from the coaches. Injured athletes don't produce wins. The looks were unnecessary, because I was already putting enormous pressure on myself. The marijuana incident of the previous spring had something to do with it. Any negative thing about me conjured up images of my past trouble. Plus, I was one of the leaders on this unit. The younger players looked up to me and I could not help the team. I felt I was letting everyone down.

We had Georgia Tech next. The atmosphere didn't get better.

We began to develop factions on the team. There are cliques on every team, but this team wasn't unified enough to discard those distractions once we hit the field. Winning teams can overcome distractions by unifying around a common theme. We hadn't found one.

The team left for Georgia Tech without me. That felt funny. I'd been on every trip since the start of the '71 season. Since I wouldn't be dressing or playing, I wouldn't be traveling with the team to Atlanta.

I went home and spent a fall weekend with my family for the first time since I'd left for school. I sat around the dining table with my dad and mom. Mama prepared a spread of fried chicken, collard greens, candied yams, and cornbread. It had been a long time since I'd been home eating Mom's cooking. It felt good to be home, to sit around the table and talk.

"Don't look to get your starting job back first game," my dad warned. "They are gonna work you back in." I agreed, but I expected to be playing.

We beat Georgia Tech 24-20 with 322 yards of offense. Winning without me made me doubt myself even more. Maybe they didn't need me. Mitzi scored on a two-yard run. There was more bad news when Randy Walls went down with a possible shoulder separation.

Houston was up next. Homecoming! They were ranked twelfth. They had the number one offense in the country. We were four point underdogs. I felt I could play. I tested the leg and wanted to give it a shot.

The team went to see the movie *Walking Tall* Friday night before the game. It was our Friday custom. Coach Jordan and Kenny Howard, our trainer and Coach Jordan's good friend, would search the movie landscape and select something inspirational. In *Walking Tall*, a lonesome, good guy sheriff in rural Tennessee whups the bad guys with a big old stick and runs them out of town. That was something we needed to see the night before playing Houston.

We recaptured some of the old magic. We got physical. We shut out Houston and its number one offense, 7-0. I played, mainly as a blocker. Rett started in front of me.

We began the second half of the season at 5-2. Still, something was different with this team. We couldn't put our finger on it, but we could feel it. Tension filled the air at practice. We started to drift away from, "All for one and one for all, " and toward, "Every man for himself."

A huge sell-out crowd of 63,429 came to see us play Florida. We had a six-game winning streak against Florida. Plus, they'd never won at our stadium. Never. I was still running second team behind Rett.

Florida scored on two touchdowns but missed both conversion attempts. We were behind 12-0. I sat on the sideline and stewed. It was painful to watch, knowing I could help. I hadn't expected my job to be given to me, but we were losing and I could help the team. Finally, late in the fourth quarter they called my name. "Gossom." I sprinted onto the field. I caught a quick touchdown from Randy, who was back in the lineup. We went for two. Randy hit me for the two-point conversion. But, it was too late. They beat us, 12-8. I scored all eight points. We fumbled seven times. We lost three of them. One of Florida's running backs had more offense than the entire Auburn team.

Things were spiraling downhill. We'd fallen out of the top twenty.

The fractures and divisions on the team started to run deep. Guys hung out in their cliques, others didn't like each other. The FCA guys began to pass judgment on those who were different. Some of the better athletes were the younger players who pushed the older guys for playing time. Injuries and mistakes constantly changed our lineup, causing teammates to leapfrog over each other weekly for playing time.

The coaches did what they'd always done. Practices got rougher. We scrimmaged, fiercely. They needed to make an example of someone, bring the fear back. Their choice was Ken Callega. "The Italian Stallion," we called him. Ken was a handsome, dark-haired, tailback. Another Florida Boy. On a memorable day, Ken was forced to run the same blocking drill over and over and over again. Fresh guys were brought in against him. Guys were brought in to double-team him. He'd fall. The whistle would blow. He'd have to line up and do it again. He was exhausted, but the drill continued. It was obvious they were trying to run him off. We cheered for him. We became defiant in urging him not to quit. Finally, he fell and didn't get up. He was done. He was physically exhausted. He crossed the psychological barrier that allowed him to just lie there. It didn't matter to him anymore. The drill was moved to another part of the field. They left him there. When he recovered, Ken walked off.

With each loss, things got tougher. One bizarre day before practice, an obviously upset Coach Jordan gave us a lecture on how to park our cars properly between the lines in the coliseum parking lot. It seems we were parking across the lines, "being arrogant. Dr. Philpott runs everything up there," he pointed in the direction of the administration buildings. "I run everything down here," he said, referring to the athletic offices.

Then came the big crackdown. Actress Raquel Welch had to go.

At an evening meal, Brownie announced that all nude or partially nude pictures, posters, and anything of this type had to be removed from the walls of all dorm rooms. That meant, for a few guys, playboy centerfolds would have to come down. But, it also meant the world's number one selling poster of Raquel Welch, all sexed up, would have to come down off the many walls she occupied. Raquel didn't do nudity but she showed plenty of cleavage in a tight bathing suit. Now, she had to go.

We responded by beating Mississippi State 31-14. Secedrick scored three touchdowns. Rusty Fuller, the fullback who'd stepped in for James, scored one. Mike Fuller returned a punt back thirty-nine yards. I caught one pass for five yards, but I wasn't playing much. My morale was sinking. Mentally, I was as low as I'd been on the field since I'd been at Auburn.

At 6-3, we were back between the hedges in Athens, Georgia. Georgia was always the biggest team we played. Their offensive line averaged about 250 pounds. One of their linemen stood six-foot-eight; another, six-foot-six. They pushed us around and beat us 28-14. Our one bright spot on offense was Secedrick. He started against Georgia and led us with eighty-three yards rushing. Secedrick became the first Auburn tailback to play every offensive snap in a game that year. Mike Fuller scored on a ninety-six-yard kickoff return for a touchdown, the third longest in Auburn history to that point.

We were now 6-4 and another problem reared its ugly head.

Betting on college football is big business in Alabama. A couple of our guys had gotten sucked into betting. It started out as fun for a few players, then it spread like a fever running rampant in the dorm. I'd never bet, but I got sucked in for one game. I was told it was a sure bet. It was the hot tip in the dorm. Guys who didn't know how to bet, like me, were betting this one game. Several guys had already won money for the season. It was exciting until we lost. The team I bet on didn't beat the spread. I lost $27.50. I paid up. I've never bet on any game since. I learned my lesson. I didn't have money to give away. For most of the novice guys, that loss was enough to quit. But, not everyone would stop.

A couple of guys got in too deep. The first, we loaned money to bail him out. I made him promise not to bet any more. The other guy, I found out about on the field. During one of our games, as other scores were called out over the intercom system, I heard him swearing. He was reacting to the scores based on whom he had bet on. I asked him, "What's the problem?" He just shrugged. I didn't want to know any more.

We had one game left in the regular season. Alabama was ranked number one in the country. If we could beat them it would change our whole season.

Before the big annual game, the usual psychological war was waged between the two coaches. Bear Bryant called us the "best 6-4 team in the country." I doubt he believed that, but he was making sure we didn't sneak up on them again. Coach Jordan praised Alabama for their number one ranking. He said we were proud to be on the field with them.

Bear Bryant wanted the nation to see this game. He was still sour from last year. He used his clout with the ABC network to get the game on television. ABC agreed to accommodate the coach. That put the pressure on the team and our coaches.

Sports pundits like to say about big rivalry games and their outcomes, "You can throw the records out. Anyone can win." That's not true in my book. The best team wins, nine times out of ten, rivalry or not.

Alabama was the better team. They smoked us 35-0 to get their revenge in front of 69,418 fans in Birmingham's Legion Field. Surprisingly, I was back in the starting lineup for the game. On our opening drive, the coaches called a quick-out pattern to me. The ball was late, behind me. Mike Washington, the Alabama cornerback broke on it and intercepted the ball. He ran it down deep into our territory. From there, it was downhill.

The coaches held the intercepted ball against me. I was taken out of the game for the next series. Perhaps our quarterbacks' psyche was too fragile to blame it on them. Maybe they couldn't take it. But, it was part of the game. Even though something may not be your fault, when the coach lays the blame at your feet, you accept it. I took the blame and went on.

It was the only game I'd ever been involved in at Auburn where I was glad when it was over. I'm sure the coaches were too. Some of my teammates didn't agree the Alabama team was superior because it was Alabama and they couldn't give them credit. Not me. In a story headlined "Auburn Players Differ on Reaction to Bama," there was a quote from me, "Wingback Thomas Gossom said that the Crimson Tide's number one rated team is a super team. 'I was proud that we were able to move the ball on them,' Gossom said."

There was another factor we blacks on the Auburn team were aware of. Although Auburn had been the first to sign a black athlete in the state, Alabama had jumped way out front in the number of black athletes on their campus. Alabama had three times the number of black athletes on their football team than we did. They probably had ten times as many black students. Black athletes filled the skill positions on Alabama's football roster. On both offense and defense, their players were much faster than their counterparts on our team.

We were now 6-5. We were offered the opportunity to go to the Sun Bowl in El Paso, Texas. Coach Jordan gave the seniors and fourth-year juniors the opportunity to vote. He said it would be our decision if we went or not. It had been a long, tiring, fractious season. I sure didn't want to go. We players met on the field. No one else wanted to go either, so we voted no. The next day it was announced in the newspapers that we were going to the Sun Bowl. We would play Missouri.

We flew into El Paso the day after Christmas. We were shocked at the beautiful green field, considering there wasn't any greenery anywhere else in town. We found out they'd painted the ground a beautiful green for television. It was as hard as a rock.

My attitude continually slid downhill. I was at rock bottom. I'd begun thinking about not coming back for my last year of eligibility. I was close to crossing that psychological boundary to quitting, giving up. In eight days of bowl practice I was thrown one pass. Most of the time, I didn't even practice. I just stood around with the subs. No one talked to me. I would run the occasional play with the second team. I was being totally ignored. But no one would tell me why or what I could do to help the team.

I'd investigated and found out that I could possibly graduate the next summer. I decided to look further into it.

We took the bus daily from the hotel to the field for practice. Freshman Coach Doug Barfield came down the aisle and sat next to me on the bus. I liked Coach Barfield. He was a player's coach, and there were rumors that Coach Lorendo would be replaced with Coach Barfield as offensive coordinator.

Coach Barfield moved past the chit chat, and treaded into the subject on his mind. "Things aren't going very well for you, huh?"

Not knowing how much to say, I didn't bother to look at him. "No," I answered.

"What are you going to do about your fifth year? " he asked. "You coming back?"

I shrugged an "I don't know."

He addressed the rumors of his taking over the offense. "If they are true, I'd like to have you on the team."

For the first time, I looked at him. He was sincere.

We kicked off on CBS television at noon central time on December 29, 1973, with Missouri favored by seven points. The game was a reflection of our season. We fumbled four times and threw an interception. Rob Spivey, our tight end, broke his leg. I sat on the bench and pouted. I'd started against Alabama, but after the interception, I was back on the bench.

There was one bright spot.

We started yet another quarterback, freshman Phil Gargis. He was doing well but needed help. Behind 21-3 late in the first half, they called my name. "Gossom." I grabbed my helmet. It had been the pattern since my injury. At the start the game, I wouldn't play. Once we were behind, I'd come in. My black teammates had taken to calling me "Super '"N" word,'" because the coaches would only put me in when we were behind and needed to score.

I ran onto the field. "A right 65 X post on 2," was the call. I ran a deep post route through the middle of the field. Phil let it go. I caught it. Touchdown. No, I was over the end line at the back of the end zone. When I jogged back to the sideline, I asked Coach Lorendo to let me run the post corner route this time. It was right before halftime, we were behind and didn't have much to lose. He agreed.

"A right 65 X post corner on 2." It was to be a very similar route to the one I'd just run, but with a twist at the end. After twelve yards, I broke to the post. The defensive back bit, trying to get in front of me. He had a safety backing him up. They thought they had me, but I broke back to the corner with the ball already in the air. I caught it. Touchdown.

I'd catch another in the second half. Deep in the third quarter, our offense was chugging but not going anywhere. Again, I jogged over to Coach Lorendo on the sideline. "I can beat this guy, Coach," I told him. "Let me go by him before the quarter ends," I said. "We have the wind." There was a very strong wind that day. It affected all long passes and any kicks.

Coach Lorendo said, "Okay."

I hustled to the huddle, relayed the message to Gargis. Phil called, "A right, 65 X streak on two."

I burst from my stance straight down the field, past the defensive back. Phil let it go toward the end zone. Both the defensive back and I jumped. I went a little higher. We both got our hands on the ball, but I came down with it. I had my second touchdown catch of the day.

We were back in the game, until we kicked off and the Missouri guy ran the kickoff back all the way. We lost 34-17.

The December 30 edition of the *Montgomery Advertiser*, under the headline, "Tigers Feel Wrath of Fighting Tigers," found a lone bright spot in the loss, "Only the passing combo of freshman quarterback Phil Gargis to junior wingback Tom Gossom kept it from being a rout as they teamed for a pair of touchdown strikes for the War Eagles."

My two touchdowns were a record for touchdown catches in the Sun Bowl. For me, it had been a nice ending to a miserable year; a miserable year for coaches, for players, for Auburn. We weren't a close bunch. We had not had much fun. The fans only look at the record. We didn't like the record nor did we like the product, both on the field and behind the scenes.

I was faced with the decision of whether to come back next year or graduate and get on with my life. Would Coach Barfield make a difference? If I came back we still wouldn't have a quarterback who could get me the ball. During the '73 season, I had broken up more wayward passes than I caught. We would need a quarterback.

Maybe we'd found one in Phil Gargis. On the flight home, sports information director Buddy Davidson told me they'd already come up with a slogan for the Gargis to Gossom passing combination for the next year, "The G Men," he called us. "The G Men." I liked that.

[ 1974 ]

# CHAPTER 17

---

# THE WALKOUT

On February 14, 1974, Valentine's Day, the article "Black Athletes Follow Rules; Reinstated But on Probation," was published on the front page of *The Plainsman*. I was again in the middle of another controversy. The following are excerpts from that story.

"'The end of the episode' is how head football coach Ralph Shug Jordan described the return of three football players to the varsity football team after a dispute over a ban on facial hair.

"'Mitzi Jackson, running back, Tom Gossom, wide receiver, and fullback Sullivan Walker were reinstated Saturday, Sunday, and Monday, respectively after they complied with the grooming regulation,' Jordan said. The regulation forbids moustaches, goatees, sideburns, and beards on football players.

"'The athletes will take part in the winter exercise program and the request for cancellation of the scholarships will be withdrawn,' Jordan noted.

"Jordan commented that grooming is part of discipline and part of being a good football team. Citing last year's football record as an indication of a lack of discipline, Jordan said he hopes the enforcement of the grooming policy will instill pride in the team.

"Jordan said he feels the affair has been grossly exaggerated."

Was it grossly exaggerated? An uncredited "Our Opinion" column in *The Plainsman* spoke for many of the students and athletes on campus.

"A sure disaster for the Auburn Athletic Department was avoided this week when fourteen black athletes ended their walkout over hair regulations. Had the black athletes stayed away, the damage to black recruiting and the athletic program in general would have been severe."

Larry Gierer, sports editor of *The Plainsman* weighed in.

"...Coach Ralph "Shug" Jordan's statement that hair rules are being enforced now as they were in 1951 is particularly damning of the rules. The whole set of values our society places on hair length has changed in the intervening 23 years; how could hair rules made then possibly apply today?

"Unfortunately when the rule came in effect the crew cut was in style and the idea of a black athlete at Auburn was scoffed at. Auburn will someday find that as the times around us change, so must Auburn."

What started as a spark rapidly became a four-alarm fire that threatened to engulf the university. National news media labeled the Auburn Hair Walkout one of the top five national stories, the day the story broke.

What happened?

Running back Mitzi Jackson, now my roommate, burst into our room, the same room James and I had lived in. I was lying on the bed reading. He grabbed his suitcase. Emptied his dresser drawer into the suitcase.

"What's up, Mitzi?" I asked. His eyes were red, teary. He wouldn't talk. He slammed the contents of another drawer of underwear into the suitcase.

I was Mitzi's big brother. We didn't hang together much. Mitzi had a steady girlfriend. He spent most of his time with her. Still, we were close.

A fine athlete from DeFuniak Springs, Florida, Mitzi was a great guy. Most people in the dorm who knew him liked him, but he didn't let many get to know him. He and I depended on each other, we liked and respected each other.

Mitzi was also the first in his family to go to college. Also, like most of us, he was from poorer circumstances. He saw an education as a step up. Once he arrived at Auburn, he never went home. Auburn became his home. He stayed at school during summers and holidays for four years.

I raised my voice, "What's up, Mitzi?"

He blurted out. "I was up waiting for the dining hall to open. Coach Jordan came over and cussed me. Told me not to come in the dining hall 'with that shit on your face.' Wouldn't let me in the dining hall." Mitzi had a light mustache. His sideburns were thick and below his ears. He had a couple of days growth on his face. Mitzi was one of the few guys that could grow a full beard at that early age of life. "Take your ass downstairs and shave," he said he was told.

You had to know Mitzi. He was laid-back, sensitive, and temperamental. He would often get mail solicitations addressed to Miss Mitzi Jackson. We would make fun of him. He did not like it and he let us know that. He didn't take a lot of shit. A good running back and a good student, he never caused any trouble for the coaches. But he could throw a temper tantrum.

The dining hall was his domain. The dietitian in charge, Mrs. Graves, a white woman, treated Mitzi like a son. She soothed him with his favorite foods when he'd had a bad day at practice. She made sure Mitzi had his ice cream. Sometimes when I was looking for him, I'd find him in the dining hall sitting with Mrs. Graves, talking.

During the time between the end of the season and winter workout, guys finally had a much needed and well-deserved break, some time for school, and a social life. During this period, we would let our hair down, so to speak. My "fro" was bigger and I had some peach fuzz over my lip, but nobody cared during this time of the year. The coaches didn't come around the dorm often. We avoided them too, letting our hair grow.

Coach Jordan must have been having a bad day. He never cussed much around me, even when he was angry. He'd let go on the field and in halftime speeches sometimes. But for the most part, he left the screaming and cussing to his assistant coaches. Of course, we'd had a bad season and Coach was already getting ready for next season. He was going back to what had always worked in his eyes, discipline. Discipline meant you had to look a certain way.

I talked Mitzi into chilling out. He put the suitcase up.

The hair issue surfaced ever so often. The last time had been in '72. It was Coach Jordan's rule. We all knew that. No one wanted to challenge him on it. Certainly I didn't.

For the first time in the dorm, I felt comfortable. We'd gone from having nine blacks in the athletic dormitory to fourteen. There were still only four blacks on the football team; the others were split between the basketball and track teams.

Of course, all of the guys were younger than me. I enjoyed my senior statesman status. I felt I had to give something back to these guys, like Henry and James had done for me. It was important to me to be a pro on the field and in school.

Many of the young black athletes were immediate stars on campus; Eddie Johnson and Pepto Bolden, in basketball; Clifford Outlin and Willie Smith in track. The majority of the new black athletes were basketball players. One of them, Emmett Thomas, was dating my sister Donna and would become my brother-in-law. These new guys had far more social freedom than we'd had. James and Henry had done the heavy lifting for them.

There were enough guys in the dorm and black students on campus to have some social life. After dinner, the black athletes would gather in one of the basketball players' rooms to talk, laugh, tell jokes, and brag on our athletic prowess. It was like I'd envisioned college being. Finally, in my last year, I'd found some peace.

It wouldn't last.

A new basketball coach had been hired, Dr. Bob Davis. Neither Coach Davis, nor the track coach, Mel Rosen had rules prohibiting facial hair on their players. The black basketball and track guys wore some slight facial hair, light mustaches, and sideburns. Nothing that was unkempt. Most of the guys were neat. Nothing about their grooming would cast a bad image on the university.

There was also a medical consequence for shaving for some young black men, like Mitzi. One that only black people knew. I could shave without any skin problems. But for a lot black men during the 1970s, including my dad, Mitzi, and several of the younger black athletes, shaving was a grueling process if you didn't want your skin to "bump," meaning that after shaving, the skin would become irritated, bumpy, and swollen. Maybe, the shaving creams were irritants. It could have been the razors. Either way, it meant walking around looking like a leper.

The solution for my dad, Mitzi, and the others was a stinky formula called Magic Shave. It was a white funky shave cream and it stank. Bad! You put it on your face and let it sit while it got hot. It literally burned the whiskers off the face. You then shaved yourself with a knife to remove your hair. It was one reason why many black men wore facial hair and even beards.

I figured Coach Jordan had walked into the dorm. The athletes were mingling outside the dining room door, waiting for the dinning hall to open. He saw several black basketball and track guys with their facial hair (one track guy had a beard) outside the dining hall. He saw Mitzi with his sideburns and tiny mustache. Some of the white basketball and football guys had long sideburns, long hair, and were unshaven. Maybe Coach envisioned a coming epidemic, the erosion of years of discipline caused by the now coming cultural change.

The next day, someone gave a directive to clean up the dorm. Brownie took action. All athletes with any kind of facial or long, unkempt hair would not be allowed into the dining hall until the athlete complied with the rules. Everyone had to get a haircut that complied with the football version of the athletic department rules. The rule was for everyone. Shave and get a haircut or you can't eat.

The basketball and track guys would follow the rules of their coaches, though. Basketball coach Bob Davis knew he could not win without his black players. The basketball team now routinely started three to four black athletes. Coach Davis decided he would go to bat for his guys. He tried to get a clarification from the athletic director Lee Hayley, but ran into a roadblock. In the meantime, the guys with facial hair were banned from eating in the dorm even though they weren't violating their coach's rule. The clean-shaven guys would sneak food up to them in their rooms, hoping the issue would be resolved soon.

The after dinner get-togethers turned bitter, angry. Some of the freshmen now wondered why they'd come to Auburn. Their coach couldn't run his own program.

I went to see assistant head football coach, Paul Davis. I relayed what was happening with the basketball players, what had happened with Mitzi, how upset he was. I explained to him the medical problem peculiar with black men and shaving. I told him of the simmering anger in the dorm. Some guys had beards and mustaches, but their respective coaches thought it was okay.

I ventured away from safe ground. I thought the rule was outdated; it had been instituted in 1951. Times had changed. "It's 1974," I said. I covered my tracks by saying the rule didn't affect me as much. This was my last year. "It's The Man's rule," he told me.

Soon, the edict came down. "All scholarship athletes must shave any and all facial hair or be removed from all athletic department facilities and dismissed from the scholarship program."

Ironically, the players' meeting on the third floor of the dormitory was held in Henry's old room. All fourteen of us came. There was no joking or playing around, just plenty of frustration. The younger guys felt betrayed by their coaches. "Why should we play for them if they won't go to bat for us?" They were more militant in their stance. They wanted to walk out, go home. Because they were freshmen and sophomores, they could transfer to other schools. The older guys tried to lobby for being reasonable.

I was near the end of my journey. I knew how much things had improved, but I also knew that socially, we were way behind not only the rest of the country, but also the rest of the Southeastern Conference and our bitter rival, the University of Alabama.

Someone called for a walkout. It was quickly agreed and voted on that if we walked we had to be in unison. The upcoming weekend track meet and basketball game would be a disaster without the black players. No one wanted it to come to that. But, we still had guys who could not enter the dining hall to eat and their coach had no answers for them. We wanted some understanding. We felt we had to stick together.

The guys agreed to meet again the next day after lunch.

I don't think any of us thought it would go much further. None of us wanted to go anywhere. Hell, I was used to the hair harassment by now. I was hoping the basketball players and track guys would be left alone. If they got a little freedom, perhaps future football players would also. I never saw myself as defying anybody. I'd had a good talk with Coach Barfield. I'd decided another year was what I really wanted. Since Coach Jordan's and Mitzi's encounter, I had avoided the dining hall altogether.

At 11:50 on Thursday morning, the warning shot was fired across the bow. While checking my mail in the lobby, Brownie told me, "The Man wants to see you, Mitzi, and Sullivan in his office." Mitzi, not having shaved, had tried to sneak into the dining hall for breakfast after Brownie left and someone told on him. "He was in the dining hall and he had facial hair."

Now we were on our way to see The Man. We let the guys know and a quick gathering convened. Everyone would hold fast and not shave. We would meet with Coach Jordan and attempt to speak with him for the entire group. If no agreement could be reached, the guys vowed to walk.

I knew my coach. Before we left, I sadly told them, "Start packing."

I walked into Coach Jordan's office with Sullivan and Mitzi. I was the oldest. I led the way. Sullivan wore his reflector shades. Mitzi had a sour look on his face. He was still angry, but he didn't want to lose his "home" at Auburn. I had some peach fuzz over my lip. Sullivan had a few strands on his chin. His sideburns were past the middle of his ear. Mitzi was the only one of us who could grow real noticeable facial hair. He had a small mustache and long side burns. The hair on Secedrick's face would not grow yet. Secedrick was not asked to come. That was not a good sign for us.

In Coach Jordan's office, Jim Hilyer was sitting in the corner. The defensive ends coach had earned a Ph.D. in psychology. He didn't say anything.

I noticed the plaque on Coach Jordan's desk, "Watch Out For Everybody."

"Coach, you wanted to see us," I said.

"Yeah, come on in," he responded.

We sat directly in front of him. He examined our faces. I imagined him counting the hairs over my lip.

I thought I'd try and talk to Coach. Explain that we were not defying him. I opened my mouth. He cut me off. "I don't want to hear anything about black power, white power, yellow power, marches, or demonstrations," he said matter-of-factly. "All I care about is Auburn power."

What was he talking about? I tried again, "Coach." He cut me off. "You got a choice," he said. "You can either shave or lose your scholarship."

I was determined. "Coach we don't want to talk about any black power. We just want to talk. There's a problem in the dorm." I said. He shot back, "What are you going to do?" It was obvious anything except blind compliance would not be tolerated.

Surprisingly, there was little anger in the room. Coach was not angry. Neither was I. We just couldn't communicate. I looked to Coach Hilyer. He dropped his eyes to the floor. We all sat in silence.

We just wanted to talk. That's all. But Coach saw it as a challenge to his authority, an erosion of discipline. I would have played anybody, anywhere, on any day for him, but my dedication to him and Auburn had nothing to do with my hair length. I wanted to have a conversation with my Coach. He wouldn't allow it. We were World War II and Vietnam trying to have a conversation. There was no way to resolve the two points of view without talking.

He looked directly at me. In a tone of finality, he demanded, "What are you going to do?" In that moment, I knew we had no chance for talk or understanding.

I made up my mind. My decision had nothing to do with a walkout. All of a sudden I was tired. Tired of fighting every day. Tired of being the racial negotiator to Auburn's athletic department. Maybe Coach was tired as well. After all the time, the sweat and tears, I gave in to myself. "Coach," I told him, "I'll just go on home."

He fired back, "I have to take your scholarship."

He turned to Sullivan and he responded, "I'm with TG." Mitzi joined in, "I'll leave too," he said.

As we started to file out, I told Coach Jordan, "One day, Coach you are going to have to listen to somebody." It was not meant in anger or defiance. It wasn't ugly. I just wanted him to hear me.

He responded to me, "Not as long as I'm the head coach."

We went back to the dorm and relayed the news of our meeting to the others. By that evening all the black athletes had left the dorm. The news of "the walkout" flashed around the country, but initially it was suppressed within the state of Alabama. Alabama newspapers, radio, and television stations worked with the athletic department to keep the walkout quiet. Associated Press and United Press International, *Sports Illustrated*, *The New York Times*, and *Jet* magazine all either ran pieces or tried to run pieces. The athletic department responded with statements similar to, "The athletic department is not aware of any walkout by our black athletes" or "Three black football players have been suspended by Coach Jordan for disciplinary reasons."

Everyone left the dorm, but most didn't get far. In Opelika, some of the track guys claimed they had a flat tire. They "reluctantly" came back to the dorm. A couple of the track guys went home, only to be talked into coming back before the track meet on the weekend. Some of the basketball players left. Others lingered until they were "convinced" by Coach Bob Davis not to leave. The walkout quickly became an, "every man for himself," scramble.

I went home immediately after the talk with Coach Jordan. Secedrick and Sullivan went home. Mitzi stayed in Auburn, he would become our spokesman.

My parents and I talked the matter over. I said I would transfer to UAB in Birmingham to finish my degree. I'd accomplished my goals at Auburn and there was nothing else to prove.

My dad in his persuasive way reminded me I hadn't graduated yet and I still had another year of eligibility. He told me I should, "fight for what was mine."

The phone rang constantly. Newspaper reporters, concerned friends, and family all called. My parents and I agreed that I would not talk to anyone but my parents. It was hard, but it turned out to be the best thing I did. My mom would answer the phone. "Nothing has happened," she would say into the phone.

But the athletic department could no longer pretend that the problem was relegated to the three black football players. Basketball player, Eddie Johnson dropped the bomb, and it hit the athletic department broadside. "I would never advise any black to come here," Eddie was quoted as saying in the Montgomery newspaper. The headlines went national.

Now the university was scrambling.

Mitzi was quoted in the local Auburn paper as saying, "The problem is in communication. No one in the athletic department will listen to what we feel or have to say. We all decided to leave because no one here cares about us as individuals. They just look on us as tools for winning games."

The pressure was mounting on the university, recruiting was being hurt. It's overall image suffered.

Two days after the walkout, I was still home when the phone rang. It was Mitzi. My mom handed me the phone. Mitzi updated me. It looked like Auburn University would have a full complement of black athletes for the weekend basketball game and track meet. All of the guys were back. That meant just the football guys were out in the cold.

Mitzi said reporters were running all over the place. The influential Montgomery alumni were trying to get Secedrick back. After all, he didn't have any facial hair and had not "walked out." He'd just gone home. But, Secedrick told them he would not be the only black athlete on the team. Mitzi met with President Philpott who made a move to end a part of the controversy and to begin to repair the university's image. He told Mitzi that we could have our scholarships back. He said, if Coach Jordan didn't want us on the team, the president would not overrule him. But we could finish school under our scholarships.

Mitzi then scheduled a meeting with Coach Jordan. He vowed to keep me posted. I told him, "I'm with you, Sullivan, and Secedrick."

Mitzi called back right after his meeting with Coach. The pressure was on. Auburn wanted this over. "We need to meet with Coach Jordan on Sunday."

I took a deep breath. Did I want to go back? I knew my parents wanted me to. I knew, deep down, I wanted to. I owed it to too many people. I owed it to myself. I owed it to Auburn. "I'll be there," I said.

Mitzi and I filed into Coach Jordan's office five days after our first meeting. Sullivan was not there. Coach smiled. Coach talked about the Auburn family and sticking together. He spoke about a team versus a group of individuals. "We all have to be for Auburn."

He explained to me in particular how he admired Bill Cosby and O. J. Simpson. "Neither one of them has a mustache." I wanted to say, "My father does," but I figured it wouldn't do any good. Coach was trying. He was not apologizing. He was still Coach. But he was trying to meet us halfway. That's all we could ask for. I appreciated it.

He went on to explain that discipline is a huge part of any successful program. We would have to be disciplined and work hard to get back on track for next season. Then he announced, "I have decided to let you boys back on the team." We thought that was it but he added, "I will make you a promise. If you decide to come back, my door will always be open to you to come in and talk whenever you need to." He asked Mitzi and I to come see him once a week, for the rest of the quarter, "to talk."

He explained that we would live in Magnolia Hall for the rest of the quarter. He would move us back into the athletic dorm in spring. It would be my second time in Magnolia and it suited me fine. I would be separated from my teammates again, but I liked living with the student body.

"Do we have a deal?" he wanted to know. We took the deal. We shook hands.

Sullivan would come back the next day. Then finally, Secedrick returned. Secedrick didn't have facial hair, but his connections to alumni and his refusal to come back and be the only black on the team was courageous and I'm sure is part of what got us back.

The next morning's newspaper headline read, "Three Footballers Disciplined – Retain Scholarships." We found out from the newspaper we were accepted back "on probation." The word had never come up in our discussion, but we didn't care. We ended up sacrificing ourselves, but the university was pushed a little further down the road of cultural change.

The rule stayed in place, but after the initial enforcement, it faded somewhat. No one enforced the hair rule for the basketball and track guys any longer. They only had to be neat.

After the walkout, I came to know Coach Jordan as well as I ever would. Our weekly meetings were brief. We didn't have long, philosophical older-man-younger-man conversations. We strained many times to find something to talk about. "How you been, Thomas?" he'd ask. "I'm good, Coach," I would respond. "How are things in the dorm over there?" he'd ask. Magnolia Hall was across the campus. "It's fine, Coach," I told him. "I kind of like it." "Are you staying in good shape?" he'd want to know. "Yes, Coach," I'd respond. "I will be ready."

The talk was superficial. We couldn't get past first base. But we were trying.

We formed a strange bond. The swirling winds of change in 1974 bound us to each other, a family. We learned to navigate around differences to common ground. Our player-coach relationship was solidified by our respect for each other as individuals. We relaxed. He'd give me a smile. I wasn't afraid of him anymore. I began to think, in a strange way, he liked me. Still, we couldn't overcome who we were to ever be close. I went out on a limb the week before I was scheduled to move back into the athletic dorm. I asked him in our weekly meeting if I could continue to live in the other dormitory. I felt I could do better away from the whole jock scene. The answer was no.

April 16 marked the beginning of the end of the 6-6 season of 1973 and the hair walkout controversy. Spring practice began. We expected it to be rough, like two years ago, but the misery of the bad season, and the controversy united us players. We all worked toward the same goal, a championship in 1974.

Coach Doug Barfield was the new offensive coordinator. Practice became different fast. He had an approach more in tune with the 1970s. Coach Barfield didn't have to be in charge to be in charge. He brought the attitude that football could be fun. The scream fests ended. You could joke and kid with him. Guys were no longer beaten down.

He loved coaching us. At the beginning of practice, he would growl, "It's a great day for the race, boys." We'd ask, "What race is that, Coach?" He'd say, "The human race." More important, he installed the veer offense. The new concept of teaching and learning was instilled across the offensive practice field. We could have fun as we learned.

We formed a special bond. I loved playing for him. He believed in me, looked to me for leadership. He asked me to look out for the younger guys. I became a leader. In particular, I made sure the younger blacks kept up with their studies.

We were reborn. Rather than go back to the future, we ventured down a new path. The 1974 team would not be like either the 1972 team or the 1973 team. We were big, sleek, fast, athletic, and smart. We had new leadership.

As camp came to an end, we knew we would be good. We were a team of talented individual athletes who were molding themselves into a unit. We got rid of the divisions and the cliques. This team would be our team. It would belong to us, the players, as much as it did to the coaches. At the end of spring training, Coach Jordan told us we'd had "a stomping good spring."

Mike Flynn, a tough outside linebacker from Miami, became a good friend both on and off the field. Mike and I were both outcasts of a sort. He'd had some legal trouble but put it behind him. He went to class regularly and didn't judge. We hung out at a house where the girl he dated lived with three other female students. I started seeing one of the women, a white woman from Birmingham. Hanging out at the house in the evenings with Flynn and the women became a relaxing way to spend my time. We watched television, had house dinners, and studied. The women were on track to graduate in the spring, giving the whole house a positive vibe.

Staying at the house meant I didn't hang out at the dorm any more than necessary. The black athletes no longer hung out as a group. I had no desire to.

In 1974, black student enrollment was about 200. There were over 15,000 students on campus. Thirty-seven black students were awarded degrees at spring commencement. Auburn had yet to graduate a black athlete.

One rare night, I'd decided to stay in the dorm. Mitzi and I didn't have a television in our room, so I went to the TV room to catch the late NBA game. As I walked into the TV room, at first, I could only catch snippets of what the sports announcer was saying. "...he died...suicide... he was depressed... Auburn's first black athlete." Henry's picture was on the screen.

The announcer kept talking. He was talking about Henry Harris. Our Henry! He kept saying over and over, Henry was dead. Dead? Suicide? How could that be? He was our friend. He wouldn't commit suicide. "God, no!" I screamed and fled to my room.

Henry had been a small-town, poor boy on his first journey into the world. He'd chosen Auburn to begin that journey. *The Plainsman* captured Henry's death.

"A young man is gone. Henry Harris, age 24, the first black athlete at Auburn University, was found dead at the bottom of the seventeen-story dormitory where he lived on the University of Milwaukee campus. Harris ...was working as a freshman basketball coach and director of intramurals at the school and at the same time was a part time student.

"Friends say that Harris was going to lose his job and had been very depressed lately. A police captain in town said that Harris had been drinking heavily and had been smoking a lot of marijuana."

Henry's eligibility had been up at Auburn since the '72 basketball season. The Houston Rockets of the National Basketball Association drafted him. Because he had a shot knee, he was a fragment of the ball player he'd been when he first arrived at Auburn. He was bitter. He hadn't graduated. He'd taken a few classes and then left Auburn. He was working as a graduate assistant and on his degree.

Several months before Henry died I received a late-night, long-distance phone call from him. He was lonely and depressed. We had been his family, his home. He said he was coming back to Auburn because he had unfinished business. He laughed a bitter laugh when he talked of Auburn. We ended with, "Later," and hung up.

I stared at the photo of a young, handsome Henry Harris standing strong in his number 25 Auburn basketball jersey and I wondered what happened.

James and I were pallbearers at Henry's funeral. Henry was our big brother. He was the first. He showed us the way. I will always remember him telling me why he chose to become Auburn's first black athlete. "I did it for the old folks."

# CHAPTER 18

---

# FIRST AND TEN

My mom lost it. She couldn't believe it. It was the only time I'd ever heard her ask the question, "Why God?" I told her I'd be home in about three hours. They would go to the hospital with me.

The latest saga began after lunch. It was the Wednesday before our Saturday opening game of the 1974 season with Louisville in Birmingham.

The three black athletes on the team, Mitzi, Secedrick, and I were given a directive at lunch to report to the student infirmary to get a test for sickle cell anemia. Apparently, a young black athlete had died at one of the universities in the Big Eight conference. It was discovered afterward that the young man had died of sickle cell anemia, an inherited blood disorder that mostly affects people of African, Mediterranean, and Middle Eastern ancestry. There is no cure for sickle cell anemia and it's possible to die from the disease.

In 1974, there was little to no information on the campus of Auburn about sickle cell anemia. The athletic department, in compliance with a directive from the Southeastern Conference or the National Collegiate Athletic Association, sent us to be tested.

I was the last to get to the infirmary. When I got there, Mitzi and Secedrick were done. Their test, as expected, had come back negative.

I can't remember the exact color the sample was supposed to turn, but my blood test refused to cooperate. Whichever was the negative color, the one that said you do not have sickle cell anemia wasn't happening with my test. The attendant and I closely watched the little vial refuse to exonerate my blood. "Do it again," I forced a laugh. He forced a laugh. We both knew it had to be mistake.

The attendant again placed the strip of metal with drops of my blood on it into the solution in a small vial. We watched the color come back. It was positive, again.

The laughter evaporated from the room. Now, we were both concerned. "Can you do it one more time?" I asked. "Okay," he responded. He pricked me again, ran the test, and got the same result, another positive. Silence filled the room.

"What does this mean?" I asked.

"How old are you?" he returned.

"Twenty-two" I answered.

He looked at me funny.

"What," I wanted to know.

"If you have sickle cell anemia you don't live much longer than your twenties," he responded matter-of-factly. "You shouldn't be playing football, flying in planes."

After that, the world fell in.

Dr. Turk came in and told me I needed to get to the athletic department right away. I chose to walk, alone. In a fog, I reached the coaches offices; I made sure there were no tears in my eyes. I was scared, but I put up a strong front.

Coach Jordan had called his personal doctor in Birmingham. They'd made arrangements for me to be admitted into University Hospital in Birmingham as soon as I could get there. They wanted to have someone drive me. I insisted on driving myself. I needed the time. Then came the hard part. I had to call my parents.

My mom's "Why God?" over the phone had been enough to break me down. I kept telling her, "I'm sorry," even though I hadn't done anything. "Hurry home," she urged.

At home, my mom questioned the unfairness of it all. She kept mumbling to herself "How could this be happening?" We packed a small bag, and went to University Hospital.

Coach Jordan's doctor was reassuring. We'd get to the bottom of it. He was certain. For two days, I was poked, prodded, and awakened from the couple of hours of sleep I could get, before someone would come in with another needle, wanting more blood. Every time I opened my eyes, my parents were there, concern and worry etched on their faces. I didn't hear from anyone at the athletic department, neither did my parents. We assumed the doctor was in touch with them.

On Thursday evening, the doctor arrived with a concerned smile, but a smile nevertheless. My parents jumped to their feet, anxious for the news. The doctor told me that I carried the sickle cell trait, but I did not have sickle cell anemia. He gave me the ins and outs of being a trait carrier. My mom and dad stood strong. They would have to be tested to see which of them was a carrier of the trait. It would prove to be my dad. My sister's tests would come back negative. We were all relieved, but mentally exhausted.

Then came the best news, the doctor told me I could check out Friday in time to meet the team at Legion Field!

On Friday, my parents, recovered from the scare, drove me to Legion Field. We had a sentimental goodbye as I left them to rejoin the team. I told them how much I appreciated them and what a great team we made. I left them standing outside the stadium.

Inside the locker room, the guys gave me an ovation. I went around the locker room shaking hands. It was the closest I ever felt to my teammates.

Approaching the first game, I also had a journalism assignment. *The Plainsman* editor, Rheta Grimsley, and sports editor, Mark Murphy had asked me to write a football column throughout the upcoming season. Joe Nathan came up with the title, "First and Ten with Thomas Gossom."

Before our first game, I predicted a return to glory in "First And Ten." "Our football team has the opportunity to achieve something great. I doubt if anybody outside of the coaches and players really realize the potential this team has."

In 1974, I recaptured the magic. I got into the best shape of my life. I weighed in at 184 pounds. I went back to playing like I had in the Heights…'cause I loved it.

We were a looser group than either of the previous two seasons. The coaches were looser. Peruse a media guide for the 1974 season and you'll notice the players' hair was longer than the previous two seasons. My 'fro was all over my head. So were Secedrick's and Mitzi's. We still had a hair rule, but it wasn't being enforced to the extreme. Times were changing.

A closer relationship existed between players and coaches. When it was time to work, we worked. But there was more joking around. We could even joke with Coach Jordan.

My position coach, Tim Christian, and I got along fine. The position coach is responsible for his players and their performance. Coach Christian had played the same position, so he knew the ins and outs of playing receiver. I didn't make a lot of mistakes. I took care of him. He took care of me.

The players enjoyed each other's company. We liked each other. Many of us would go to The Tiger in the hour between the end of our meetings and dinner. We were as close to teammates off the field as I had ever felt.

We also had the most fun I had while playing at Auburn.

We developed a season-long tradition at our warm-up workout on Fridays. It started as a joke before the first game. We'd take the field in our shorts, t-shirts, and helmets. We'd check out the turf, loosen up. The offense would run about five plays against the defense. We'd cover the length of the field. We'd turn it around and run another five plays back. We'd run the last play from the five-yard line going into the end zone. As a joke, we lined up at different positions than our own for the last play. Giggling, we'd break the huddle. I would be quarterback. Everybody got a kick out of it, players and coaches. I did too. I made a big deal of calling the play. I'd bark the signals. The play was always the same. I would throw a pass to Lee Gross, our captain and center. He would line up at tight end. For superstition purposes I had to make a good throw and Gross had to catch it. The defense couldn't interfere. It would be bad luck. When Gross caught the ball, a huge roar would go up amongst the players. We'd then start clapping rapidly as we gathered around Coach Jordan. It was a testament to the new attitude on the team.

After getting out of the hospital, I begged Coach Barfield to call my number on the first play of the new season. "Let me go deep on the first play of the game, Coach. Come on Coach," I said. "Let's show everybody we're back." "We'll see," he growled.

We had no national pre-season ranking and three of the teams on our schedule were ranked in the top twenty in the country. We were picked to finish sixth in the conference. According to Coach Jordan, we were right where we wanted to be. "We had the whip hand."

On the very first play of the 1974 season, new offensive coordinator Doug Barfield, in his first play call ever for the Auburn varsity called my number. It wasn't the deep route, but a quick screen to me. I caught it, headed up field, got great blocking from the offensive line, and turned it into a twenty-one-yard gain. We went on to take Louisville 16-3 in front of a small crowd of 25,000. It was a typical first game. We were sporadic on offense. We couldn't move the ball consistently.

The small crowd didn't help. We were too eager on offense. We made mistake after mistake. But, there were signs we could be special. Phil Gargis, in his first game running the veer offense, ran for a hundred yards. He was fearless. Secedrick ran for fifty-two yards. I caught three passes for thirty-five yards. The defense held them to less than 100 total yards. It was evident our defense would be special.

We crushed Chattanooga for the eighteenth consecutive time, 52-7, in front of 42,000 fans at home in Auburn. It was what we needed, an easy win. Our senior safety, Mike Fuller, personally outscored the entire Chattanooga team. He had punt returns of fifty-five, fifty-five, and sixty-three yards and two touchdowns. He also returned an intercepted pass twenty-seven yards and a kickoff twenty-nine yards. I scored on a three-yard pass from Gargis. Secedrick ran for ninety-two yards, Mitzi for twenty-seven.

Dr. Philpott visited the locker room after the game.

He was one of the last people to congratulate Shug on his 164th victory as Auburn coach. "The season begins next week," he said.

We all understood. The season did begin next week. It was time for Tennessee. Auburn home games against Tennessee were always played in Birmingham's Legion Field. Finally, in 1974, President Philpott and his administration got Tennessee administrators to agree to play us in Auburn.

On a historic day in Auburn, a sellout crowd of 64,293 fans packed Jordan-Hare stadium. For the first time ever, the University of Tennessee was playing Auburn in Auburn. Everyone on the team had this game marked on their calendar. Tennessee would be a grudge match. They'd embarrassed us in '73 by punting to us on first down and shutting us out, 21-0. After they'd beaten us in the rain, their fans had showered us with whiskey bottles, ice, and beer cans. We hadn't forgotten. We had no doubts about winning. We wanted to embarrass them. We wanted Coach Jordan to punt on first down, just one time.

We were not ranked. Tennessee was ranked fourteenth in the country. They were four point favorites. In his offensive meeting before the game, Coach Barfield, described the game as a "Daddy" game. "Your daddy will appreciate you if you win, " he told us. "You know your mama always gonna tell you, you done good. It doesn't matter if the team is Chattanooga and you beat them, 52-7. But Tennessee is a Daddy game, a big boy game," he preached. "You do it today, your daddy gonna congratulate you."

Secedrick, Mitzi, and I called it, "a three black game." Meaning we would all need to be in the starting lineup for this game. Privately, between us, we felt we were a more powerful offense when the three of us were on the field at the same time. We had more speed. We could score from anywhere on the field.

It was hot that day, Auburn in September, hot. After a play in the second quarter, the Tennessee defensive back and I jogged back to our respective huddles with sweat pouring off of both of us. "Man," he said, "I don't see how you all stand this heat."

We shut them out, 21-0.

In the *Opelika-Auburn News* Coach Jordan praised the teamwork. "It always seems redundant to say a game like this was a team victory, but it was in every sense of the word. We whipped them physically. We just put it all together today. Our offense really helped the defense by giving it quite a bit of rest. I was well pleased with the effort of the entire team. After that thing up in Knoxville last year, this had to be a real big one for us."

At one point with the game secure, several of the guys begged Coach Jordan to punt on first down. "Come on, Coach," we asked. He wouldn't do it. He told reporters afterward, "The thought of doing the same to Tennessee never crossed my mind."

The next week, we recorded our second shutout in a row. Miami went down 3-0 in their own stadium, the Orange Bowl. The wind blew unmercifully, with gusts up to twenty-eight miles per hour. We ran the ball and dominated the time of possession thirty-eight minutes to twenty-two. One time-consuming drive ended with Wilson missing a thirty-seven yard field goal. It was unfortunate for him. Our other kicker, Greg Gillis, was called on to kick the game winner in the third quarter. We only threw two passes all night. On one, I was wide open for a touchdown but Phil's throw didn't reach me. It was intercepted. The errant throw prompted a comment from Coach Jordan for which he later apologized. Coach said, "Gossom was wide open, all he had to do was throw it." After watching the film, Coach felt the comment was harsh and apologized.

We learned a lot about talking shit during this game. I was not much of a shit talker during games, but I started jawing with this guy from Miami. The level of discourse quickly disintegrated to the "your mama" level. After a play, I gave him a "your mama" and headed back to the huddle. Secedrick overheard and joined in. "Your mama," he shouted back at the guys from Miami. Trouble is, Secedrick was running the ball on the next play. He hit into the line and didn't get up. You could hear his screams all the way to the sideline. He lay moaning, writhing in pain, on the turf. He was grabbing his knee. The trainers rushed to the field.

You never think about getting hurt. You block it out. With Secedrick lying there moaning, it was hard not to think of your own vulnerability. But you have to let it go quickly. "Lets' get them for Secedrick," became the cry.

In Miami, there were two very pleasant surprises for me. The woman I'd dated back at the house with the three girls in Auburn had graduated the previous May and moved to Miami. We hadn't seen each other and agreed to date other people, but we stayed in touch by phone. She came to visit me at the hotel. It was good to see her. I got her and her roommate tickets to the game. Only Fat Daddy, Flynn, Mitzi, and Secedrick knew that we'd ever dated. I kept it that way in Miami.

Also, when the busses pulled up to the Orange Bowl the day before the game, we spotted the Auburn brothers from Omega Psi Phi. Henry Ford, George Smith, and the others had rented a Winnebago and driven down to the game. It was the first time we'd had any of our black fans on a road trip. Although Henry and George had told me they would come, seeing them was heart-warming. When I'd first started playing, there wouldn't be any black fans in the stands at home games, other than the building and grounds guys. Now we had guys renting Winnebago's and driving all the way to Miami. It was indicative of the spirit of the few blacks on campus. We were determined to carve out a place for ourselves at Auburn.

After Miami, we lead the nation in total defense. We allowed 136.5 yards per game and 2.5 points per game. None of our opponents had scored a touchdown from scrimmage. We shot up to number ten in the AP poll. The top ten were:

Ohio State

Oklahoma

Alabama

Michigan

Nebraska

Notre Dame

Southern California

Florida

Texas Tech

Auburn

We took Kentucky next, 31-13. Going into the game, we had the nation's best rushing and total defensive team. The *Opelika-Auburn News* reporters wrote we "were destined to wear the mantle of greatness before the season comes to a close."

We were winning but we were having trouble passing. Gargis was an outstanding veer quarterback. He took a lot of punishment and it affected his throwing. Against Kentucky, we completed four of nine passes with two interceptions.

I couldn't get the ball. It was frustrating. Either I'd break open and the ball would fall short or we wouldn't pass out of fear an errant pass would be intercepted. I was happy for the team, and not satisfied at the same time.

It started to show in my on-the-field attitude. I'd have the occasional outburst on the sideline. During one such outburst, I threw my helmet against the fence, causing everyone around to give me my space, including the coaches.

The bowl scouts came out in force for the Georgia Tech game. Representatives of the Cotton, Sugar, and Gator were on hand. We spanked Tech, 31-22. Secedrick scored the clinching touchdown, a five-yard run with twenty seconds left in the game. I scored on a twenty-yard pass on their All-American, defensive back, Randy Rhino. I handed him the ball as I crossed the goal line. Mr. King got a picture for me. Halfway through the season we were ranked fifth in the country.

---

Governor Wallace, in an Auburn orange blazer, was on hand for Homecoming 1974. He presented the Homecoming Queen Cup from his wheelchair to homecoming queen, Debbie Day. She responded by giving the governor a hug and a kiss. The governor got a mixed round of applause.

The Confederate flag still flew over the stadium during games. The flag would be lowered in a ceremonial salute at the end of the third quarter. George Smith decided he'd had enough.

"The first thing I saw when I came into Auburn as a freshman was the KA house with that huge Confederate flag they hung outside. It shocked me. Like many of the black kids who came to Auburn in that time, I'd never seen the campus. Then I saw the flag flying over the stadium for football games. My first two years, I never went to a game.

"When we had the march on President Philpott's office, I told him we were going to take that flag down over the stadium. He said it was part of the heritage. I told him it represented everything I thought was evil. So for me it was years of frustration.

"I was sitting with the fraternity brothers at a game, my last year, and I told them, I'm going to do it. I'm going to take that flag down. One of the brothers said, 'Okay, let's do it.' He went with me, and we took it down. We ran home with it.

"The next week they had two Confederate flags flying, one at each end of the stadium. I went to get them, too. Only, they had black guys guarding the flagpoles. I couldn't believe it. I believe when Barfield came in as head coach, they took the flags down. It's kind of hard to recruit black guys with confederate flags flying all over campus.

"Oh, yeah, I kept the flag. I still have it."

After the game, Governor Wallace visited our locker room where he was presented the game ball. Governor Wallace had started to tone down his racist rhetoric. He would later say he did what he had to do in order to get elected in Alabama. After one of our games he wheeled up next to me in the locker room and said, "Believe it or not, I'm on your side." I still don't know what he meant.

On another occasion, we were flying out of Montgomery and the governor had come to the airport to see us off. Individually, we filed by him and shook his hand. My teammates had fun betting whether or not I'd shake his hand. Of course, I did. I felt confused, but he gave me a smile.

Although incremental progress had been made, racial issues continued to plague Auburn. The Health, Education, and Welfare (HEW) department of the federal government stuck it to Auburn with a blistering report on the lack of racial and gender progress.

The October 8, 1974 HEW report stated: "There were no black players on the tennis, swimming, golf, or baseball teams." There was no minority athletic staff in the men's intercollegiate program. The report requested that the university submit a plan for affirmatively recruiting black or other minority (athletic) staff. Another issue raised was the discrepancy in expenditures between men's ($2.4 million) and women's athletics ($3,000).

We began the second half of the schedule with Florida State. I loved playing against them because they had two secondary guys that were projected high NFL picks. It got my juices going, to prove myself against the best.

Before a crowd of 58,709, we turned up the offense, gaining over 400 yards. With the score 7-6 at halftime, we exploded and crushed them 38-6. I had my best statistical game of the season, catching four passes for eighty-five yards, one a forty-three yard touchdown that broke the game open.

Now 7-0, we flew to Gainesville ranked number five in the country. Florida was number eleven. We were favored to win by three and the game would be televised on ABC. It would be our first time on television all year. Coach Jordan told the newspapers, "If you like competition, this should be competition at its best."

It would be a physical game. It would be a challenge and we had not been challenged in a while. In addition, many of the guys on our team were from Florida and they had a little extra incentive.

I summed up the stakes in my "First and Ten" column, "This year's game will attract as much attention as any we play. It will be regionally televised. It will attract bowl scouts. More importantly, it is a big stepping-stone to the Southeastern Conference Championship."

It was the largest crowd ever to see a game at Florida Field, 64,912. We fell behind 7-0 for the first time all year. Wayne Fields, Florida's starting safety started yapping. He'd yap the whole game. "Gossom, you ain't catching nothing today. I got you." I'd smile at him, especially if I knew we had something planned for him. And that day, we did.

We came right back. Secedrick ripped off two long runs to get us down the field. Gargis clicked with Ed Butler on a six-yard pass for the first touchdown. Wilson came in and kicked the extra point.

In the second quarter, Florida rammed the ball down our throats. They went ninety yards in sixteen plays for another touchdown.

It was my time. Gargis called X streak. I blew past the defender. I had at least seven yards of space between us. A photo in the next day's paper captured the action. I was five yards behind the guy but waiting for the ball. The ball hung. It would not come down. I stopped and waited. Finally it settled into my hands, but by then the Florida defender caught up to make the tackle at the seven-yard line. The play had carried from our forty-yard line to Florida's seven-yard line, fifty-three yards. The first person I saw when I stood was Wayne Fields. "Yeah, you got me, you got me," he said. He game me some skin. I grinned at him, slapped his hand.

It took us four plays, but Mitzi took it in on fourth down from the one-yard line. We were ahead 14-13. With a few seconds left before halftime, we outsmarted ourselves. The instruction came in to kicker Greg Gillis to pooch kick the kickoff, a safe kick before halftime. It was not a safe kick. A Florida running back caught it on the dead run and nearly scored. They scored before halftime and we went into the second half, behind.

It was a rock-em'-sock-em' game. In the third quarter, a trick play on third down almost gave us the spark we needed. We drove the ball down deep into Florida's territory. A touchdown would give us the lead. We called a fake sweep play. Mitzi would take the ball on a fake sweep right. Mike Gates, our tight end on the play, and I would fake blocks on our defenders and slip out for the pass. Mitzi would have his choice of who to throw it to, either Mike at the goal line or me deeper in the end zone. It worked perfectly. We were both open. Mitzi chose Mike and let it go. It hit Mike's hands around his waist. Sadly for us, the ball fell to the ground.

Wilson subsequently missed a thirty-yard field goal. Florida then followed with a long fourth quarter touchdown drive. It sealed the win for them 25-14. It was a helluva game. Later, Florida's Coach Doug Dickey described the game: "This was the most spirited football game I've been involved in, in a number of years. I was proud of our team for taking the pressure of this very big game and never cracking. The same is true of Auburn."

Our record was 7-1. We dropped to number ten in the polls.

The next week's "First and Ten" was the most difficult one I'd had to write all year. Up until this column, I'd had fun. My columns were being read campus wide. I'd written about teammates and pre- and post-game information that could only come from inside the team. But, I couldn't muster up much.

I didn't have much to say in "First and Ten," but I was being written about and quoted in the local newspaper.

"The major beneficiary of the recent passing development has been senior split end, Thomas Gossom, of Birmingham. After six games, he had caught only nine passes for 99 yards. In the two past games, he has caught seven passes for 169 yards, bringing this season's total to 16 catches for 268 yards. He caught a 43-yard touchdown pass against Florida State and a 53-yard grab against Florida. All of a sudden, Gossom has gained a place of importance in the Auburn offense.

"'I think the coaches realize now that we are going to have to pass more,' Gossom said. 'The last two weeks, we have worked like hell on our passing game, but to do any good, we have to use it more in games.

'I feel like I can get open most every time and I have enough confidence in myself that if we are going to pass, I want it to be thrown to me,' said Gossom.

'But I'm not that dissatisfied with the veer. Scoring touchdowns is not that big a deal for me. The best thing is just helping the team move the ball in any way I can.'"

I was a long way from being dissatisfied because we were winning. But I wanted to do more. Not out of selfishness, but because I could. However, I was on a great team and that had to suffice.

Mississippi State was up next. We jumped out to a comfortable lead, 17-0 at the half. We got too comfortable. According to Coach Jordan, Mississippi State manhandled us in the second half. "We had the whip hand," Jordan continued, "but Mississippi State took it away from us. We were just hanging on at the end."

Coach Jordan pitched a fit over the Mississippi State fans cowbell brigade. Every time we had the ball in the second half their fans would ring cowbells, making it impossible to hear the quarterback signals. The bells didn't bother me much, but several thousand fans ringing cowbells can cause confusion. Several guys made offensive mistakes because of the ringing bells. After one mistake filled play, Coach Jordan ran onto the field to appeal to the official. However, the more he complained the louder the fans rang the bells. The official motioned to the crowd to stop ringing the bells. Instead, they rang them louder and louder. We had to hold on at the end to win it. We beat them, 24-20.

We were ranked number seven in the AP poll after the win. Georgia was next.

During the Christmas holiday season of 2007, my wife and I made a visit to a housewarming for our new neighbors and my former teammate Sherman Moon and his wife Vicki. It was an old home week celebration. Ken Bernich was there. So was Jackie Burkett from Coach Jordan's 1957 team. On a wall in Sherman's office was a photo from the game program for the Georgia game taken of the twenty seniors on the 1974 squad. Coach Jordan is kneeling in the middle of the AU logo. The twenty seniors kneeled on one knee in a semi circle with Coach Jordan at midfield. Bernich looked at the picture, said to me, "Which one are you?" We both laughed. We understand the joke. We also understand the seriousness behind the joke. Sherman walked in; saw us looking at the picture. Before I could tell him the joke, he says to me, "Which one are you?"

A new Jordan-Hare stadium record of 64,748 fans showed up for the Georgia game. We were still in the running for the Southeastern Conference Championship. Georgia had an outside shot. It would be another classic Auburn-Georgia matchup.

We whipped Georgia 17-13. Fat Daddy would kick a thirty-six-yard field goal that would prove to be the winning points. On offense,

Secedrick ran for 119 yards. Gargis played his best game, running for 160 yards. Despite his passing deficiencies, Gargis was fearless. He never backed down. We all liked him and respected him. Gargis was named AP Southeastern Back of the Week. I caught three passes for twenty-two yards.

How did I feel about my last game at Jordan-Hare? I wrote my feelings in "First and Ten":

"Thinking back through the years… I will always remember the thousands of little kids that swarm the field after every game searching for sweat bands, chinstraps, and autographs. …I will always remember playing in Jordan-Hare before a partisan crowd. …I am sure the other nineteen seniors will agree with me when I say we want to win this game to end our era in Jordan-Hare on a sweet note. Our record in Jordan-Hare over the past three years is fourteen wins and two losses.

"When the game is over Saturday, I will run over to say a word or two with the opposing players. Then I will make my way to the dressing room through all the little kids pulling and tearing at anything they can get their hands on. I will go in and sing "War Eagle" with the team. We will say a prayer to the Lord in thanks for the opportunity. I will thank him for the moment at hand and for the past four years because he has made them four years I will always cherish."

We were now 9-1 and heading for a nationally televised battle with Alabama in Birmingham's Legion Field. If we beat them we would win a share of the conference championship. It had also been made official, we were going back to the Gator Bowl for Auburn's seventh straight bowl appearance. We would be playing on *Monday Night Football*. Our opponent had not yet been determined.

We were excited about being on *Monday Night Football*, but first, there would be another memorable battle with our cross state rival, the number two ranked Alabama Crimson Tide.

# CHAPTER 19

---

# THE GOSSOM INCIDENT

The letter is dated December 4, 1974. It is addressed to Dr. Harry M. Philpott. The letter is from Geo. Mattison Jr. of Birmingham, Alabama, a man I never knew. He was inquiring about a controversial play I made against The University of Alabama.

Dear Harry,

I was proud of our boys last Friday afternoon and I would like to replay the game any Saturday.

I would like an honest statement from someone who was in position to "see the play" or who has seen the film adequately to make an "honest" call on the reputedly bumping out of bounds of Gossom on the disputed touchdown play, which Auburn made against Alabama. I saw the play of course as I was sitting in your box at Legion Field, but I didn't see anybody bump Gossom out of bounds. Sunday afternoon I watched both the Alabama Bear Bryant replay of the game and likewise the Auburn version... and on neither of these replays could I see any indication whatever of anyone being on the line or outside the line on that play when Gossom ran for a touchdown. I did see an official follow Gossom down the field and raise hands in a touchdown signal. The play indicating the infraction apparently came from across the field.

...do you have "evidence" on this?

Cordially yours,

GEO. A. Mattison, Jr.

Dr. Philpott responded on the 6th of December.

Dear George,

Your letter about the officiating last Friday has been received and I felt that you would be interested in a couple of points of view concerning the Gossom Incident. Up until the present, we do not have any firm evidence one way or another, which would give us the facts without a reasonable doubt. A number of Auburn people have been convinced from the television replay that the call was correct and that Gossom stepped out. Others have maintained that they were not able to see this. From what I have gathered, we will just have to go through life without knowing for sure.

… Once a call is made, right or wrong, and the game is over there is no possible way of rectifying the situation. I suppose we have to recognize that officials are human and will make mistakes, but that the mistakes become part of the game itself.

It was good to see you and hope our paths will be crossing again in the near future…

Sincerely yours,

Harry M. Philpott

President

Mattison wasn't the only one who was confused and angry. For years Auburn fans complained about "The Gossom Incident." How could an official in the middle of the field make a call at the far sideline? Even today people ask me about it.

"Are you the Thomas Gossom who scored a touchdown against Alabama and it was called back?" "Yes, that's me," I respond. The questioners, Auburn fans, respond, "They lied." "He pushed you." "I saw it, you weren't out of bounds."

Even Alabama fans have asked. A few years ago, my next-door neighbor, Carter Coleman, now an Alabama grad, but then an inquisitive fourteen year old came over to question me, "Someone told me you scored a touchdown against Alabama and it was called back. Is that true?"

When my old friend and teammate Mike Flynn heard about this book, he sent word to me through Wilson: "Ask him if he's going to tell about stepping out of bounds against Alabama. If he doesn't step out of bounds we win the damn game."

––––––––––––––––––––––

The 1974 version of the Iron Bowl was played on a Friday afternoon, on national television. That afternoon, the city of Birmingham virtually shut down. Businesses were minimally staffed with unlucky workers who brought televisions and radios from home. The entire state of Alabama was either at the game, in front of a television, or listening to a radio.

Seventy-one thousand, two hundred and twenty-four fans crammed into Legion Field. Alabama was ranked number one in the UPI poll and number two in the AP. Auburn was ranked number six in UPI and number seven in the AP poll. Alabama was a 15-point favorite.

In our white road uniforms, we ran onto Legion Field to cheers and boos. In the Legion Field days before the game was moved to the school's respective campuses, half the stadium would be orange and blue, the other half red and white. It was an awesome atmosphere; the energy in the stands electric. Fans worked themselves into a tizzy.

The game would be a "three black game." We would need all the speed we could get. The trouble was, our speed was on offense. We had good athletes on defense, but could we stop the fast Alabama halfbacks from getting around the corner on us? Since James' signing in 1969,

Alabama had raced past Auburn in the quest to sign black athletes. There were at least a dozen black football players on the Alabama squad.

Alabama scored first. Halfback Willie Shelby caught a swing pass and outran our guys to the corner of the end zone. We couldn't match his speed. Alabama led 7-0.

In our next possession, Coach Barfield tried to strike back by calling my number on a deep route. I got a step on the Alabama defender, but the ball was under thrown and he broke it up.

They kicked a field goal and went up 10-0. Secedrick and Mitzi lined up in the backfield and our offensive line went to work. Secedrick ripped off runs of twenty-one and nine yards. Mitzi went for twelve yards. Secedrick took it in for the score. Wilson kicked the extra point. He had not missed an extra point all season.

That day, our defense played the wishbone as well as we'd ever played it.

But we couldn't totally shut it down. In the third quarter, Alabama's big wishbone cranked up again. This time they drove eighty yards for a touchdown. It was 17-7 Alabama.

We fought back. Gargis broke a big run. Two plays later it was my turn on the stage.

We'd planned to run the play for a year. We knew Mike Washington, the Alabama cornerback, was aggressive. He'd intercepted the pass a year ago that had gotten me benched. We also knew he would bite on a fake.

The ball was set on the hash mark near our bench on Alabama's forty-one yard line. Coach Barfield called the play with a formation that would set me into the short side of the field, which wouldn't leave a lot of room to navigate.

I ran the route perfectly. Mike bit on the fake. He was beat and he recognized it. But he wasn't an All-American for nothing. He made the only move he could. He threw his body at me. He would take an interference call rather than give up a touchdown.

I was later told that my big toe came down on the line. I didn't go out of bounds and come back in. However, there was not a good instant replay angle, which was what made the play controversial. I never saw any film of the play other than the coach's view from the press box. From that angle, you can't see where I landed.

I caught the ball on the dead run. I had only Alabama safety, Ricky Davis to beat. I sped down the sideline. Davis steamed across the field. He had the angle. When we met at the ten-yard line, he threw his body across my legs. I gave him the old Rosalind Heights limp leg. He knocked one of my legs into the air, but I came down on my hand and balanced on my other leg. It's a great photo, one leg in the air, the hand on the ground. Ricky Davis slid past me out of bounds. I ran into the end zone.

The Alabama cheerleaders were lined up across the end zone. In an unplanned act of spontaneity, I looked to the Alabama cheerleaders, spiked the ball, and pointed to them and said "Fuck Alabama."

It was the best catch and run we'd had all year. It was beautiful. We celebrated like crazy. We had new life. Orange and blue pom-poms by the thousands shook all over the stadium. The score was now 17-13. We began to line up for the extra point.

Then confusion broke out on the field. Coach Jordan came halfway out on the field to protest. We followed the officials back up the field to the original line of scrimmage, in disbelief. I went from the top of the world to the bottom in a few seconds.

We went from euphoria to fourth down and four. We didn't get the touchdown. Nor did we get the interference call.

At that point is where most peoples' memory of the game stopped. But it was still not over. There was more ball to be played. We had to gather ourselves. We had about six minutes left in the third quarter, and the entire fourth quarter.

Alabama tried to put us away, quickly. They marched sixty-eight yards to our one-yard line. On fourth down, Coach Bryant changed his mind about going for a field goal. They took a time out. Coach Bryant decided to go for the dagger, he wanted the touchdown. On the play, our defense led by Bruce Evans and Mike Flynn trapped the Alabama quarterback, Richard Todd in the backfield. We held.

The game rolled on. There were a series of near misses for both teams. They tried a field goal. The kick fell short. We tried passing. I drew double coverage and Ricky Davis intercepted. Our defense held again. We had the ball again. But it was now late in the fourth quarter. We had to score twice.

Our offense had sputtered since the called back touchdown. Some of our guys had gotten spooked. Big game. Huge crowd. Adversity. Doubt had crept in. A heroic effort by Mitzi brought us back. Mitzi checked into the game, joined the huddle, and slapped Lynn Johnson, our biggest offensive lineman, across the headgear. "Damn it, let's go," he commanded. He looked at all of the offensive linemen. "Block, damn it. Put your damn hands in here." We all joined hands in the middle of the huddle. "Let's go."

Mitzi took over. He ripped off three big runs; seven yards, twelve yards, and twenty-five yards. Secedrick slashed for a big run. A couple of plays later, Gargis took it in. We had marched seventy-two yards and never attempted a pass.

Coach Jordan made his statement. We would go for two. If we made the two-point conversion, and we got a shot at a later field goal it would be to win the game, not tie it. On the two-point play, Gargis's pass fell short in the end zone between halfback Rick Neel and me.

Still we were energized. Momentum was back with us. They were in a flux. We'd physically whipped them on the last drive. Our line regained its confidence. Would we have time to win the game?

We kicked off and held, forcing Alabama to punt. We got the ball at midfield with 1:07 left. We hungrily ran onto the field. I was hoping for another shot at the big pass. The first down call was an end around to our tight end Dan Nugent. Mike Dubose, the Alabama linebacker broke through and disrupted the slow developing play. He knocked the ball out of Gargis' hand and fell on it. Game over.

It was a shitty end to a great game. We wanted to go down swinging. But we had to watch them run out the clock. They beat us 17-13. We would not share the conference championship. We'd played every one of the top teams in the conference. No other team had done that. That would have to be our consolation prize.

After the game, reporters gave me the star treatment. They wouldn't leave me alone. They asked the same questions over and over regarding the now controversial play. I answered as best I could.

"I thought I had a touchdown and the next thing I knew they were bringing it back. The referee said I was out–that's the only thing that matters. I don't know whether I was or not."

I'd finish and I'd get asked the same thing. I'd answer again.

"I don't know if I was out of bounds. He (Mike Washington) pushed me. I was concentrating on the ball."

Mike Washington confirmed he pushed me.

"That was about all I could do," he said, "and I had to leave my feet to do it. When I looked up and saw him catch that pass it scared the devil out of me. I wasn't sure the official had seen him go out of bounds."

In the next day's newspaper, a photo of me streaking down the sideline ran under the headline, "Controversy."

As upset as he was, Coach Jordan refused to get involved in any controversy in the newspapers, even though he was angry, stomping around. We were all angry, feeling we'd been robbed. The sideline official didn't make the call. He trailed me all the way down the field and signaled touchdown. The official who made the call was from the backfield.

In the end, the play didn't count. It became controversial because people wanted it to be. Some may have needed it to be. As a player, you recognize the refs are part of the game. They're right most of the time. There's always a shoulda, woulda, coulda in a ball game, especially a big ball game. This one just happened to involve me. I let it go after it was over.

Four years later, the NCAA changed the rule that called back my touchdown. The current ruling says an eligible offensive player can "return inbounds immediately after being blocked out of bounds by an opponent." My teammates and friends called it "The Gossom Rule."

We would move on to the Gator Bowl in one of the top matches of the bowl season, Auburn against Texas. The hype around the match-up was huge. We were still ranked sixth in the country. They were unranked at 7-3, and we were a 7-point underdog.

The game was played on ABCs *Monday Night Football*. We were pumped. Texas was not. They had expected a better season. They felt we were not up to their caliber. That played into our hands because Coach Jordan relished being the underdog.

There were 63,811 fans in attendance. During my introduction, I did a "Hi Mom" before the ABC cameras. The Gator Bowl would be the last game we seniors would play for Auburn. We wanted to go out as Gator Bowl Champions. We crushed them, 24-3.

I finished the season with twenty catches, 294 yards, and three touchdowns. I was invited to the American Bowl Game in Tampa, Florida.

The bowl game was a different experience for me. First of all, it was the first time I'd ever been on a team with more than three black players. It was the first time you could not just look out on the field and pick me out from everybody else. It felt good to have that spotlight off of me.

Also, we were treated like men, like pros. We were divided into two squads, North and South. Vince Dooley, of Georgia, was the coach of our South Squad. We only had three days to practice and practices were pretty loose. We ran basic plays using simple offensive formations. We were all timed, measured, and weighed. I was officially five feet, eleven and three-quarters inches and weighed 187 pounds. I'd suffered a slight hamstring pull before the Gator Bowl, but still I was timed at 4.4 for forty yards. After my sprint, I felt the hamstring tighten up even more. It was still sore and tender. I rested as much as possible in practice. I started for the South Squad on a bad leg. I had one catch and run for thirty yards. We won, 30-22.

After the game, I met Coach Ray Perkins, of the New England Patriots. He'd been a receiver for Alabama and the Baltimore Colts in the NFL. Growing up, I'd followed his career. We chatted briefly. He told me he'd watched me throughout the year. He said he thought I could play at the next level. Before we departed he said, "Okay, get that leg well. We may be talking to you before the draft."

[ 1975 ]

# CHAPTER 20

# GRADUATION

A week after the big game, I met Pam, from Tuskegee Institute. Pam never got to see me play at Auburn. It was fitting and symbolic of my life moving in a new direction, away from football and to whatever was next. Pam became my girlfriend, we clicked. Once I finished my classes, I'd take off for Tuskegee. We'd either hang out on her campus or go back to Auburn and study together. On weekends, we would hang out at the waterfall in Chewalca State Park. Although I'd had a couple of good relationships, Pam was probably the first girlfriend with some permanence. My life was slowing down.

My last quarter on campus was one of my best. After the season, I moved into a small, one-bedroom, red brick apartment, two blocks from campus. It was furnished with free cable. Most of the seniors whose eligibility was up had moved out of the dorm. It was standard procedure. We could enjoy some time on campus without the restrictions of football. It was an opportunity to live the life of a normal student. The past summer, I had traded my Chevy and bought a VW bug. I then sold the bug to Mike Gates. I bought a VW van, with curtains and carpet in the back.

I felt great. I was now a former Auburn football player. I wanted to make the adjustment and move ahead with life. I stopped shaving and worked on my long awaited mustache. I let my 'fro grow. I saw very few of my former teammates with the exception of my close friends and the guys I worked out with. Wilson had fallen in love and would get married that spring.

I enjoyed school and being a student. For the first time since elementary school, I was a student and not a student athlete. I needed only one class to graduate, a speech class. I had time to hang around on campus, hold long philosophical conversations.

I was no longer writing "First And Ten." I was given the opportunity to write other stories but declined. I was having too much fun.

Auburn had begun observing Black Heritage Week on campus. I went to see black Congressman Louis Stokes speak. I had time now to do all the things I'd missed throughout my five years playing football.

One rare afternoon, I ventured over to the coliseum to play basketball with some teammates. One of the coaches pulled me to the side and whispered that I should go home for the weekend.

"Someone is going to set you up to sell some marijuana," I was told. I looked at him in confusion. I replied that I didn't sell marijuana, nor did I have any, so I wasn't worried. He explained that one of the guys on the team would ask me for a joint. If I gave him one, he would give me a dollar. I would then be busted. I was in shock. I didn't have a joint. If I gave the guy one, I would have had to get it from someone else to give it to him. Who would want to bust me? That scared me. I asked the coach to tell me more. He told me the guy's name. That further shocked me because I hardly knew the guy, even though he was a teammate. He was somewhat of an outcast who didn't play a lot. Maybe this would be his way of getting himself in, accepted. The coach told me that was all he knew.

I hauled ass for home that weekend. There was a bust on campus, mainly students with small amounts of marijuana. Three black guys were busted. They were small potatoes. Only one was actually selling "dope." A "friend," someone they all trusted, set them all up. One guy was eventually sentenced to fifteen years in prison for one joint.

There was a feeling of paranoia among many of the black guys on campus. The "friend" who was ratting people out had been one of the biggest mouths on campus. He'd been one of the early rulers of "the 'N' word" Corner. Apparently he'd gotten into some trouble and agreed to set up innocent people. I made a conscious effort to stay out of everyone's way. I just wanted to graduate and leave. Most of my time was spent either in class, with Pam, or working out for football scouts in hopes of getting drafted.

Professional scouts were all over campus to work out us seniors with NFL potential. Our prospects were Bernich, who had been named an All-American, Mike Fuller, Lee Gross, Dan Nugent, and myself. I ran a 4.41 forty-yard dash for the scouts.

Like most ballplayers, I wanted to play pro ball. From the little buzz I was getting from scouts, it looked like I might get drafted. How high? It would depend. I didn't have gaudy numbers. I had effective numbers. I could move the chains for first downs. Certainly coming from Auburn would give some testament to my toughness. What kind of recommendations could I get from my coaches? Would negative recommendations from my coaches hurt my pro chances? Would "my attitude" scare teams off?

On draft day, a photographer for the local paper staged a photo of the five of us who might get drafted as we "waited for the phone call from the pros" to come. My teammates' calls came the first day of the draft. Mine didn't. Bernich, Gross, Fuller, and Nugent all went within the first five rounds. I limped home, my tail between my legs.

On the second day of the draft, I waited alone in my apartment. With my name still not called, I resigned myself to the fact that I wouldn't get drafted. I started to plot which teams I would try and sign with as a free agent. That meant walking on again.

At 3:18 on the afternoon of the second day of the draft, my phone rang. I was walking out the door, not feeling too well about not being drafted, on my way to Tuskegee. The phone rang three times before I moved to answer it.

"Hello," I answered.

"Is this Thomas Gossom?" came the question. "Yes it is," I answered. "This is Ray Perkins of The New England Patriots. We just drafted you." "I'm glad someone did," I blurted.

New England had drafted me in the fourteenth round of the seventeen round draft. I was the 353$^{rd}$ player chosen. Coach Perkins and I chatted for a minute. He told me the Head Coach, Chuck Fairbanks would be calling me. Said they would be back in touch.

All my dreams were coming true. I'd been drafted and I was nearing graduation.

Three weeks away from graduation, feeling good about my new life, the hair controversy tried to rear its ugly head again. This time it would involve guys who were no longer playing at Auburn.

I stood before Coach "Shot" Senn. I needed my last monthly check to pay my rent. "Boy, I can't give you your check until you shave. Those are my orders and I can't give you a check," he reiterated. I just stood looking at him. He had already pissed me off with that "boy" shit. But I held my tongue. He continued with his game of solitaire. "Who do I need to go see, coach?" I asked. "The Man," came the reply.

I didn't want to go see Coach Jordan. I'd tried that. I went to see Coach Haley, the athletic director, to find out what was going on. I explained to him that I was no longer eligible. I was graduating in three weeks. I didn't want to cause any problems and I didn't want to be a negative influence on the younger guys. I told him I'd gotten three checks that winter and nobody had said a word. I didn't understand. "I'd just like to get my check, pay my rent, graduate, and move on," I said. He responded, "A rule is a rule." He explained that all athletes must shave regardless of whether they have eligibility remaining or not. "If you don't shave you, can't get an athletic department check."

I went home to shave. I was tired of fighting. My phone rang. It was a reporter from The Plainsman. "I'm calling about the latest hair incident," he said. He informed me that four senior football players had been warned by Coach Jordan to shave all facial hair if they wanted to continue receiving scholarship aid. The guys, All-American Ken Bernich, Dan Nugent, Johnny Sumner, and Charlie Boyd had all celebrated the end of their football eligibility, by moving out of the dorm and growing their hair and beards. Apparently, that did not set well with someone in the athletic department. I was included, even though I had not seen the other guys.

We all complied and shaved to get our checks.

Still, *The Plainsman*, ran an article, entitled "Facial Hair: Five Athletes Must Shave or Lose Scholarship." Quotes from me were included.

"Last year, they told us if you lived in the dorm you couldn't have a mustache, but if you moved out, you could. I guess the rule has changed.

"It is really ridiculous just two weeks from graduating and I have to get disenchanted with the whole thing."

Although far less of a controversy than the black athlete walkout, the hair controversy again made national news. Within a week, an anonymous person mailed me an editorial, "Splitting Hairs" from the *Chicago Tribune*.

"Coach Shug Jordan's rule and theory about hair length has always been a little silly.

"Now the matter is causing a ruckus again, this time as five seniors were threatened with the loss of scholarship checks until they shaved their facial hair. Three of these athletes have signed with pro teams and one is only two weeks away from graduating.

"Discipline during the demanding football season is necessary, and if Coach Jordan feels demanding haircuts and shaves constitutes discipline then we can agree the silly rule should be followed if the athletes have previously agreed. However, enforcing a hair policy during post season quarters, especially upon players who will no longer represent Auburn University on the playing field, seems a mite ridiculous.

The five players involved are grown men who will soon be changing their life styles to fit with other rules, probably having nothing to do with the length of their hair.

"The threat of no more scholarship money seems to have persuaded the athletes to bow once again to the unchanging Jordan... We admire the coach's record, his obsession with discipline, and even his determination to stick with unpopular policy. ...Quit splitting hairs, coach, and let grown men live a little."

As I prepared to leave Auburn that winter of 1975, the university signed the largest number of black players it had ever signed. Of the thirty football scholarships allotted for the next year, seven had been awarded to black football players. That would give Auburn eleven black players in the fall.

Four of the five starters on the basketball team that year were black. There were five black track runners and three more signed for the next year. I thought back to the dark ages of my freshman year when Henry, James, and I had to count the janitors among our few friends.

More black students were on campus than ever before, but still the numbers of black students were miniscule in comparison to overall university numbers of close to 20,000 students. There were a couple of black classes, a couple of black professors, two black fraternities, and Black Heritage Week.

There were still issues to be dealt with. *The Plainsman* would again take on the issues of black students on campus.

"Vernell Barnes who is rush chairman for Omega Psi Phi, hints that although there is now no Greek integration, that integration could someday conceivably break down the barrier of segregation formed by strong prejudicial Greek walls. 'We hold an open rush,' explains Barnes. 'We have advertised on bulletin boards, on signs and on WEGL, and so far in two and one half years we have had one white appear at one rush smoker.'

"Barnes says that if a white wished to join his fraternity there would be no color consideration of the application.

"At present, there are no white members of either of the black fraternities nor are there any black members in any of Auburn white social fraternities."

Those cultural changes and locked doors would now be someone else's battle. My time was up.

Before I left my apartment for graduation, I pulled the small piece of paper out of my wallet that I'd placed there five years ago. "To Play Football At Auburn University." I'd surpassed my dreams. I tossed the paper in the garbage.

In my cap and gown among thousands, I waited for my name to be called. A swirl of emotions raced through my body. I felt pride, gain, loss, courage, faith, friendship, anger, and even love. I'd been through them all.

On the field, I'd been successful. I'd walked on and won a scholarship. I started for Coach Jordan for three years. We'd produced a three-year record of 26-9. We'd finished number five in 1972 and number eight in 1974. We went to three straight bowls. I finished my career with forty catches, a fifteen-yard average per catch and nine touchdowns. In another era, I could have done so much more.

My off-the-field legacy would equal or surpass anything I did on the field. Life is built on more than statistics. People counted on me. Henry, James, and I, along with the other early black students at Auburn University, not only walked a path less traveled, we had to create a path. We were not radicals, but we had come to make a difference. People ask, "Why didn't you leave? Just quit and go somewhere else." They don't understand. In that era, especially in the South, we were raised to make a difference. We were connected to those who'd gone before us and aware of our relationship to those who would come after us. "Take that ball life handed you Thomas, and run with it," was the message society gave me. The people in Rosalind Heights, the black guys in B&G who were made to sit on the wooden bleachers, the Auburn fans and administrators who recognized that change was coming, the black people in the state of Alabama who prayed for it to come, my parents, and the generations to come, in my mind, they all stood on the sidelines of life hollering at me as though I was Forrest Gump. "Run, Thomas, Run!"

At my graduation, I sat and waited with pride. The robed students lined the stage. Several hundred had gone before me. Several thousand waited their turn. I focused totally on President Philpott, standing in the center of the stage. He had that grin on his face as he handed out degrees. Mine was up there.

Doc, Cat, Donna, Kim, and Pam sat in the stands. A quiet pride enveloped them. We'd all done it. It had been a team project and we'd all played our part. My mom, the encourager, her dreams instilled in me. My dad, the rock, every day he'd gone out and cleared the path to manhood for me. My sisters, supportive, even when my celebrity unfairly invaded their lives. I would be first, but both my sisters would go on to graduate from Auburn, as well as a future niece. Pam now gave me peace of mind.

I had so much to be proud of.

I would be Auburn's first black athlete to graduate. It had been stressful. College was supposed to be fun. Of course there is some stress associated with grades and studying, but I was drained from more than that. I felt worn out. I felt relieved as much as celebratory. I'd honored Henry and James. They made it better for me. But we were kids playing adult games. They resigned themselves to their fate and played the cards they were dealt. But they'd looked out for me. I'd tried to give direction to the younger guys and had now handed that baton off to them.

I was proud of those Auburn fans who had truly embraced us and had tried to make us part of the family. I was proud that I discovered *The Plainsman* and that *The Plainsman* discovered me. It gave me an identity beside that of a jock.

When my turn to walk across the stage came President Philpott awaited me. I was grinning like a Cheshire cat. So was he. I marched straight to him. He took the degree in its vinyl case and handed it to me. We shook hands, smiling. There was a small smattering of applause. We posed for the photographer. I believe Dr. Philpott was as proud as I was.

My red, white, and rusted VW Bus chugged up I-85 to Montgomery, headed for Birmingham. I was done. The pomp and circumstance was over. I was ready for whatever new Rover Boy adventure awaited me.

[ 2002 ]

# CHAPTER 21

---

# AMAZING AGAIN

The morning following the thirty-year reunion reception of the 1972 team, the sun shone brightly on the beginning of my new relationship with my alma mater. The night before I'd had as good a time with my teammates as I'd ever had. All the positives that had been used to describe us on the field, special, amazing, men of destiny, and teammates for life, now applied to us off the field.

We met at 9:20 the next morning for the "Tiger Walk." The Tiger Walk is a traditional pre-game walk by the team through thousands of Auburn fans from the athletic dormitory to Jordan-Hare Stadium. In 1972, it was more informal. Today it is still traditional, but much larger and more intense.

With car traffic blocked, we walked down the middle of the street to the stadium. Thousands of Auburn fans, cheering, screaming, and hollering "War Eagle," stood on either side of us. They were excited. It was a gauntlet of goodwill. We slapped hands, held babies, saw old friends, and signed autographs. Sandy Cannon, a fellow wide receiver on that team, reminded me that he and I had always walked to the stadium together. We continued our tradition walking side by side. James was in front of me, Wilson walked right behind me. I'd forgotten how quickly the adrenaline of getting ready to play a game could return. I was pumped as I walked into the stadium.

We lined up in alphabetical order. I lined up between fellow receiver Mike Gates and center Lee Gross. Gates gave me a hard time about the Volkswagen I'd sold him. It was a lemon. I reminded him, I did tell him it burned oil. He says I didn't. I tell him if it is any consolation, the VW bus I bought with the money wasn't any better. We laugh about it.

The announcer asks the crowd to welcome the 1972 Auburn football team, "The Amazins." He tells the crowd of our 10-1 record and number five ranking in the final AP poll. He tells of the miraculous 17-16 win over Alabama. The fans give us a standing ovation. We walk to midfield. We stand there and bask in the sunshine of love and praise the crowd rains down on us.

I look for joyce. I find her standing along the fence, all smiles, pride, and love. I would not have been there that day if not for her and our son Dixson's encouragement. Buried hurts and emotions still would be buried. Scars would still be unhealed.

I drift. I scan the thousands of fans. I recall my flight out of Los Angeles on my way to the reunion. I was wearing an Auburn cap and a man of about forty stopped me, asked me my name. I told him. He told me he was from Birmingham, and as a ten-year-old, he'd been at the Tennessee-Auburn game in 1974. "After the game, I stormed the field with hundreds of other kids," he said. "I asked you for your sweatbands and you gave them to me. I still have them," Not knowing what to say to him, I thanked him. On the plane, as I made my way down the aisle of the airplane, a woman I didn't know saw my cap and sang out, "War Eagle" as I walked past her.

I thought about my biological family and their inclusion in the Auburn family. My mom saved all the photos from my playing days. She died in 2000. My dad never misses a televised Auburn football game. My sisters Donna and Kim graduated from Auburn. My brother-in-law, Emmett Thomas, played basketball for Auburn. My wife and son are Auburn converts.

Auburn is now working on its second generation of blacks. Donna and Emmett's daughter, Tippi, is an Auburn grad. George Smith's son is an Auburn grad. Henry Ford's daughter currently attends.

I think of Coach Jordan. I played for the man for four years, but I hardly knew him. Circumstances didn't allow that to happen. We were old South and new South, constantly bumping heads.

We respected each other. We didn't understand each other. But, in the language of team, we were for each other. We won games together. Whether willing or not, we advanced the cause of Auburn integration together. Coach Jordan made it possible for me to receive a great education with little financial impact on my family. He made sure I got the best care with my mistaken sickle-cell diagnosis. He taught us about dignity, teamwork, and class. But he never let me express to him who I was. He never got to know me.

I was the coming change in society. He was the status quo. We couldn't cross the bridge to our mutual humanity. I ran into Coach Jordan at a professional football exhibition game in Birmingham after I'd finished playing. We were face to face before either one of us could get away from the other. He pulled me into a vacant bathroom and he gave me his home phone number. He told me I was one of his boys, and I should call him if I ever needed him. He meant it. I thanked him. I meant it.

I think about Henry. How unfair it had been that the university did not prepare to welcome him, accept him, and help him to assimilate onto the campus. He gave his life to Auburn. I think about James and his loneliness. James gave his life as well. They both belong in the Alabama Sports Hall of Fame.

The night before, at the reception, I stole a private moment with James and asked him, "Would you do it again?" He gave the question a lot of thought. Then he started to ramble. His answer was both yes and no. He concluded for some things the answer would be no. He says, "On the field, I could have done so much more. Been so much happier." Off the field, he thinks Auburn prepared him for his ministry. "Auburn taught me about handling adversity, building character, and integrity. I made lifelong friends, and I have had occasion to minister to teammates."

Within four months of the reunion, Jay Casey, our starting guard, died. James, Henley, and others would attend his funeral and assist his family. James tells me, "When our guys have problems, the other guys look out for them. That's a beautiful thing."

Standing there that day, I asked myself that question. Would I do it again? My answer is longer and more rambling than James'. It can't be wrapped up in a neat, meaningless sound bite. It's complicated. Very complicated.

I looked up and down the line at my teammates. Most wore smiles of contentment, proud to be on the field one more time. I thought of how far we'd come. Roger Mitchell is the first one I know of to use the phrase "teammates for life." He sent me a letter and signed it "your teammate for life." It touched me. Stayed with me. Made me proud.

Some things in life are destined. Auburn didn't choose me. I chose Auburn. Something about Auburn resonated with me in that far, far away world of Rosalind Heights. Something about Auburn made me think attending Auburn would be just another Rover Boy adventure. In some ways it was. The evolutionary change of the civil right's movement needed to come to that small segment of the world. The fewer than 100 hundred black students who journeyed there during the first ten years of Auburn integration and graduated became the vessels of that change. The five black athletes who played for Coach Jordan, made it possible for those who followed.

I took the baton that James and Henry handed off to me and did my job both on and off the field. Of the five black athletes who signed with Auburn on my watch, four of them graduated.

That day on the field, I began the long journey back to bridging the gap between my alma mater and me. As we walked off the field, the fans gave us a long continuous ovation. I took it all in. "War Eagle," I thought. I held my head high.

[ 2016 ]

# CHAPTER 22

---

# THE BILLION DOLLAR MAN

The request came as a simple one. "Would you give me a copy of your resume? " I was asked. Carolyn Reed, an Auburn alumna from Birmingham, made the request. She didn't say why, I didn't ask. I've often gotten requests for my resume. I generally comply. This would be different.

The invitation to join the Auburn University Foundation Board came shortly thereafter. If timing is essential to success, this timing was right on. I joined the Board in 2008.

That fall, *Walk-On* hit the bookstores. It created a dust-up for me as I was featured on television news, radio, in newspapers, the fledging social media scene, and in bookstores and libraries. I traveled across the country for regional book signings in the Southeast and national signings in Los Angeles and Chicago. I spoke at Universities and Colleges from Texas to New Jersey. Walking into an airport bookstore and seeing *Walk-On* displayed in prime shelf space made me proud.

I would serve two four-year terms on the Foundation Board. I served on the Development and Directorship Committees, which I enjoyed. My background in Communication and Marketing assisted me with Development as my training background did with Directorship.

Also, in 2008, the University began the silent phase of a one billion dollar comprehensive campaign for the benefit of four major areas of the University: students, faculty, programs, and facilities. The one billion dollar goal would be historical for the University. No University or college in Alabama had ever reached for such a lofty goal. Auburn

University was stepping up to the plate. I was honored and glad to play a small part.

In 2015 and 2016, I served as Chair of the Foundation Board. My tenure coincided with the public announcement and public phase of the campaign. There were articles, campus events, and many alumni events that joyce and I attended.

I became the face of the campaign.

Having been an actor and speaker for three decades, what the University needed from me was right up my alley. It was great casting. My talents and skills lined up perfectly for the role. And, I could serve my alma mater.

It ended up being a blast!

Thom Gossom Announces the "Billion Dollar" Goal at Auburn's "A-Day" Spring Practice Game

With an A-Day attendance of 62,143, and backed by some of Auburn's finest and most generous Alumni, I blurted, "One Billion Dollars," to the excited crowd. "That's Billion with a B." The applause came in waves.

The "billion" word, "with a "B," gave me strength. Courage. Boldness. I did my best to inspire the crowd. I told them, "We are undertaking a lofty goal that will make us all proud." It made me proud!

*Because This is Auburn,* the campaign for Auburn University, was unprecedented and game-changing. It was designed to propel the University forward to meet unique 21st century challenges and opportunities with well-researched and innovative solutions. The campaign would be the catalyst moving us forward.

The live events were the frosting on my cake. We took the campaign to Auburn alums and friends across the United States. Produced by the Communication Department of the Development Office, led by its Assistant Vice-President Jason Peevy, the live events featured talented students and brilliant faculty and attracted hundreds of Auburn alumni and friends at each event. After the first couple of events, I was installed as the host for the live events. It was again perfect casting.

Taking the campaign on the road, in a live 90-minute presentation, we were able to feature the wonderful and innovative discoveries taking place at the University. There were many "gee whiz moments" and "gee whiz" people. We were a hit in Atlanta, Dallas, Huntsville, Nashville, Tampa, Birmingham, Houston, Mobile, New York, and Washington DC.

A highlight for me was getting to work with my good friend and fellow actor, Michael O'Neill. Michael, a consummate professional actor, is an Auburn grad. We attended the University at the same time and lived within five miles of each other in Los Angeles. It was special for both of us. After over 30-years in the business, we were able to work together for the first time.

Another highlight was involving our African American Alumni as active participants in the campaign. Because the University came late to the integration party there are only two and one half generations of Auburn black alumni. We challenged all of our alumni to get involved in the process.

We involved our black alumni in ways they had not been engaged before. The Development Department set a goal of getting at least 1,964 African American alumni donors in the campaign to commemorate the year (1964) when Harold Franklin, Auburn's first African American student, enrolled in the University. The effort was hugely successful with 2,341 black alumni giving $4.3 million to the campaign. More importantly, we expanded our giving base. Those alumni will continue to be involved as we go forward.

In August of 2016, we surpassed the $1 billion dollar goal with more than 16 months remaining in the campaign.

A new Performing Arts Center, an Engineering Student Achievement Center, Small Animal Teaching Hospital, and a beautiful remodeling of the campus library are all improvements that now or will soon grace the campus as a result of our efforts.

There was more… Alongside serving on the board, I was an ambassador for the University out of President Jay Gogue's office. It was an exciting time. I was involved in the recruitment of the Edward Via College of Osteopathic Medicine locating a branch of their medical college on the Auburn campus. Other issues included, Diversity and Inclusion initiatives across the University campus, agreements for The University's Vapor Wake Technology, bomb-sniffing dogs; and a reemphasis on Kinesiology leading to the campus being named an Olympic training site designation. I enjoyed working with the outstanding administrators and faculty.

What an experience!

From walking onto the football team in 1970 to leading the cheers in raising a billion dollars, it has been an incredible journey of history, living, learning, and believing I could make a difference in a university's history. Quite a ride!

Family isn't a word I throw around lightly. Mine is a mixture of biological, step this, step that, African American, Caucasian, Native American, and Latin. But we're all cool. We enjoy each other's company. I love them all.

Family became a word that was tossed around a lot during the campaign, specifically "The Auburn Family." Were we all family through our connection with the University? "Hesitant," is the word I'd use to describe my feelings. Yes, the University is more open, more willing to thrust itself into an inclusive, diverse world.

But…sometimes it comes down to one-on-one.

The young college graduate traveling through New York's LaGuardia airport broke through my protective guard. As I reached for my bag, she approached me and said, "I've been waiting to see whose bag that was. I saw the Auburn luggage tag on it. I'm a new alum, just graduated. War Eagle." Her grin, filled with so much promise, lit up the terminal.

"War Eagle," I smiled back at her!

. . . . .

Thom Gossom Jr. will receive the Auburn University, Lifetime Achievement Award on March 2, 2019.

# ACKNOWLEDGEMENTS

I knew I'd write this book, even during the dark days of living through the biggest cultural change of the twentieth century. I am grateful to all who helped make it happen. I am particularly grateful to print this second edition.

Much love and many thanks to my wife, Dr. joyce gillie gossom. Everyday from loving partner to proofreader, to trusted friend she is there for me with patience, love, and a smile. Thanks to my dad and mom for encouraging me to dream, and a special thanks to Mom G. (Marcella Gillie).

Thanks to Amanda Bennett for her tireless energy in assisting the Best Gurl team.

Thanks to Brad Ashmore for his great photos.

Thanks to the Auburn family and everyone who has read *Walk-On* and come away with a better understanding of our mutual humanity.

And, hello to my good buddy, Carter Coleman.

Also a big thanks to "Little Emily," The Communicator, for her work on the 10th anniversary edition of *Walk- On*.

# ABOUT THE AUTHOR

Born in Birmingham Alabama, THOM GOSSOM, JR. received his Bachelor of Arts in communication from Auburn University, and a Master of Arts in communication from The University of Montevallo. Gossom began his career at Bellsouth in the office of Public Relations. In 1987, Gossom struck out on his own, starting his own PR Firm to supplement his writing and acting adventures.

In addition to *Walk-On* Gossom has penned a collection of short stories, *A Slice of Life*, *Another Slice of Life* and *The Rest of The Pie*. He also produced, wrote and directed the documentary *Quiet Courage, The James Owens Story* about the trailblazing football scholarship athlete who integrated major college football in Alabama, Mississippi, and Georgia.

An accomplished actor, Gossom has appeared in *Fight Club*, *Jeepers Creepers 2*, *NYPD Blue*, *Containment*, and *The Quad*.

He and his wife live in Fort Walton Beach, Florida. They have one son.

Visit the author's website:

www.bestgurl.com

Also by Thom Gossom Jr.
*A Slice of Life*
*Another Slice of Life*
*The Rest of The Pie*
*Quiet Courage*